SAILING INTO HISTORY

SAILING INTO HISTORY

GREAT LAKES BULK CARRIERS
OF THE TWENTIETH CENTURY AND THE
CREWS WHO SAILED THEM

FRANK BOLES

MICHIGAN STATE UNIVERSITY PRESS • EAST LANSING

⊛ The paper used in this publication meets the minimum requirements
of ANSI/NISO Z39.48-1992 (R 1997) (Permanence of Paper).

Michigan State University Press
East Lansing, Michigan 48823-5245

Printed and bound in the United States of America.

25 24 23 22 21 20 19 18 17   1 2 3 4 5 6 7 8 9 10

LIBRARY OF CONGRESS CATALOGING-IN-PUBLICATION DATA
Names: Boles, Frank, 1951–
Title: Sailing into history : Great Lakes bulk carriers of the twentieth century and the crews who sailed them / Frank Boles.
Other titles: Great Lakes bulk carriers of the twentieth century and the crews who sailed them
Description: East Lansing, Michigan : Michigan State University Press, [2017]
| Includes bibliographical references and index.
Identifiers: LCCN 2016001748| ISBN 9781611862232 (cloth : alk. paper) | ISBN 9781609175085 (pdf)
| ISBN 9781628952803 (epub) | ISBN 9781628962802 (kindle)
Subjects: LCSH: Bulk carrier cargo ships—Great Lakes (North America)—History—20th century. |
Ore carriers—Great Lakes (North America)—History—20th century. | Sailors—Great Lakes (North America)—
History—20th century. | Shipping—Great Lakes (North America)—History—20th century.
Classification: LCC VM393.B7 B65 2017 | DDC 386/.540440977—
dc23 LC record available at https://lccn.loc.gov/2016001748

Book design by Charlie Sharp, Sharp Des!gns, East Lansing, MI
Cover design by Erin Kirk New
Cover image of Frank Glowacki, porter, smoking cigarette on the stern of the Steamer
Pontiac while watching another ship pass (1941). Image from the Albert A. Bartlett
Collection, Historical Collections of the Great Lakes, Bowling Green State University.

Michigan State University Press is a member of the Green Press Initiative and is
committed to developing and encouraging ecologically responsible publishing
practices. For more information about the Green Press Initiative and the use
of recycled paper in book publishing, please visit www.greenpressinitiative.org.

Visit Michigan State University Press at *www.msupress.org*

For Matthew,
who loved the water.

CONTENTS

PREFACE

In 1942 Walter Havighurst published his history of nineteenth-century shipping on the Great Lakes. *Long Ships Passing* was a title with deep resonance. In 1900 approximately 2,400 cargo vessels plied the Great Lakes. In 1938, as Havighurst began his work, 308 U.S. flag bulk-cargo boats were operating. As the twentieth century drew to a close, only about 55 American-owned cargo vessels continued to sail. The twentieth century saw the passing of the long ships. Over the course of a century, Havighurst's ships had become much longer, vastly more capacious, and dramatically fewer.

This volume tells the twentieth-century history of Great Lakes bulk commercial shipping, with a particular concern for those who served on the vessels and the reminiscences they left behind. Shipping on the Great Lakes is a vast enterprise that includes both the obvious and the unlikely. It is the story of brave crew serving on well-built boats; but it is also the story of accountants ensuring the profitability of the ships, government aiding and regulating commerce, technology interacting with all aspects of the business, and labor-management relations.

There are many existing histories about the ships that sailed the Great Lakes, but a large number are written by sailors for sailors, or by devotees of the lakes for others that share their passion. These books simply assume that anyone reading the account will be familiar with the ways and terminology of sailors. This book does not assume a familiarity with Great Lakes vessels or the nature of cargoes on the lakes. Thus, it devotes many pages to explaining the tools sailors used to accomplish the tasks they were assigned, from the giant ships themselves to the things sailors used daily in their jobs.

If this volume devotes much of the reader's attention to learning the business of sailing and the sailors' tools, the book spends little time on the weather, particularly bad weather. It is not that weather is unimportant. Weather mattered. Ship schedules were affected by the moods of nature; ships' crews were inconvenienced or frightened when nature's moods turned ugly; and in the worst conditions, lives were lost when nature's forces overwhelmed ship and crew. But while the literature about the Great Lakes is scant in some areas, the one subject that has been written about is weather, especially the weather preceding a shipwreck. I leave for others often-repeated tales such as the Big Blow of 1913, the Armistice Day Storm of 1940, or the sinking of the *Edmund Fitzgerald*. This book sets a course for less-traveled waters.

The book I have written tells the story of an industry that served the nation, and how the workers in that industry labored to render that service. It is about why the ships existed, what they moved, how they were designed to render service, and how their crews made it happen and made a life for themselves and their families. In the end, it is about perseverance, season after season, over the course of a century.

As an armchair deckhand with a stomach not well suited for the sea, I have learned most of what I share in this volume from the existing body of literature about the Great Lakes. For almost every story told in this book, I likely can point to someone who knows more about it—or, if they are no longer among us, knew more than I. Thus I have tried to leave a thoughtful trail of footnotes for those inclined to learn more about a specific subject. If this volume has virtue, it is not in its depth, but rather in its breadth. It seeks to bring together a sometimes highly specialized literature and share it in an accessible way with a general audience. I suspect some will be unhappy with the result. But to those who say, with a touch of justifiable condescension, "well, not exactly," I trust the broader purpose of the volume will lead them to forgive what I hope are minor inaccuracies that result from the desire to summarize the experience of hundreds of commercial ships and crews that sailed the Great Lakes in the twentieth century, and a large list of secondary sources, into one small volume.

Let me also thank four individuals for their help in preparing this work. Robert W. Graham at Bowling Green State University has been unfailingly helpful. Susan

Paton offered invaluable assistance in copyediting the final version of the book. Mistakes that remain are entirely the result of my stubborn insistence on certain expressions and punctuation, not her wise advice. My son Nick and wife Valerie also deserve praise. Although their contributions were many, perhaps the most important was a semi-private reading of an earlier draft of the book during a very long car ride, at which I was not present. They graciously later claimed to be laughing with me and not at me. I rather doubt that, but their comments after the trip, as well as many other acts of assistance, are greatly appreciated.

CHAPTER 1

REMAKING THE LAKES TO MOVE THE CARGO

There is no ore in the world as beautiful as Lake Superior specular hematite.

—Chase Osborn, *The Long Ships Passing: The Story of the Great Lakes*

Each year as the ice begins to melt on the Great Lakes, work begins on the bulk carriers anchored at their winter berths. During the darkest days of winter, the ships were entrusted to a few watchmen—or shipkeepers, as they are known in the trade—placed on board largely for insurance reasons. The shipkeepers made their rounds, checking ballast tanks and bilges, making sure the mooring lines were secure, and guarding against unauthorized persons coming aboard.[1] But as spring approaches, the shipkeepers are joined by new faces, sailors who are often old friends. The galley crew comes first, to prepare the kitchen in order to feed everyone who follows. Next comes the engine crew to inspect the engines, make any needed adjustments, and ensure that the ship is ready to make way. About ten days after the engine crew begins work, the deck crew is called back to prepare the rest of the ship. If all goes well, about a week later the vessel is ready to sail.[2]

At ports throughout the lakes, cargo is waiting. The reason for all the preparation and all the work is to move cargo. To do it, huge ships have been built and sailed;

even large engineering projects have been undertaken to remake the lakes in ways that have both benefited and defined those ships.

The Great Lakes are an inland sea, creating a vast waterway that stretches from deep within North America to the Atlantic Ocean. But unlike the deep ocean, capable of accepting any ship that could be imagined and constructed, the lakes as they were left by nature imposed clear limitations on vessels. Three geographic features defined the size of ships in the Upper Lakes[3]—the St. Marys River Rapids and other navigational impediments in the lower St. Marys River, the St. Clair Flats between Lake Huron and Lake St. Clair, and Lime Kiln Crossing in the Detroit River near the city of Amherstburg, Ontario. These established natural limits on Great Lakes shipping.

The most spectacular barrier to navigation on the Upper Lakes was the falls at the St. Marys River. The mouth of the St. Marys River is seven miles wide at the point where the waters of Lake Superior first pour into it. But the river quickly narrows, and at Sault Ste. Marie the river drops 22 feet in less than one-half mile.[4] A brave person in a canoe could shoot the rapids in three to five minutes, but doing the same with a ship of any size was virtually impossible. Without locks, a ship could not be sailed through the St. Marys River between Lake Superior and Lake Huron. The only way to move cargo was to unload it and carry the cargo around the rapids.

South of the falls, the Lower St. Marys River again limited shipping. Two miles below the rapids, the river divided into two streams, the "old" channel that passed through Lake George, and a second passage through Lake Hay. The Lake George passage was longer, winding, and shallow. The maximum draft of a ship using the passage could be no more than 9 to 12 feet, depending on water conditions and weather. Despite this, the Lake George passage was preferred to the Lake Hay passage. The Lake Hay passage was similarly shallow, but with the added danger of jagged rocks on the bottom and the sides, especially near the "Little Rapids" at the north end of the river. Although both passages were difficult to navigate, the Lake George passage was more forgiving of mistakes.[5]

The St. Clair Flats, located at the mouth of the St. Clair River where the river flows into Lake St. Clair, is the largest freshwater delta in the United States. Covering approximately forty square miles, the delta creates both an ecological paradise and a huge obstacle to shipping. Channels in the Flats are winding and shallow, often being less than 10 feet deep. Storms or heavy spring runoffs frequently caused the channels to change.[6] Each transit of the Flats required a captain's full attention in order to avoid running aground. The only saving grace to the Flats was that the delta was almost devoid of large rocks. A ship aground in the Flats, while inconvenienced and often in need of assistance, was rarely damaged.

Lime Kiln Crossing across from Amherstburg, Ontario, near the point where the Detroit River enters Lake Erie, imposed a final challenge for sailors. A narrow channel with a rocky bottom and a typical depth of 14 feet, the Crossing was always traversed carefully. A ship that hit bottom here usually experienced damage. However, what earned Lime Kiln Crossing the name "Hell-Gate of the West" was not so much the narrow channel or rocky bottom, but rather the extreme variability in the water's depth.[7]

This variability was the result of Lake Erie's susceptibility to extreme seiches. Seiches are phenomena observed in all bodies of water in which persistent wind can "pile up" water at one side of a lake while causing the water level to drop on the lake's other side. Seiches occur on all of the Great Lakes. For example on June 22, 1954, a seiche struck Chicago beaches, raising water levels from 5 to 25 feet and drowning thirteen.[8] However, the rectangular west-to-east shape of Lake Erie, the lake's relatively shallow average depth of only 70 feet, and the predominant west-to-east winds in North America make Lake Erie susceptible to extreme seiches.[9]

Stories about Lake Erie seiches are legion. According to legend, in 1904 a recently purchased ship docked in Buffalo was found by its new owner sitting on the shore. Apparently a seiche had lifted the ship over the dock and deposited it on the land. The new owner was furious and sought out the ship's seller for restitution. Fortunately for everyone, the next morning the ship was found back in the water. A second seiche had again raised the water level and refloated the ship, but this time the vessel was conveniently placed in the lake.[10] Although this story may be apocryphal, the extreme variance in depth at each end of Lake Erie has often been recorded. On January 31, 1914, Buffalo experienced a 9-foot seiche, and on January 2, 1942, the water in Buffalo measured 13 feet higher than the water in Toledo.[11] At the western end of the lake on January 14, 1950, a seiche caused a 5-foot drop in water level at Put-in-Bay, Ohio, and an estimated 6-foot drop at Toledo.[12] For a ship's captain, the real concern was not ending up on a dock in Buffalo, but rather striking the rocks in Lime Kiln Crossing as the water drew rapidly away from the western end of Lake Erie. A seiche could bring the Crossing's rocky bottom unexpectedly close to the ship's hull.[13]

The combined effect of the St. Marys River, the St. Clair Flats, and the water level at Lime Kiln Crossing created natural limits on the size of ships sailing the Great Lakes. No matter what size was technologically possible for naval engineers to build, any ship that drew more than about 11 feet of water would likely run aground in the Flats, and if a seiche developed in Lake Erie, stood a good chance of striking rock in Lime Kiln Crossing. In the same way, if the lake passages were left in their natural state, it would be unthinkable to routinely sail a vessel of any size in the St. Marys River between Lake Huron and Lake Superior.

Until the middle of the nineteenth century, all this information was merely the stuff of an evening's conversation. An eighteenth-century French voyageur's Native American–designed canoe was at best 40 feet long and 5 feet wide, and drew only a few inches of water.[14] Eighteenth- and early nineteenth-century European-designed vessels were also sized to make passage possible through the St. Clair Flats or Lime Kiln Crossing. Indeed, in the 1850s a uniquely designed and widely copied lakes sailing vessel with a hinged centerboard allowed a significantly larger vessel to obtain stability in open water but draw only about 6 feet of water when passing through shallow areas.[15]

But by the middle of the nineteenth century, the amount of waterborne commerce sailing on the lakes called for more than clever modifications of old ship designs. The desire for larger vessels made the lakes' natural limits the topic of vital economic discussion. Businessmen wanted to bring the lakes to "maximum service," and to do so, Great Lakes shipping interests began lobbying the federal government to modify the natural characteristics of the lakes, or in the word still used today, make "improvements" that would allow larger vessels with a deeper draft to sail unimpeded by nature's limitations.

America's pre–Civil War federal government, although it would invest in port improvements and aids to navigation,[16] was generally unwilling to fund improvements to the lakes' waterways. In part the objection was based on principle. The Democratic Party, which usually held sway in one way or another, understood the federal Constitution in a very literal way. Because the Constitution did not specifically enumerate "internal improvements" as being among the powers of the Congress, many Democrats argued that the federal government lacked authority to undertake such projects. In the words of Democratic president Franklin Pierce, "The springs of industry rest securely upon the general reserved powers of the people of the several states."[17] As far as Pierce and many other Democrats were concerned, if roads, canals, and navigable waterways were to be improved, the responsibility for the work rested upon the individual states, not the federal government.

A second, less-principled motive limiting pre–Civil War improvements on the Great Lakes was regional politics. With federal money for internal improvements hard to come by, congressional representatives from the more populous states facing the Atlantic Ocean did all that was in their power to see that whatever money was available was spent on the East Coast. Regional politics led projects in the Great Lakes to be ignored or underfunded, something that Midwestern members of Congress regularly complained about by the 1850s.[18]

And there was a great deal of work the Midwestern members of Congress would have liked to have the federal government undertake. The first federal proposal to improve navigation in the upper Great Lakes (in contrast to proposals to improve ports or build lighthouses and other aids to navigation) was made in 1842. The Army Corps of Engineers recommended dredging a 500-foot wide, 12-foot deep channel through the St. Clair Flats.[19] The rationale was straightforward—the Flats represented the major navigational obstacle in the increasingly important trade between the western shore of Lake Michigan and the eastern ports of Lake Erie—particularly Buffalo, where cargo could be placed on barges and travel through the Erie Canal to eventually reach New York City. The proposal made business sense, but was not successful politically. It failed in Congress.

As time passed, the need for dredging at the Flats became ever more obvious. Before the Civil War, it was said that there was almost always at least one ship stranded in the Flats, and in November 1854 the *Detroit Inquirer* claimed that a severe storm had left 150 vessels stranded. Whether or not the paper exaggerated the storm's effect, in 1854 Michigan senator Lewis Cass, in advocating work on the waterway, reported that "fourteen vessels, steamboats and others are constantly employed in lightering vessels and in towing them through this difficult pass."[20] Cass's comments made clear that whatever the exact number, there were plenty of boats in the Flats that needed help—and a small fleet ready to assist them, for a price.

Although improving the St. Clair Flats was often discussed by Congress, the first major project undertaken to improve lake shipping was the construction of a new canal at Sault Ste. Marie. Michigan had long wanted a canal at the Soo. Among the first acts of the newly established Michigan legislature was to employ a surveyor to go to the Soo and plan a canal around the rapids. A plan was created and preliminary funding was voted by the Michigan legislature in 1839, but nothing came of the state's effort. In 1839 the Michigan congressional delegation supported the state's effort with the first request for federal assistance to build a canal at the Soo. In speaking against it, Senator Henry Clay of Kentucky summed up congressional sentiment when he declared that he could see no reason to spend money on a place "as remote as the moon." No federal funds were made available for the project by the Twenty-sixth Congress of the United States.[21]

What made spending money worthwhile in such a remote place was the mining of copper and iron ore along the shores of Lake Superior. Vast quantities of material upbound for the newly opened mines and even larger quantities of downbound ore began to move past the Soo. The land-based portage system that carried cargo around the rapids was completely inadequate to deal with the volume of commerce created by the mining industry. At the end of the 1851 navigation season, 12,000 barrels of supplies remained in the Soo, unable to be shipped onward to the mines. The portage was not only hopelessly slow, it was expensive. In 1846, when the copper boom first began in Michigan's Upper Peninsula, it cost $8.50 per ton to move copper ore from Lake Superior to Buffalo. Of that cost, $1.00 per ton was spent in the mile-long portage around the rapids.[22] Although the Soo might be remote, with considerable investment being made in Lake Superior mining activity by people along America's Atlantic Seaboard, Michigan's congressional delegation gained important political support for a canal. A good rate of return on investments in Michigan mines made by New Englanders required a good canal at the Soo. In 1852 Congress gave 750,000 acres of federally owned land to the State of Michigan. The state was to sell the land and use the money received to pay for building a canal at the Soo.[23]

In 1855 tandem "State Locks" were opened for use. The State Locks were each 350 feet long and 70 feet wide, and had a minimum depth of about 11.5 feet. The state-constructed locks were not only considerably longer than what was required by the federal government, but considerably longer than any ship that could reach them. In its natural state, the St. Marys River was unnavigable by a 350-foot ship.[24] But the financial logic of building larger ships to achieve the greatest economy when moving cargo had taken hold. Shortly after the locks were opened, Congress authorized deepening the shallow portions of the St. Marys River near Lake George from a natural depth of from 10 to 14 feet to a uniform depth of 16 feet. Rock was also removed from the East Neebish Rapids, a much smaller rapids within the St. Marys River that was located south of the canal at the Soo, where the canal bypassed the most important rapids.[25] This was the first channel work paid for by the federal government on the Great Lakes.

In 1852, a federal improvement project was finally authorized for the St. Clair Flats.[26] Federal funds and additional dredging work paid for by private shippers, who were allowed to "borrow" a federally owned dredge, created a channel in the

Flats with the nominal depth of 13.5 feet. The new channel, however, followed a line determined by the easiest path to dredge, not the easiest course to sail. It quickly proved a challenge to navigate. Added to this inconvenience, captains quickly learned that the work had made the Flats only marginally deeper. Under low-water conditions, the channel's actual depth could still drop to as little as 8 feet.[27]

The 1850s was a decade of intense political turmoil and change. One small aspect of that change was in Washington's attitude toward "internal improvements." Unlike its literal-minded and often parsimonious political predecessors, the new Republican Party had an 1860 platform that promised generous federal funding for internal improvements to increase the commercial value of the nation's rivers and harbors. Although the Civil War made immediate implementation of this promise impossible, after the war's conclusion, the now politically dominant Republicans made good on their pledge.[28] The party of Lincoln was generous in allocating funds to improve the Great Lakes.

The first postwar projects focused on the St. Clair Flats. In 1867 Congress approved dredging a new 1.5-mile-long channel with dikes on either side to hold back silt. This channel was opened unofficially in 1870 and officially in 1871.[29] Beginning in 1870, and for more than a decade after, appropriations for dredging in the Flats became an almost annual part of the federal budget.[30] Over time, various dredging projects deepened the navigable channels to 16 feet, creating demand to build a new lock at the Soo, where the State Locks' 11.5-foot depth made it impossible to build ships that took full advantage of the deeper channels. The State of Michigan, which had been able to undertake construction of the first Soo Locks only with federal aid, continued to lack the resources to undertake such a large project. To make the lakes usable by larger ships, the federal government directly financed the construction of a new Soo lock and assumed full financial responsibility and complete control for the operation of all locks on the St. Marys River. Federal control of the Soo Locks, assumed by the Army Corps of Engineers, began in 1881 with the opening of the newly constructed lock. Named in honor of Civil War general Godfrey Weitzel, the Weitzel Lock was 515 feet long, at least 60 feet wide, and had a minimum depth of 17 feet. Although its purpose was economic, newspapers of the day were more interested in the sheer size of the project. When it opened, it was the largest lock in the world.[31]

As in 1855 when the State Locks opened, the Weitzel Lock anticipated serving a boat that was too large to successfully navigate through the existing St. Marys River. In 1882 Congress appropriated funds to dig a new channel in the lower St.

Marys River through Lake Hay. Although not completed until 1894, the 300-foot-wide, 20-foot-deep channel marked a significant improvement in the waterway's commercial use.[32] It shortened the journey through the river by eleven miles, significantly straightened the course, and included the first navigational lights to be placed on the river, allowing for safe nighttime navigation. In 1902 work was begun in the St. Marys to widen the channel to 600 feet and deepen it to 21 feet.[33]

As important for commerce as the ongoing work at the Soo was, more important was the realization by the Army Corps of Engineers that the Great Lakes should be considered a single integrated navigational system. The Corps' objective changed from solving problems at a specific location to establishing a dependable depth throughout the lakes to accommodate commercial vessels of a standard size. In 1892, the Corps adopted the first comprehensive plan for lake navigation,[34] establishing a minimum navigable depth of 20 feet throughout all the lakes' commercial channels.

The centerpiece of this first comprehensive plan for lake navigation was another lock at the Soo. This lock, named in honor of Civil War general and outstanding Great Lakes engineer Orlando Poe, was opened in 1896. The economic need for the new lock was clear. A boat waited, on average, five hours to lock through at the Soo.[35] But the Poe Lock did much more than just reduce waiting time by creating an additional lock. The new 800-foot-long, 100-foot-wide lock was, like its predecessor, the largest in the world. Although newspapers of the day again made much of the lock's size, what was perhaps most important for commerce was that the lock's minimum depth of 22 feet made it compliant with the Corps' updated master plan for lake navigation, which had been revised to call for a minimum 22-foot depth for all commercial channels. In the early years of the twentieth century, two additional locks were placed in service at the Soo by the United States. The Davis Lock in 1914 and the Sabin Lock five years later both had a minimum depth of slightly more than 23 feet.[36] An additional, but smaller, lock was opened in 1895 on the Canadian side of the St. Marys River by the government of Canada. It was known simply as the "Canadian Lock."[37]

The natural resources needed to fight World War II led to a new, larger lock at the Soo. With the United States straining to obtain every possible pound of iron ore from northern Minnesota and Michigan's Upper Peninsula for the steel mills on the south shores of Lake Erie and Lake Michigan, the new lock was built in record time. Authorized on March 7, 1942, a twenty-four-hour-a-day construction schedule led to the lock opening on July 11, 1943. Named the MacArthur Lock, at 800 feet long, 80 feet wide, and 29.5 feet deep, the lock was designed to allow larger and more heavily loaded vessels to pass through the St. Marys River.[38] In 1968 the rebuilt and enlarged Poe Lock was opened at the Soo to shipping. It was 1,200 feet long, 110 feet wide, and 32 feet deep. It also allowed for bigger and more capacious freighters.

In the early years of twentieth-century shipping, companies focused on persuading Congress to fund increasing the uniform depth of channels, which the Corps of Engineers had first set at 20 feet in 1892. Shipping companies were particularly interested in obtaining deeper levels for the downbound channels, frequented by heavily loaded boats carrying iron ore. By 1929 downbound channels had been deepened to 24 feet, while a depth of only 21 feet was maintained upbound. On May 21, 1956, President Eisenhower signed into law Public Law 434 increasing legal minimum depth in the lakes' navigable channels to 25.5 feet downbound and 21 to 25.5 feet upbound.[39] By the end of the century the standardized depth was 27 feet.[40]

Unlike massive canal construction projects, dredging the lakes' navigable channels and harbors was a never-ending task. Over time, nature inevitably filled artificially deepened channels, eventually returning them to their original depth. Channel deepening created a constant cycle of work, and by the end of the twentieth century the Army Corps of Engineers was responsible for dredging sixty commercial and seventy-nine shallow-draft harbors on the Great Lakes, for a total of 139 ports, as well as six hundred miles of navigational channels. Approximately 3 to 5 million cubic yards of sediment was removed each year.[41] That is enough soil to raise the height of a square mile of land 3 to 5 feet.

The money spent to improve Great Lakes navigation was justified by the bounty of natural riches for which the lakes proved the most convenient form of transportation. The foundation of American Great Lakes shipping in the twentieth century rested on three fundamental cargoes: iron, coal, and stone. Grain was the fourth major cargo, but more often it moved on Canadian vessels.[42] The amount of iron, coal, and stone carried on American ships transported over the course of the twentieth century is so vast that it is hard to find meaningful comparisons. Between 1900 and 1999, some 6,629,051,456 tons of iron ore and taconite pellets moved across the lakes; 3,797,126,962 tons of coal were transported; and 1,911,711,568 tons of stone found their way into and out of the holds of Great Lakes bulk carriers. Combined, this amounted to 12,337,889,986 tons of cargo.[43] Finding a comparison for this amount of material is almost impossible. The 1,451-foot-tall Willis Tower in Chicago (formerly the Sears Tower) weighs 222,500 tons. The iron, coal, and stone moved over the Great Lakes in the twentieth century equals 55,451 such buildings. The five-mile-long Mackinac Bridge, which connects Michigan's two peninsulas at the Straits of Mackinac, weighs 1,024,500 tons. The cargoes of iron, coal, and stone moved over the lakes during the twentieth century equals almost 12,043 identical bridges. The Hoover Dam, which holds back the largest water reservoir in the United States, weighs an estimated 6.6 million tons. The iron, stone, and coal moved across the lakes in the twentieth century could create 1,869 Hoover Dams. These are numbers so large that it is difficult to understand them.

During the twentieth century, iron ore was the principal cargo found aboard Great Lakes freighters. "Iron ore" was a simple term for a complex substance that had many grades and variations.[44] At its finest, ore was a beautiful red color, something new crew members often noted.[45] Ore was the principal cargo because of the United States' voracious appetite for what it made: iron and steel. By 1894 America had become the leading manufacturing economy in the world, producing more than Germany and Britain combined, and much of that manufacturing depended upon steel.[46] Through a quirk of geology, Michigan and Minnesota iron ore was especially well suited for nineteenth- and twentieth-century steelmaking.

The Bessemer process revolutionized steelmaking in 1855, reducing the cost of iron and steel production to one-sixth of earlier techniques. Because of its vast cost savings, this new process was rapidly adopted by steel manufacturers. In addition to its cost advantage, the Bessemer process also burned off unwanted additional minerals found in iron ore. It removed carbon and silicone impurities; however, it left behind phosphorus impurities, and steel contaminated with phosphorus was hopelessly brittle. Ore from Pennsylvania, previously used extensively by American steelmakers, was full of phosphorus.[47] Phosphorus-free ore, however, was abundant in both Michigan's Upper Peninsula and Minnesota, making ore from these two regions the first choice of most steel manufacturers.[48]

Soon enough, huge quantities of iron ore from the northernmost part of the Great Lakes region were being sent south to America's steel mills. In 1899, twenty-two ore docks on the Upper Lakes handled 12.5 million tons of ore—70 percent of the total American iron ore produced that year.[49] Iron ore was also the heaviest bulk commodity carried over the lakes, a net ton filling only 16 cubic feet.[50] Iron ore was so heavy, no ship could be filled with it to the top of the cargo hold without sinking. Special loading techniques were developed so that a ship at the dock would not be damaged or even sink from the weight of too much iron ore being suddenly dumped into the hold.

Coal, the second largest cargo on the Great Lakes, first began to move across the lakes in quantity around 1851.[51] At the beginning of the twentieth century, coal was brought by railroad from mines in Pennsylvania and West Virginia to the same ports on the southern shores of Lake Erie where great quantities of iron ore were being delivered. Freighters that had emptied their holds of ore often filled up with coal for the return trip.[52] In addition to usually traveling in the opposite direction of iron ore, coal was the mirror image of iron ore in many other ways. No sailor ever commented on the beauty of a ship full of coal. Coal was a dirty cargo that only an accountant, sitting in a clean office far removed from the dock, could appreciate. Unlike iron ore it was also a light cargo. A net ton of coal occupied 42 cubic feet.[53] Because of this, a ship was frequently filled to overflowing with the stuff and, had space allowed, could have easily carried more. Toward the end of the century, a market for western coal produced a new pattern of transportation in which coal moved from ports on the northern and western shores of the Great Lakes to ports at the southern and eastern ends of the lakes.

Limestone was necessary in the steelmaking process, and was also used as aggregate material for building and construction, in cement, and in agriculture. Thus "stone" made up a significant quantity of the cargo carried on the lakes. Stone, however, had its own pattern of commerce, different from that of iron ore or coal. Most stone came from the Alpena, Michigan, area.[54] Alpena limestone, also known as dolomite, was used in blast furnaces because of its chemical purity, and because the nearness of the quarries to lakeside docking facilities made it easy to transport.[55] Because stone was often delivered to relatively small ports, specialized ships were often used to move stone. Limestone falls between iron ore and coal in the space needed to transport it, requiring about 29 cubic feet per ton.

Finally there was grain. The rich harvests of both the United States and Canada moved from the farmers working on the western prairies to the people living in eastern cities beyond the lakes. The first grain shipment on Lake Michigan was transported in 1834 from St. Joseph, Michigan.[56] By 1860, there were 69 million bushels of grain moved out of Lake Michigan ports, 50 million bushels from Chicago alone. A pattern was quickly established: grain was usually shipped from port cities on the western shore of Lake Michigan to ports on the eastern shores of Lake Erie, and from there further east by train or canal. In 1899 the fleet moved 200 million bushels of grain.[57]

The Lake Michigan grain trade peaked in 1921. By World War II, grain shipments had stopped entirely from all but two Lake Michigan ports. The decline of grain shipments on Lake Michigan, however, did not indicate a decline in the commodity's importance, but rather a relocating of the principal shipping ports. Increasingly grain moved east from the westernmost point of Lake Superior rather than from ports along Lake Michigan.[58]

These cargoes—iron ore, coal, stone, and grain—were at the heart of America's economy for much of the nineteenth and twentieth centuries. Because of their centrality to the nation's welfare, the ships that moved this cargo, and the navigational system that enabled these ships to sail swiftly, efficiently, and safely from port to port, also became a national priority. As a result, the lakes were reshaped from the way nature had left them to accommodate this commerce and its ships. A vast, nationally subsidized program of canal building, channel reconstruction and deepening, and harbor construction was undertaken. The U.S. Army Corps of Engineers intervened whenever "God didn't make it right"[59] along the Great Lakes, or at least failed to create in a way that facilitated safe and reliable movement of needed bulk commodities across Lakes Superior, Michigan, Huron, and Erie.

CHAPTER 2

THE CREW

For a century that common trade [seafaring] has given men a character in common: endurance, enterprise, imagination, patience.

—James Oliver Curwood, *The Great Lakes and the Vessels That Plough Them: Their Owners, Their Sailors, and Their Cargoes*

M uch of the writing about life aboard a Great Lakes freighter portrays a crew of sturdy men, dutifully performing an often dangerous job in the face of a sometimes unforgiving sea. James Oliver Curwood, an influential fiction writer in the first years of the twentieth century, who occasionally rode on a freighter as a passenger during the pleasant summer months, was one of many writers who helped create a vision of the enduring, enterprising, imaginative, and patient Great Lakes sailor.[1] In creating this image, Curwood, and others, injected a considerable amount of romance into their prose.

In his 1943 novel *November Storm*, Jay McCormick took aim at the romantic bubble created around lake sailors. McCormick creates a scene in which a ship's fireman is read a heroic poem written by a passenger describing the work in the boiler room. The reading completed, the fireman bursts out laughing and says:

You don't honest to God think Tony or old Tom or anybody down in the fire hold
thinks about how he's making the boat go or how he's hot as fire or strong as
steam, do you? You think Polacks and Greeks and guys like me think that way? . . .
We don't. We shovel coal and haul ashes. Somebody hangs a dollar watch up on a
pipe and when we get a breather we go and look to see how much longer till we
can get the hell out of here.[2]

Patrick Livingston summed up his changing perceptions about the romantic literary
tradition regarding sailors and the reality of life and work aboard a lake freighter
this way:

Years ago, around the age of ten, one of my chief preoccupations was to gaze at
the steamboats rounding Belle Isle [in the Detroit River] and to fantasize them as
valiant guardians of a glamorous era past when ships were the principal commu-
nicators that linked different modes of thought and life about the earth. Since I
have begun gazing at Belle Isle from their steel decks, I have discovered that these
steamboats have lost much of their allure.[3]

Much can be said about Great Lakes sailors, but their true experience focuses
inexorably on each ship. Although the fleet may have collectively created a community of sailors, the crew of each vessel created a largely isolated neighborhood. Each
ship was a very, very small town where unique individuals lived in close quarters
with little change in their daily routine and even less distraction from one another.
It is wise to remember that each ship had its own stories and legends, and that as
crew moved from vessel to vessel, those stories were retold, enhanced, appropriated,
and sometimes changed beyond all semblance of truth.

Rather than trying to debunk such stories, a task as futile as it would be mirth-
less, what this chapter seeks to do is to create an appreciation of shipboard life as
a way to understand these stories. Understanding some basic characteristics of the
crew, such as education, and the nature of the crew's work, and daily life in such a
close environment helps explain the colorful tales that eventually found their way
ashore and into magazines and books.

One of the most important issues for sailors was education. For crew members,
formal education was relatively unimportant. The basic work on any Great Lakes
ship was given to the deckhands up top or, until about 1960 when technology
eliminated the jobs, coal passers and firemen deep inside the vessel. The principal

qualification to work in either place was a strong back and common sense. The work was physical and demanding, but it rarely involved tasks that called upon learning gained through formal education. A high school education was enough, and for much of the century more than enough. Most of the crew had schooling and a job very similar to that of the employees who worked in the many factories that ringed the lakes.

At the beginning of the century, officers also needed only a minimal formal education; however, over time the education of officers changed dramatically. In the early years, an officer's primary qualification was experience. For many decades, the common wisdom was that experience was the best teacher, and the typical career path for a bright young man was from the deck or the fire room to an officer's berth either in the wheelhouse or in engineering. As one old-timer noted at the beginning of the twentieth century, when it was common for a fireman to work his way up to become an engineer, "This was rightly considered a better training."[4]

Statistics compiled during World War II documented the many years of officers' experience. In 1944 the average captain had been on the water for thirty-two years. Officers in lesser positions did not have as much experience as the captain, but still had served many years aboard ships. First mates averaged twenty years of experience, and first assistant engineers usually had eighteen years of work on their résumé. Second mates and second assistant engineers respectively had fourteen and twelve years of experience. Most junior officers, third mates, and third assistant engineers were young but not inexperienced. They averaged nine and seven years of service respectively.[5] Well into the 1950s, experience mattered more among officers than academic diplomas, and it was not uncommon for a captain to have ended his formal education after graduating from high school. Ray McGrath, a long-serving captain, ended his formal academic career in 1935, his high school diploma in hand. His remaining book learning revolved around winter courses designed to help him pass various certification examinations administered by the United States Coast Guard.[6]

What ended the dominance of on-the-job officer education was changing technology. As early as 1945 the apprentice system was failing engineers. Older engineers could be completely flummoxed when they came upon a "newfangled" device. One sailor reminisced with considerable bitterness about an engineer who could not perform the simplest maintenance on the galley's refrigeration units because he had no experience with them, no training regarding their operation, and no interest in learning what he needed to know to fix them.[7] More important than changes in the galley were changes to the ship's engine. The basic design of a ship engine, which had remained essentially unchanged since the beginning of the century, was being replaced in the years preceding World War II by propulsion systems employing entirely new techniques. These new engines could mystify engineers whose training consisted solely of on-the-job experience with increasingly outdated propulsion technology.[8] After World War II, technological change in the pilothouse created similar problems among deck officers. Tools derived from completely new technology left little opportunity for hands-on training.

Shipboard conversations in the last half of the twentieth century often simply assumed that officers had always learned their craft by observation and working their way up the ranks. However, this was not true. Job-specific officer education began just prior to America's entry into World War I. The fleet was expanding rapidly, and there were not enough experienced sailors available to fill the number of officer berths created by the fleet's expansion. To cope with this problem, shipowners created nautical schools to teach ambitious young men the skills required to be an officer.

The first of these schools was organized in 1916 by the Lake Carriers' Association (LCA), the trade association of Great Lakes shipowners. Held during the winter when the ships were laid up, there was no tuition charged for the classes, although students were responsible for their own room and board. The first school was dedicated to navigation. In 1918 the LCA added courses in engineering. The objective was to train sailors to pass the necessary tests administered by the government (after 1939 the Coast Guard) to be certified as a deck or engineering officer.[9] Later, industry groups sponsored schools to help crew obtain lesser licenses. As technology evolved, so did the curriculum. When gyrocompasses or radar were placed on board, the LCA organized new classes to teach officers how to use them.[10]

With the advent of successful unionization in the 1950s, unions began to play a role in education. Often in competition with the LCA, unions offered off-season educational programs designed to help members qualify for higher shipboard ratings or perform duties more effectively. Union-run schools intentionally stood outside of the existing "management" process and offered members an alternative to company-run schools. Union-run schools were not just for the "laboring classes" among the crew, as officer unions also became involved in education. In 1984 the Marine Engineers' Beneficial Association (MEBA), a national organization with strong Great Lakes roots representing licensed engineering officers, invested in

Great Lakes training simulators and opened a state-of-the-art student training center. A student using the 6 million dollar simulator at the heart of the program had an experience that was just like sailing a ship but with several additional advantages. The student could be quickly put into any point on the lakes, the size and characteristics of the ship could be changed at will, and mistakes only resulted in a poor grade.

Toward the end of the century, the LCA and the unions ceded most educational responsibility to government agencies. For example, in 1975 the government-owned Great Lakes Radar Training Center was opened in Toledo to replace a course in radar offered by MEBA. The center was run by the Coast Guard and was designed to assist deck officers achieve the five-year recertification required in radar systems.[11] The center expanded rapidly. By 1978 it had added courses in Loran-C-based locational systems, gyrocompasses, automatic depth finders, radio direction finders, and fathometers.[12]

If in the 1970s the federal government was taking over continuing education, a different model was developing to educate new officers. In 1947 Great Lakes shipowners first experimented with employing cadets enrolled in college-level merchant-marine maritime academies.[13] In the late 1950s and early 1960s, the LCA wrote with great enthusiasm about the promise offered by newly added engineering classes at the U.S. Merchant Marine Academy at Kings Point, New York.[14] The academy, which opened just prior to World War II, offered a four-year program leading to a bachelor of science degree. Approximately 18 percent of the academy's students came from the Great Lakes region, and many were interested in careers on the lakes.[15]

What the LCA really hoped for, however, was a merchant marine academy located on the Great Lakes and focused on educating officers for lake vessels. In 1965, the Ontario Provincial Institute of Trades and Occupations established in Toronto the first four-year naval academy focused on Great Lakes vessels. On the American side of the water, in 1969 Northwestern Michigan College in Traverse City, Michigan, announced plans to form the Great Lakes Maritime Academy (GLMA)—plans that the LCA wholeheartedly endorsed. By 1978 the LCA was encouraging aspiring young officers to attend the GLMA, and had established a scholarship program to help make this possible.[16] At the same time, the LCA abandoned that part of its winter educational program designed for obtaining an officer's license. The GLMA offered its students college degrees, first at the associate's level and subsequently at the bachelor's level.[17]

GLMA's goal was to graduate one to two hundred new students annually, 60 percent trained in engineering and the remainder trained as deck officers, all of whom would be capable of successfully passing the necessary Coast Guard licensing examinations. The necessary enrollment to accomplish these goals was first reached in 1979. Despite problems finding jobs for graduates in the 1980s, the GLMA continued into the twenty-first century and remained a key pathway to an officer berth aboard a laker.[18]

These college-educated officers were not always welcome. Crews often engaged in heated discussions over the merits of officers who had worked their way up the ranks compared to officers freshly graduated from college. Graduates, some crew members claimed, lacked the practical skills of the old-timers. But other crew members responded that the graduates could take full advantage of the latest technological knowledge that improved both safety and economy. After a long night of discussion, most crew members ended up agreeing that the "good ones" among the academy graduates could pick up the practical skills they needed in a few years sailing, although talk then continued the next day about how many "good ones" actually came out of the academies.[19]

While the change in an officer's education was largely invisible to the casual observer's eye, what was much more obvious was the change in gender among the ship's officers. For the first three quarters of the twentieth century, sailing was a man's business. On the rare occasion that a woman was employed aboard a ship, she invariably worked in the galley.[20] This strict gender division among officers ended in the late 1970s, caused by women who had graduated from maritime colleges. In 1977, Marjorie Murtaugh boarded the freighter *John Dykstra* and became the first female officer to sail the Great Lakes. She was a graduate of the maritime academy at Kings Point, New York. In October 1979, eleven women were enrolled in the Great Lakes Maritime Academy in Traverse City, and by 1982 about 10 percent of the students enrolled in the GLMA were women, a level that was fairly constant for the rest of the century.[21]

Civil Rights legislation enacted by Congress in the 1960s also introduced women onto the decks of American lake freighters, often in the crew's quarters. Both management and union representatives were rather sanguine about their compliance with these laws, but anecdotal information suggests that gender was a factor in how unlicensed crew were treated.[22]

One woman wrote that after three years working on the ships, from 1973 to 1976, she was generally accepted, although a few people "made her initial employment period very difficult."[23] In 1976 two other women, both of whom served as porters at different times aboard the same boat, complained. One wrote, "I have tried very hard to please the Steward and Captain, which is almost impossible because they don't want women working on the boats. They talk to you rotten and treat you like a dog and are very beneath them."[24] A second female porter, ordered from the ship while it was docked at Detroit's Zug Island, contacted the company's home office to learn what she had done to be fired. She reported to her union that "Mr. Gilmore told me no, I had a very good work record but the steward didn't want no women on the ship."[25] It should be noted that the steward in question had a reputation as being hard to work for, and one of the women, while complaining about unfair treatment based on gender, did go out of her way to state that she worked with "some very nice gentlemen."[26] Despite a somewhat self-congratulatory attitude regarding the issue by management and labor, comments as late as 1997 suggest that employment problems relating to a person's gender did continue to appear on American boats.[27]

Canadian boats were more accommodating to women, perhaps because women had remained in the galleys of Canadian ships long after men had replaced women in the galleys of U.S. flag vessels. The first female captain on the lakes, Lillian Kluka, was appointed to a Canadian laker, the *Comeaudoc*, in 1986.[28] Serving as the ship's captain led to more than a few interesting stories. Captain Kluka recalled an early conversation with a shoreside official:

> "I'm here to see the captain," announced a dry dock representative. "I'm the Captain," she replied. "No, I mean the real Captain." "Am I not real enough?" "I'll come back later when there's someone here with more authority."

Another story told by Kluka was of passing through a lock in the Welland Canal and hearing a voice from shore say, "Look, there's a woman in the pilot house! She must be the Captain's wife." Added to these stereotypical observations was another from her crew. Notwithstanding her gender, the crew of the *Comeaudoc* still referred to Captain Kluka as "the old man," the term reserved for captains aboard most lake freighters. Despite her ability to see the humor in her situation, Kluka noted more seriously that when she assumed the "old man's" job, she, and other pioneering female officers, had to perform flawlessly. As she put it, if her ship had an accident, the story told around the lakes would not be about an unfortunate happenstance, but rather that "Lillian hit the wall."[29]

Whatever their education or gender, the number of individuals aboard a ship was always small. In the early years of the twentieth century, a typical American Great Lakes bulk freighter had a crew of about thirty-five to forty.[30] By the end of the century, the typical American crew had been reduced to about thirty or less.[31] Canadian ships at century's end tended to have a crew only about two-thirds the size of an American registered vessel, and the increasingly frequent tug-barge combinations that operated on the lakes did so with even fewer people aboard.

Whatever the exact number, crews divided into four broad categories, based on their responsibilities. In the early days of the century, the crew in the wheelhouse (forward) consisted of the deck officers—that is, the captain and the mates—as well as the wheelsmen who steered the ship. The ship's aft housed Engineering. Counted among this department were the chief engineer and his assistant engineers, oilers, firemen, and coal passers. In between were the watchmen and the deckhands, who helped load or unload the ship and did the day-to-day cleaning and maintenance that did not involve the engine. Also in the aft, but distinct from Engineering, was the galley with the chief cook (usually called the steward), assistant cooks, and porters. A ship with a self-unloading mechanism would usually have an additional four crewmen to operate and maintain that equipment.[32]

GALLEY

The steward ran the galley; he was the chief cook, supervisor, and person responsible for the paperwork. In addition to the steward, ships had a second cook, who was generally responsible for breakfast and was in charge of salads and desserts for the other meals. In the first half of the century, a ship usually carried a third cook to prepare a fourth full meal called the "night lunch," but in the 1960s the job fell to the second cook, who, before he left the galley for the evening, stocked a refrigerator with an array of late-night food, which might include sandwich fixings, various kinds of salads, potatoes, several kinds of meat for grilling, and everything a crew member might want for a breakfast.[33]

Galley porters helped with simple food-preparation tasks, such as peeling potatoes or vegetables and cleaning up after the meals. They washed the dishes and mopped the floors. Porters also made up the officers' rooms at least weekly.[34] On those boats built in the first three quarters of the century, separate dining rooms were constructed for officers and crew, with porters serving meals family-style. Aboard ships built after about 1970, the crew's dining room changed to a cafeteria.[35]

Though galley was often considered the lightest work aboard ship, the galley crew's day was long and often hot. One steward in the late 1990s reported working from 6:00 A.M. until 5:30 P.M. every day, with little or no breaks.[36] On a hot summer's day, anchored next to a roaring steel mill, with the stove going and the porter's hands in hot dishwater, the galley was a very uncomfortable place.[37] On the worst days, even the crew ate quickly to get away from the galley's heat.[38]

But everyone aboard knew that the galley crew mattered. As one wag had it:

You can live without friends,
You can live without books,
But you can't sail a ship
Without good cooks![39]

The quality of the table the steward set was something endlessly debated. Some writers claimed that the cooking on a freighter equaled that of a fine restaurant. As Jacques LesStrang put it, "Good food on the Great Lakes [is] a tradition that has grown with the maritime industry. It is a well known fact that many chief stewards are widely known throughout the Great Lakes for their excellent meals and enjoy the prestige and status near that of a chef in a fine hotel."[40] Certainly some stewards had the temperament of a great chef. One young porter described what happened when a steward who did not like to be interrupted began what she called "the ceremony of baking bread." A "hush fell upon the galley. Nobody dare speak."[41]

Were Great Lakes stewards really expert chefs? The reputation of Great Lakes stewards as being the equivalent of fine restaurant chefs was undoubtedly aided by those lucky enough to find themselves cruising during the summer months in the guest accommodations aboard the Ford freighters. The Ford fleet's flagship, the *Henry Ford II*, hosted frequent cruises by Henry Ford from 1924, the year the ship was put in service, until Henry Ford's death in 1947. To serve this role, the *Henry Ford II* was not only built with unusually luxurious passenger berths in the forward part of the ship, it was also equipped with a separate forward galley that was often used by the personal chef of Mr. and Mrs. Ford. Despite the frequent presence of their own chef, Mrs. Ford developed a fondness for cookies baked by the ship's regular steward, Isaac Syria. She was so fond of the cookies that an elaborate process was created so she could enjoy them, freshly baked, when she was at the Fords' home in Dearborn, Michigan. Ford engineers created a custom container for Isaac's cookies that was placed aboard the *Henry Ford II*. When the ship neared the Soo, Syria baked fresh cookies and placed them into this container. While the *Henry Ford II* locked through, the container was put over the side, where a waiting truck would whisk the container with its special cargo of cookies to a nearby airport. There, a waiting company airplane would immediately fly the delicacies to Dearborn.[42] It would not take many such deliveries to create the impression that if even the cookies were of such quality, the rest of the cooking must be superb.

Those who rode as guests on a freighter only added to the mystique surrounding the meals. Guests frequently commented on the quality of the food. As one wrote in the guestbook of the *William A. Irvin*:

> The food is marvelous never ending;
> Any dish you may desire;
> Willis will cook and feed you full;
> Without a crane you can't retire.[43]

Another guest wrote in the same log:

> The galley, the haunt of Willis, Dave and James
> With most fantastical cuisine,
> The fanciest appetite it tames
> But on this voyage there's no chance
> of you're keeping lean.[44]

It was also noted by the crew that when guests boarded any vessel, the quality of the food improved. As one sailor put it, "You really ate when the passenger season was on."[45]

In truth, the comparison between the food in a freighter's galley and that found in a fine restaurant was exaggerated. On some ships, the cook was unimaginative. One sailor recalled how on his ship the menu was usually meat, potatoes, canned peas, and canned carrots.[46] Another sailor wrote home in 1938 that while he had enjoyed a good chicken dinner, supper consisted of "wieners."[47] As for fresh-baked goods, most ships converted to store-bought bread in the 1930s, and as frozen products became more available, crews tended to get more and more food from the freezer.[48] One of the most novel complaints made to their union by a crew in the 1960s was a demand for better meals and fewer leftovers.[49]

Another reason to question the luxuriousness of the menu was the method by which stewards were promoted. Cooking skills were rarely the primary reason for promotion, which was usually based on seniority and attendance at a mandatory cooking school. Some alleged the only rule for galley promotion was that "if you didn't poison anyone" you got the job.

Indeed, stewards with hopes of offering a more inspirational menu were often frustrated by changes in procurement practices and the traditional tastes of the crew. A steward who prided himself on his skill longed for the "bygone days" when the supply boat included such luxuries as fresh meat so that he could actually handpick the cuts he planned to serve.[50] The luxury of picking one's own supplies, however, had an unexpected downside. Another steward reminiscing about the "old days" recalled that stewards were very competitive and would sometimes sabotage another man's cooking. A visit to the supply boat was not only an opportunity to handpick meat, but also a chance to slip salt into the flour destined for another vessel.[51] And perhaps one should not make too much out of the steward's ability to handpick groceries, since sailors in the 1930s gave the supply boat at the Soo the rather unappetizing moniker of the "gut tub."[52] In later years the ship was referred to by the equally unappealing name of the "garbage boat."[53]

The creative side of an exceptional steward could also be stymied by the choices of the largely working-class crew, who often had very traditional tastes. A steward who prided himself on his culinary ability was very unhappy when he found himself cooking on a ship crewed mainly by men from Presque Isle, Michigan. He served innovative stir-fries and other low-fat options. The crew ignored these dishes, instead eating the Polish sausage, raw hamburger with lots of onion and peppers in it, and pickled bologna that they had grown up enjoying.

Regardless of the steward's skill, certain meals were traditions on Great Lakes vessels, such as fish on Friday and steak or prime rib on Saturday. Some shipping companies also had their own unique food traditions. On one line, pickles were served only on Sunday, and stuffed olives only appeared when turkey was served. But regardless of the shipping line or the steward, the Thanksgiving meal was a feast that represented the high point of the galley crew's season.[54]

A typical 1941 Thanksgiving meal included freshly roasted turkey and roasted goose, as well as baked ham. The meat was served with peas, squash, brussels sprouts, and corn. Dessert included a choice of pumpkin pie with whipped cream, mince pie, apple pie, plum pudding with brandy sauce, or fruit cake. Before the meal began, the crew was offered a little something to whet the appetite: tomato juice, shrimp cocktail, royal asparagus salad, celery hearts, or stuffed olives. For beverages, the crew could choose between port wine, apple cider, coffee, tea, or milk. When the dinner was finally over, the men were invited to sit back and enjoy mixed nuts, fruits, candy, cigars, cigarettes, and an after-dinner mint. It took two to three days to prepare this extravaganza, and the galley crew looked forward to it as a day to shine.[55]

If anything, the Thanksgiving feast expanded after World War II. In 1947 the galley crew of the *Louis W. Hill* served their shipmates roast suckling pig, turkey, goose, duck, chicken, and ham (each with its own unique dressing); three different pies: apple, pumpkin, and mincemeat; and all the trimmings.[56] The 1976 Thanksgiving dinner on the *Charles M. White* included six appetizers; four entrees, including lobster tails; and a baker's dozen of choices for dessert.[57]

Stewards did not take kindly to anything that interfered with their moment to shine. In 1942 the Thanksgiving meal was laid out on the *George W. Perkins* when unanticipated rough seas literally tossed the food onto the deck. The crew ended up eating turkey sandwiches and the steward refused to talk to the captain for almost a month, clearly believing that the "old man" should have known about the heavy weather and, more importantly, told the steward about it.[58]

Serving meals in bad weather was a challenge. Wet tablecloths tended to keep the plates from sliding, and in truly rough weather "rolling bars," half-inch pipes that came up over both the edge of the tables and the stove, were used to try to keep things in their place.[59] Stories abounded, particularly in the early decades of the century, of how in bad weather the "forward" crew would be cut off for days from the "aft" galley, leaving them with little or nothing to eat. A partial solution to the problem was a "lifeline," a metal cable strung a few feet above the deck from one end of the ship to the other. A sailor could "clip" a short rope tied to the sailor's waist to the lifeline and make his way forward or aft.[60] However, in very heavy seas someone would need to be "a brave man or damned fool" to risk the trip even if clipped to the lifeline.[61] Stories regarding crews isolated forward by weather became less common after the late 1930s, when new ships were built with "tunnels," passages for the crew below deck that ran from bow to stern and were placed between the cargo hold wall and the ship's outer hull.[62] But in rough weather the tunnel still was something to which a new crew member needed to adjust as the ships were designed to bend, causing the tunnel to also bend, twisting and swaying like a wet noodle.[63]

The size of the Thanksgiving feast did, however, reflect a standard that existed on almost every boat: the quantity of food available was prodigious.[64] It was often, in fact, too plentiful, and the crew frequently gained weight while onboard. This tendency was not helped by practices such as steak-eating contests. One sailor recalled eating five or six T-bone steaks at a sitting, but losing to a fellow who could down six or seven.[65] Another sailor recalled skipping one meal a day to keep from putting on extra pounds.[66] Occasionally a company might try to address the problem by ordering reduced portion sizes, but whether the change was designed to help the crew be healthy or, as the crew more often thought, to save money, crews disliked ships known to be "poor feeders."[67] As one sailor recalled of the 1920 season, "Older sailors knew every ship that passed, who the 'old man' was, and above all the quality of the food it served its crew."[68]

The galley was a place about which everyone on board had an opinion. It was always a topic of conversation, and if a crewmember didn't like a meal, it was obvious who to blame.[69] Of course stewards had their own take on the complaints. As one tartly noted, "If they don't like what I've prepared, they can go next door."[70]

ENGINEERING

Sharing the stern of the boat with the galley was the Engineering Department. Engineering's job was deceptively simple: keep the ship moving. The Engineering Department usually consisted of a chief engineer, three assistant engineers, three "oilers," and in the spring a complement of "wipers" who helped complete any cleaning that could not be finished before the ship first sailed in the spring.[71] By act of Congress, the chief engineer and his immediate assistants had been declared officers in 1896.[72] Also within the engineer's jurisdiction were firemen and coal passers who, when coal was the fuel of choice, stoked and maintained the fire in the ship's boilers.

The chief engineer had overall responsibility for all of the ship's mechanical systems, the most important of course being the ship's propulsion system. As time passed, the position became more and more administrative. Watch assistants were responsible for day-to-day operation of the equipment, performing routine maintenance tasks, and supervising the oilers and wipers. The chief engineer kept the paperwork, oversaw what happened in the engine room, and dealt with the most severe problems.

When a crisis did occur, the chief engineer often showed great resourcefulness. One sailor recalled that as his ship was passing through the Detroit River, a critical bearing in the engine began to overheat, a problem that inevitably would cause the bearing to fail. When the bearing failed, the engine would stop and the ship would be adrift in the narrow river channel, almost inevitably causing an accident. Faced with a critical problem and with no time to implement a proper solution, the quick-thinking engineer devised an unorthodox fix. Undoubtedly to the captain's great concern, or more likely without telling the captain, the engineer shut down the engine long enough to thread a fire hose above the critical bearing. After restarting the engine, the engineer turned on the fire hose, creating a steady stream of cold water that poured onto the bearing, cooling it and keeping the engine operating until a proper repair could be accomplished.[73]

If the chief engineer was the person in charge, oilers and wipers had the opposite status. An oiler, later known as a "Qualified Member of the Engine Department" (QMED), was the person who made the rounds, checking, cleaning, and otherwise making sure the engine was properly running. In the early years of the century, about once every half-hour an oiler would literally touch various key parts to make sure nothing was overheating—or as one sailor described it, "tickling the cranks and shaking hands with the crossheads."[74] Tickling cranks and shaking hands with crossheads was a job not to be done carelessly, since it often meant reaching through moving parts to touch the critical bearings.[75] As time passed, however, automation and remote sensing equipment replaced the sailor's hand.

At the beginning of the twentieth century, most cargo ships used coal to fire their boilers. A 600-foot-long vessel, a "top-of-the-line" ship at the beginning of the twentieth century, would consume 320 to 350 tons of coal on a typical seven-day voyage.[76] It took six railroad cars full of coal to completely fill a freighter's fuel bunker.[77]

Once the captain called for steam, the "Black Gang" went to work. Stoking the boiler's firebox with coal was hot, dirty work, and temperatures in the work areas could reach 140 degrees Fahrenheit.[78] The heat, ash, and fumes made the boiler room a place many men avoided.[79] As James Oliver Curwood, in one of his less romantic observations about life aboard a freighter, expressed it:

> the din is fearful, the heat of the furnace-room insufferable, and when once each
> half-minute a furnace door is opened for fresh fuel, and writhing torrents of fires

and light illumine the gloomy depths, the tenderfoot passenger looks up nervously to where his eyes catch glimpses of light and freedom far above him.[80]

A contrary view of the workspace, however, was voiced in early spring and in late fall. During the cold months, the one sure warm place on a metal ship covered with ice would be the boiler area.

On many ships the Black Gang consisted of a fireman working with a single coal passer, but some ships required two firemen per watch. The decision was usually based on the size of the ship's engine, as an engine that could generate more than 1,500 horsepower generally required two firemen to fuel its boiler.[81] The fireman's craft, while physically backbreaking, was also an applied art. A good fireman did not simply hurl coal into the firebox; he placed it strategically within the firebox so that the fire burned evenly. The objective was an even fire throughout the firebox that would keep the steam pressure constant. An uneven fire most often resulted in one of two problems. Either too much steam was created, only to be wasted as it was released without use through the emergency pressure valve, or too little steam was made, causing the ship's speed to decrease. Either way, it was the fireman's fault and he was sure to hear about it from the chief engineer. Although every fireman had a steam gauge available to keep track of the pressure, a good fireman rarely looked at the gauge—he could tell if things were right from the look of the fire itself.[82]

Firemen also were concerned about the quality of coal used. If a ship had a load of bad coal, more of it was needed to keep the fire burning properly. Bad coal also meant that the firebox would have to be cleaned twice as often.[83] Bad coal often meant the fireman couldn't keep up a full head of steam, but neither the captain nor the chief engineer were inclined to accept the fireman's plea that he could not maintain pressure because the coal was substandard. Thus for several reasons firemen kept track of which ships tended to save money by purchasing cheaper coal.[84]

Because of the quantity of coal that needed to be moved, firemen were assisted by coal passers or shovelers, who brought the coal from the storage bunker to the waiting fireman. Gravity made coal flow down a funnel from the bunker above into the boiler area. The passer filled a wheelbarrow full of coal at the funnel and rolled it to the waiting fireman, who then shoveled it into the boiler. As the bunker began to empty, coal would pile up on the sides and often became stuck. When this happened the passer had to go topside, enter the coal bunker, and shovel coal into the middle of the bunker, where it would fall downward. He then rushed down to the boiler area and moved the coal from the chute to the fireman.[85]

In addition to shoveling coal into the boiler, two or three times a day the fireman had to clean ash from the firebox and see to it that it was removed from the ship. Cleaning the fire meant the fireman knocked the coals out of half of the box while keeping the ship at full steam with the other half. Firemen did this by "winging over" the still good coals onto the half of the firebox being left undisturbed, and then use a hoe-like device to pull still hot 200-degree ash out of the other half of the firebox. As the waste came out of the box, the coal passer hosed water on it, and for a few moments it looked like fog rolling into the St. Marys River. When the fog lifted, the fireman was already standing back. If he had been quick enough, he had avoided burning himself. After one side of the box was clean, the whole process was repeated on the other side.[86]

Once the ash was removed from the box, the passer shoveled it aside and broke up any large pieces, called "clinkers." The passer then used the "ash gun" to blow the material overboard. The gun was simply a six-inch pipe that exited the vessel above the waterline. A pump forced hot pressurized water or live steam into the pipe. As the passer shoveled ash into an opening in the pipe, the hot water or steam shot it out of the ship's side. All went quickly and well if the passer had completely broken up the clinkers. However, a large clinker would plug the ash gun, shooting hot water or steam back at the passer. If the pipe was plugged, the pump was shut off, and the passer used a metal bar to dislodge the clinker. Cleaning a clinker out of the pipe could be tedious. Little sympathy was offered to a man who might have been burned by the hot water or steam, and although a few clinkers were almost inevitable, a fireman had no patience for passers who wasted time by repeatedly plugging the pipe.[87]

Because of the nature of the work, recruiting men for the Black Gang was often difficult. Coal passing was particularly onerous. The job was so disliked that the LaFollette Act of 1915 outlawed pressing deckhands into service as coal passers. Deckhands signed on to a job that involved a great deal of physical labor, but passing coal was not something deckhands readily agreed to do.[88] Indeed the work was so hard that as a concession, on some ships, where the usual work schedule was "six hours on, six hours off," the Black Gang worked only "three on" and "six off."[89] Under the best of conditions work in the boiler room was a hard job, but when the weather became rough and the ship began to pitch and roll, it could become almost impossible to move coal or shovel it accurately.[90]

Advances in technology would eventually replace the Black Gang with machinery. In the late 1930s automatic stoking machines began to move the coal from the storage bunker to the boiler, thus eliminating the passer's work.[91] In the 1950s fuel oil began to replace coal as the principal fuel used by lake boats, eliminating altogether the need for firemen.[92] The transition away from coal occurred quite suddenly. As late as the 1950s, there were 107 hand-fired vessels sailing the lakes. However in 1964, only one hand-fired vessel remained in service.[93]

DECK CREW

Deckhands required very little experience. A sailor who hired onto his first ship in March 1904 recalled being concerned because he had absolutely no qualifications for the job. To his surprise, the officer on board asked him only one question: "Can you scrub?" A quick "yes" got him the job.[94] If there was ever a shortage of deckhands on a Ford boat unloading iron or coal at Ford's Rouge plant, the problem was solved by recruiting a volunteer from the plant's dock to fill the vacancy. No experience on a ship was required. Anyone capable of working on the dock was equally qualified to work as a deckhand.[95]

Deckhands performed several basic jobs on the boat, all of them built around the need for manual labor. They helped load or unload the ship, which included opening all the hatches as the ship approached port, and then closing the hatches as the ship began to make way. When not working with the hatches or otherwise involved in loading or unloading, deckhands kept busy cleaning or performing basic maintenance tasks, such as painting.

Loading and unloading was work to be done in the quickest and most timely way possible. The process began before the ship reached dock and often continued well after the ship was underway—whether that was 3:00 P.M. or 3:00 A.M.[96] The process began and ended with the hatch covers. Covers had to be removed as the ship approached port to load or unload, and put back as the ship got underway. In the pre–World War II era, ship hatches evolved through three distinct generations: wooden, telescoping, and solid metal. For much of the century, a deckhand might find any of the three types aboard a particular vessel. Whichever type was used, the process was arduous. Solid metal hatches were the easiest of the group to handle, telescoping fell in the middle, and wooden hatches involved the hardest physical work. If firemen rated ships by the quality of coal used, deckhands ranked ships by their type of hatch. Just as it was claimed that firemen knew all about a ship's coal before boarding, it was also claimed that experienced deckhands knew the ships with wooden hatch covers by name and avoided working on them.[97]

Late in the season, ice would freeze the hatch covers in place, adding a new complexity to an already tedious task. The only solutions were to chip off the ice with axes or use hot water to melt the ice. Chipping was harder work, but a sure thing; using hot water was a gamble. If it failed, the crew not only still needed to chip ice off the hatches, but they were now working on a deck coated with a new, smooth layer of ice, much like a skating rink.[98]

Working around open hatches was dangerous. Falling into the hold was a common, and sometimes deadly, mishap. If a deckhand was lucky there was a "soft" cargo to cushion the fall, but if not, he or she could fall fifty feet onto a steel deck. But a deckhand need not fall into a hatch to be injured. There were many other ways to be hurt. Once lines had been thrown over the side and attached to the dock, a sudden movement of the ship could cause lines to jerk violently, throwing a man onto the deck or into the water.[99] Freak accidents also occurred. One unlucky person broke his leg on a brutally cold day in Chicago. He had been assigned to stand on deck and call out the distance as the ship approached the dock, but to keep warm he kept darting into and out of the ship. Without his realizing it, as he stood outside, the half-melted snow on his boot froze to the deck. When he turned to run back inside, the frozen boot proved more firm than his leg bone.[100]

As a ship was docking, one crew member was given a job generally disliked by all: being put over the side of the ship in the bosun's chair to catch the ship's lines as they were thrown from ship to shore. Even if the ship approached a dock with workers, it was the ship's crew who had the responsibility for handling the lines, not the dockworkers. To do this, a deckhand sitting in a chair attached to a crane would be suspended over the side of the ship. As the crane's boom came over the dock, the deckhand would be lowered to the ground. As one sailor described it, "In a few seconds I had cleared the railing and was over the cold dark water. I looked down as the wind buffeted me and it looked like a long way down. When I was over the pier I hollered to Frank, and he answered, 'Okay, here ya go.' I dropped like a rock. [Frank] Gable stopped the running line just as my feet hit the pier. I stopped with a jerk and jumped off the chair."[101] Once on the dock, the crew member would catch lines thrown from the vessel to make the ship fast.[102]

Although the bosun's chair was disliked, it was a considerable improvement over past practice. Prior to its introduction, a line with knots tied every two feet or so was simply tossed over the side, and a crew member was expected to climb down the rope and jump onto the dock. Unsurprisingly, climbing accidents were common. In bad weather the unlucky crew member ordered over the side frequently lost his grip. The bosun's chair was first used by Canadian ships in 1912 and appeared on the U.S. side of the lakes in 1915.[103]

After a ship was loaded or unloaded and the hatches made secure, it was usually necessary to wash down the decks.[104] Almost every cargo required deck cleaning. Iron ore, for example, was claylike and sticky, clinging to everything.[105] Coal was always the dirtiest cargo. One galley crew member complained that when the ship was loading coal, he could wipe a plate clean and within five minutes there would be enough dust to write your initials on it.[106]

When cleaning, the deck crew would usually divide themselves into two groups, with one starting at the front of the ship and the other at the back. New deckhands often found "hosing" to be fun at first, but it was hard work that quickly became repetitive. After several hours of washing, a person's shoulders would ache.[107] In bad weather it was very difficult, and in winter it was dangerous and sometimes impossible as the spray washed back on crewmen and froze to both them and the deck.[108]

Depending on the next cargo, the crew might also have to wash out the hold, as cargo contamination was a serious issue. If a cargo of coal followed one of iron ore, the hold needed to be thoroughly cleaned, since coal was not supposed to contain ore. The job was a bit like cleaning out a high school gymnasium, top to bottom.[109] Self-unloading ships would also clean the gates that opened up in the bottom of the hold and the conveyor belts that moved the cargo from the hold up to a boom and over the side, to ensure that each load of cargo was not affected by what had preceded it.[110]

After the deck was washed off from cargo, deckhands began a round of respon- sibilities that included general cleaning, preparing metal for paint, or painting.[111] General cleaning was often done using a concoction called "soojie." Though spelled many ways and created using as many recipes, soojie usually began as a mix of about two dozen bars "of the hardest, darkest, vile-smelling soap I had ever seen" mixed into pails of hot water. The hot soapy water was poured into a barrel, where it was mixed with more water and a quart of turpentine. A steam pipe was "injected" into the barrel and the brew cooked for about thirty minutes before being ready to use.[112] After cleaning, the soojie was either washed off with a firehose or, if inside, rinsed off with a mop and a pail of clean water.[113] The longevity of the formula proved that it cleaned very well, but it was also brutal on the skin of the deckhands. Even when crew wore rain gear to keep the material off of their bodies, the liquid would inevitably run down their arms when they worked overhead. After a day using soojie, a person's arms would be red and raw from the chemicals.[114]

Perhaps the only advantage of cold weather was that it brought to an end most painting and cleaning. The weather made it impossible for outside work to be done, and thus deckhands often found themselves with little or nothing to do as the ship traveled from one port to the next. One deckhand recalled how, in desperation to find something for him to do, he was assigned to crack nuts for the cook who was making fudge. When even kitchen help was unneeded, a deckhand might be told by an officer to "go change light bulbs," a code for disappearing from view until the next meal.[115]

At the beginning of the twentieth century the watchman did exactly that: he would stand at the bow of the ship looking for hazards and alerting the captain or mate in command. In the century's early days the watchman's role was vital, and brutal. While on some days he might stand in glorious weather, the watchman also stood outside in rain, sleet, gales, and ice spray.[116] With the invention of radar and other navigational aids that appeared after World War II, the job was largely eliminated. At the end of the twentieth century, a watch was only posted when the ship was in narrow waters, primarily to look for small recreational boats that might come near the ship.[117]

THE PILOTHOUSE

The captain, the deck officers, and the wheelsmen spent much of their day in the pilothouse, which on lake freighters was traditionally located at the ship's bow.

The lowest-ranking member of the crew was the wheelsman. The wheelsman steered the ship, which was a physically demanding job. On older boats, moving the wheel took muscle. In 1964, on the vintage *Douglass Houghton*, it took two hands to turn the 6-foot steering wheel. Although the rudder itself was turned by a small steam engine, the system used cables that ran the length of the ship from the wheel to the steam-powered device that moved the rudder. Not only were there several hundred feet of cable to move, but as it got cold the grease on the cable got sticky and the wheel became even harder to pull. In cold weather even a strong wheelsman would be worn out by the end of a watch.[118]

Technically the wheelsman's responsibility was only to follow orders, but a good wheelsman could make any captain or mate's job much easier.[119] Maneuvering a ship through the busy, narrow channels on the lakes took experience and skill, which a well-seasoned wheelsman usually had.[120] One retired captain remembered that when he became a third mate and was just learning the job, "he learned a great deal from him [the wheelsman] and respected him."[121] Looked at another way, many a new wheelsman found himself receiving invaluable training for a deck officer's license by observing an experienced captain or mate.[122] As one gruff old captain told a "youngster" who was nervously eyeing an approaching vessel, "Don't you worry about that boat. You just steer that course I gave you. If we're too close to that boat it's my fault."[123]

The wheelsman, however, also could take the blame when something went wrong. One wheelsman recalled how on a foggy day near the entrance of the St. Marys River the captain had a sixth sense that something was amiss. He ordered the engine stopped, which proved a wise decision. Minutes later the slowing ship grounded on a sandbar, roughly a mile off course. The unhappy captain questioned the wheelsman carefully regarding the compass headings he was holding. Eventually both wheelsman and captain realized that the problem was a large metal wrench left very near the magnetic compass. The metal from the wrench had thrown the compass off ever so slightly—but in the narrow channel the difference caused the ship to run aground.[124]

Learning to steer a freighter took practice. Because of the vessel's size, the ship was very unresponsive to the wheel. A good wheelsman learned to anticipate the ship's response and often corrected course before the ship had actually responded. Another problem was "slack" in the chains that connected the wheel to the rudder. Slack could vary, and thus the exact response of the rudder to the wheel could vary. Because of challenges such as these, it took time to learn the craft. New wheelsmen invariably overcorrected, or used "too much wheel," which caused the ship to wobble back and forth rather than sail in a straight line.[125] A truly experienced wheelsman might learn several tricks, such as standing backwards when leaving a port and lining the ship up with the port's receding range lights, which were designed to guide ships into the harbor. It was a clever trick, provided the wheelsman also remembered to do everything backwards from the way it would be done if he were looking forward.[126] A wheelsman also had to learn to compensate for the ship's load. A heavily loaded ship was much more sluggish at responding to the wheel than a ship riding in ballast. One wheelsman commented about an overloaded ship sailing during World War II that "It handled just like a log."[127]

For all its challenges, the wheelsman's job also had its delights. Fred Dutton described the view from the wheelhouse in poetic terms:

It was always fine to steer a steamship up the St. Marys River on a dark, clear night—an exhilarating thing. Tonight it was at its best. A small north breeze rippled the water, humming in the rigging. The moon was setting over the dark pines to the west while the northern lights flung their eerie banners flaring the northern sky. All else was dark, except for the line of buoys blinking on either side and the brilliant gleam of the range lights ahead and astern. You felt as though you were in another world. It was strong wine.[128]

The principal job of the mates was to stand watch and operate the ship in the captain's absence. Most first mates were also responsible for the loading of the ship. This was no small responsibility. The basic task was to make sure that the maximum amount of cargo was loaded and that it was properly distributed. Too little cargo and fuel was wasted and money lost. Too much cargo and the ship would ride too deeply, making it impossible to pass through the shallowest channels on the lakes. Placing too much cargo on one side or the other would cause the ship to list. A ship could also bend.[129] Too little weight in the middle and the ship would "sag," bending downward at the bow and stern. Too much weight in the middle and the ship would "hog," bending upward at the bow and stern.[130] The first mate not only took all this into consideration but also needed to be aware of the preferences of the ship's wheelsmen, many of whom preferred just a bit more weight in the stern. This caused the boat to settle, sinking the rudder a little deeper in the water, and, in the opinion of many wheelsmen, made the ship steer better.[131]

For the first third of the twentieth century, when the mate loaded the ship he was also responsible for maintaining a safety margin. Everyone agreed that to sail safely a ship required a certain amount of "freeboard"—that is, the distance between the waterline and the main deck. Should the ship begin to take on water, the "freeboard" served as an emergency reserve of buoyancy. Everyone also knew that iron ore was so heavy that if a ship's hold was filled to the top with it, the ship would quite literally sink. But what was not clear was when a ship was overloaded. Early in the century, the amount of freeboard to be maintained was a matter of judgment made by each captain and mate. In 1919 a "Shore Captains" committee was formed by the LCA, which issued recommendations on the subject.[132] In 1936 the Coast Guard wrote into official regulation an elegant solution to the problem adopted by the English sixty years earlier. A maximum load line, or "Plimsoll mark," was painted on every ship. It was a violation of Coast Guard regulations for a ship to leave port if the line was not visible.[133]

The junior officers, particularly the second and third mates, often learned much about their craft from a good captain. Bill Wilson, who eventually became a captain in his own right, first signed on as a third mate in 1950. The ship's master was a crotchety fellow with a sharp tongue but great skill. Sailing without radar he could thread the St. Marys River when fog stopped virtually every other ship. He proceeded slowly, found each navigation buoy, and made turns at the proper locations by memory. He could also dock his big ship without the aid of tugs, a rare accomplishment in those days. "That guy could do it," Wilson remembered. "You learned by watching that."[134]

As Wilson and many others who served aboard the ships noted, captains stood apart. Their primary responsibility was to deliver the cargo on time, within costs, and without damage to the ship. For much of the century, how they did it was up to them. Most were soft-spoken men who nevertheless conveyed authority. Most were also somewhat aloof.[135] A few ran to personal extremes. Regardless of how easygoing or eccentric he was, the captain was the "old man," and the crew tended to avoid him.[136] This isolation, coupled with the huge responsibility placed on his shoulders, made the job emotionally difficult. Always on call, captains were paid to worry. As one person observed, "they became nervous and gray-haired at the age of fifty."[137] Few captains managed to avoid this fate, but as even a captain who apparently dealt well with stress said, "It's a great way to make a dollar; 99% boredom, and 1% pure hell."[138]

Most days the captain of a ship with a good crew could merely watch with satisfaction as jobs were well done. But that seemingly easily made money was tempered with the knowledge that everything ultimately rested on the captain. Sooner or later "pure hell" would test every resource he or she possessed, with the fate of the ship and the crew resting on a decision made in seconds.

Captains were also, by nature, a competitive group. Quick trips and even quicker turnarounds were ways the "home office" measured a good captain, and captains would resort to various tactics to achieve them. Competition was a constant feature in a captain's life throughout the century.[139] As one captain put it, "caution may be rewarded, but it won't hang up records."[140]

Summer passengers tended to see the captain in a noble light. In 1950, Mark Murphy described the captain of the *Harry Coulby* this way: "Captain Saunders is a stocky, growling, wholly pleasant man of sixty, and he knows the lakes, their traffic lanes, shoals, rocks, harbors, weather and vagaries better than he does the streets of his home town of Buffalo."[141] Crews, however, who sailed with a captain not only during the pleasant summer but also in the hard spring and winter, often saw things differently. What most crew members observed, recalled, and endlessly told stories about were the captains' idiosyncrasies. Captain stories were unending. A few of them serve as archetypes, and others simply deserve repeating.

Some captains were deeply religious. One was known to deliver a virtual sermon in the form of a prayer before meals. Officers, who could not begin eating until the captain's invocation was concluded, watched their food grow cold as the ship's master prayed:

> O Lord, lift up our feet from the rough road of life and help us to safely cross the gangplank of temptation into the ship of salvation. Let the hand of prudence guide our helm, the winds of love fill our sails, and the Good Book be our compass. And Almighty God, whose patience with humanity is everlasting, keep all hidden rocks of adversity off our course; let our bow cut clean the fresh waters of righteousness; steer us clear of Satan's derelicts; and may the bright rays of hope never die out of the lighthouses along the shore that we may make the run of life without disaster. And, oh Lord, if it be thy pleasure, let the tides bear unto us in letters of gold the true meaning of the Ten Commandments, that we may be mariners worthy of thy blessing. Let not our eyes be darkened by fogs of evil; keep ringing loud for our guidance the bell-buoys of faith. And when at last we have sailed into and anchored in the very port of death, may the good skipper of the universe say: "Well done, thou good and faithful mariner, come and sign the log and receive eternal happiness as your salvage reward."[142]

Other captains were more inclined to consign their troubles to alternative salvage. Captain David "goddam-it-to-hell" Huser got his unusual nickname from his seeming inability to speak a sentence that did not include the phrase.[143]

If Huser could sound like a petty tyrant, some captains acted out the role. A sailor recalled two captains who were more than demanding regarding their meals. One captain demanded pie daily, served with whipped cream on Sunday. Another captain wanted a sausage sandwich for breakfast. When the cook delivered a bacon sandwich with the explanation that there was no sausage left, the captain hurled the unanticipated meal to the deck, and in clear language well suited to a ship's deck, but not to a book for general readers, informed the cook that he wanted sausage, whether there was any onboard or not.[144]

Other captains used their authority to settle old scores. One sailor told the story of a Saginaw, Michigan, grocer who regularly boarded the ship to sell his goods and brought presents for the captain and scorn for everyone else. Eventually the often-scorned first mate inherited command of the ship. When the boat next docked at Saginaw and the grocer arrived with his usual gifts, the now promoted first mate ordered the grocer off the ship.[145]

Tyrants, however, occasionally had to deal with minor rebellions. When one sailor was promoted from porter to second cook, the captain complained long and loud about a "college boy" getting the job. The steward stood firm, firing back that he was tired of covering for drunks who missed the ship, and wanted as his second cook a sober "college boy" who could be counted on to do his job. In the end the steward got his way and the college boy got the job, although he seems to have also retained some of his porter duties, among them making up the captain's quarters. On his last day aboard, the college student took advantage of this latter responsibility to get a bit of revenge: he short-sheeted the captain's bed before going over the side to begin the fall semester at school.[146]

A few captains drank excessively. One sailor from the 1960s recalled serving on a ship where, after docking, the captain frequently led his crew into port for "pizza, pizza, pizza," which was code for heavy drinking at the nearest sailor's bar. When they returned, the captain and most of the crew were drunk. Fortunately, the captain was a jovial drunk who understood his limitations. Ordering the ship to cast off, he ceded responsibility to the usually sober first mate and retired to his quarters.[147] Another sailor from a generation earlier recalls a heavy-drinking captain who, when asked when the ship would reach Saginaw, responded, "in about six cans of beer."[148]

And a few were just plain lucky. Edward Perrine recalled the stories his father, a chief engineer, told about Alfred Revenew. On paper, Captain Revenew was a model officer. But one day, when young Edward asked his father about the captain, he was surprised by the answer. "No son he is really a poor captain, but he is simply the luckiest man in the world, and luck wins over ability every time." Revenew was a poor boat handler. When docking he seemed to make all the wrong moves and ran around the wheelhouse screaming. His propensity for doing the wrong thing at the wrong time, but somehow getting away with it, was so well known that whenever he was about to dock the boat, various off-duty members of the crew would assemble quietly to see what piece of luck would save him this time. Revenew was no more capable on the open lake. Once, running at full speed on a very foggy Lake Superior, a clearly dangerous decision, the inevitable happened: another ship appeared out of the fog on a collision course. The crew of both ships used the few seconds available to them to prepare for the crash. The boats came so close together you could shake hands with the other crew, but Revenew's luck held—they missed. Revenew's luck also played a part in saving his ship from another disaster.[149]

One night Captain Revenew arrived at the entrance to Duluth harbor in a raging storm. Revenew's only choice was to run his ship back and forth in front of the narrow harbor entrance, hoping that a short break in the storm would let him slip into port. But Revenew's fabled luck took hold. Although the storm blew strong, the wind shifted suddenly and the ship rolled out of a trough perfectly in line with the harbor entrance. The captain called for full power and ran the ship for the harbor entrance. When a ship suddenly increases to full steam, for a few moments it actually loses power—which in these circumstances could have caused a fatal wreck. For a moment it appeared that this would happen, but luck again intervened; a huge wave slammed the stern, burying the propeller in water. The wave gave the ship's engineer just enough time to get up to full steam. In fact for a brief period, the skillful engineer managed to run the engine at double its rated horsepower. Although the chief couldn't keep the engine revolving at such a wild pace for long, he managed to hold both the power up and the engine together long enough for the ship to shoot safely into the harbor.[150] Luck indeed won out.

Although captains were often portrayed as men of deep thought, most were not great conversationalists. A captain knew everything there was to know about his boat, but having spent most of his life learning those critical details, he often lacked the capacity or interest to discuss anything else.[151] Captains who were asked to take passengers as guests on their boats often looked for a way to escape from their charges. Captain Harry Anderson, who commanded some of the finest ships in the Cleveland-Cliffs fleet, left standing orders that if he had not appeared in the wheelhouse a half-hour after dinner with the guests, the mate on duty should place a call to the guest's lounge, requesting the captain's presence.[152] Guests were not unaware of this tendency among captains. One wrote in the guest log of the *William A Irvin*:

Captain Whit waved goodby,
To his crew gave a whistle,
And the *Irvin* receded like the

down of a thistle.
But we heard him exclaim ere he
hove out of sight,
"God, now they have gone;
I guess they're alright!"[153]

Over time the captain's job evolved from that of being primarily a mariner to one that combined nautical skills with those of a plant manager. Shipping companies had always looked at how economically a captain ran his boat.[154] But prior to 1945 the economic measures of a captain's success were fairly simple: the home office wanted to know how much was hauled, how long it took, and a few figures about coal consumption and the cost of the galley. After World War II, many companies put ever more stringent cost-accounting measures into place to judge the effectiveness of ships and their captains. According to the then manager of the Ford fleet, when quantification was introduced by him in 1945, it did not sit well with the "old-timers."[155] In 1960, the Pittsburgh fleet established elaborate managerial standards by which a captain's performance would be judged. The Pittsburgh fleet measures took cost accounting to new levels, and made clear to its captains that the bottom line was economic, not nautical.[156]

LIFE ONBOARD

Whatever his or her job, a sailor's entire life revolved around the ship. Unlike employment in a typical office or factory, a job onboard a lake freighter uniquely defined the sailor's companions and world. Before the era of inexpensive electronic communication, a sailor's life was measured by the 500- to 600-foot length of the ship. It might be supplemented by the occasional letter or package delivered by the post office, the happy sight of a loved one shouting greetings at a point like the Soo Locks, or perhaps a trip "up the street" if there was time in port as the ship was being loaded or unloaded. But getting away from the ship was hard. The story was told often of a captain or crew member who spent the entire season without getting a haircut, simply because there was never enough time for a trip to a barber shop.[157] Daily life for months at a time consisted of whatever could be done or found within the ship itself. Most of the season, day and night, was spent with the same thirty or so people.

The work day on a Great Lakes freighter was divided into watches. Although the captain and the chief engineer were on call at all times, the rest of the crew had a fairly regular schedule. In the early years of the century, crews worked a twelve-hour day, "standing watch" six hours "on" and six "off."[158] Usually the first watch was from 6:00 A.M. until noon and the second from noon until 6:00 P.M. In the evening the first watch reported back at 6:00 P.M. and stood until midnight, when the second watch completed the day by serving from midnight until 6:00 A.M.[159] This schedule was put into question with the passage of the LaFollette Act in 1915. The act generally created an eight-hour workday on ships, thus laying the groundwork for a three-watch system. The change, however, from two watches to three took many years. As late as 1936 there were still legal exemptions for some licensed officers. However, in 1934 the LCA finally approved a three-crew plan for the majority of its ships.[160]

Under the three-watch system, crew served four hours "on" and eight "off." Eventually the first watch, which was the most desirable, served from 8:00 A.M. until noon, the second watch stood from noon until 4:00 P.M., and the third watch, usually reserved for the most junior crew, served from 4:00 P.M. until 8:00 P.M. In the evening the pattern was repeated, with the first watch beginning at 8:00 P.M. and ending at midnight, the second watch commencing at midnight and continuing until 4:00 A.M. and the third watch beginning at 4:00 A.M. and ending at 8:00 A.M.[161] Corresponding to the three watches, most ships carried a first, second, and third mate as well as a first, second, and third engineer, who during their watch had responsibility for the ship or the engine room in the absence of the captain or the chief engineer.

Watch hours, however, were not guaranteed. When a ship pulled into port, loading and unloading operations began immediately. Deckhands reported to their stations and stayed there until the job was done. In contrast, Sundays were generally considered a day of rest. The minimum crew necessary to ensure safe operation of the vessel was maintained, and deckhands usually had the day off.[162]

The real question for most crew members was not what to do during their watch, but rather how to spend their off time. Rooms were for sleeping and little else. Although crew quarters evolved over time, reflecting the growing expectations of a new generation of crew, the quarters were always utilitarian, and sometimes bleak. Accommodations for crew at the beginning of the century set a very low bar. A seaman's personal quarters in 1900 were described as a "desolate, cell-like room." Four to six men shared bunk beds in a tiny room with a single porthole, called a "deadlight," for ventilation.[163] Headspace was so limited in the top bunk that a female steward recalled that if she rolled in her bunk, her hair would be caught and pulled out by the rough plywood ceiling above her.[164] In 1895 some new vessels were bunking only two men per room; however, newly constructed ships did not routinely and systematically adopt this practice until the 1950s.[165] By mid-century a typical crew member described the "stateroom" he shared with one other crew member as having a bunk bed; linoleum-covered steel floor; two large closets, each with a lock; and a wash basin.[166]

The newest American boats on the lakes, built during the 1970s, featured rooms with a desk, recliner, and air conditioning. Canadian ships took luxury a bit further, including gyms, saunas, and even swimming pools for the crew's use. However, because of the long life of most Great Lakes freighters, crews of one era often lived in rooms built in a preceding generation. In 1996 Mark Thompson sailed on the *Calcite II*, a ship launched in 1929 as the *William G. Clyde*. His onboard accommodation was a room 10 feet by 10 feet, with an attached 6-foot by 6-foot bathroom. The room had three portholes for ventilation and exposed electrical wiring. It was furnished with a double bed, a vintage five-drawer dresser, and a two-drawer file that served as the office space where he kept the paperwork required of the chief steward. Overhead hung a life jacket and a survival suit.[167]

Although the crew's quarters were utilitarian, one might expect that sleep would come easily as the ship passed through the cool water of the open lake. Sleep, however, was often difficult. Newcomers had a hard time finding rest. The water itself made noise, and as winter came, ice endlessly pounded against the hull.[168] Loading and unloading operations were noisy.[169] The steering mechanism was loud. A Vietnam veteran compared the sound made by the steering mechanism to that made by helicopters passing overhead.[170] When the ship was docked in the lower lakes, the heat could be intense. One sailor recalled a steward who would simply pick up his mattress, haul it onto the deck, and try to sleep there rather than in the hot cabin.[171] Another recalled the small fans he tried to use to pull air in through the porthole, and "windjammers," funnels that could deliver a breeze directly to your bunk if the ship were headed into the wind.[172] Bad weather also made sleep hard. One sailor compared lying in his bunk on a night with 6- to 8-foot waves on the water to the sensation of driving an old truck with bad shock absorbers down a bumpy road. The ship's movement would literally roll him over in the bunk.[173] Fog only made sleeping harder. The fog whistle, three short blasts repeated once a minute, was something about which new crew members invariably complained.[174]

The ship itself was not a pleasant place to be when off duty. Those who made a summer trip as a company guest usually had a romantic view of the crew's off hours. As Mark Murphy, who took a pleasant cruise on the *Harry Coulby* in 1950, wrote in the *Saturday Evening Post*, "In the evening, crew members congregate in the galley aft, to drink coffee and swap tales of the lakes and their wartime experiences."[175] The idyllic evenings spent by content sailors that Murphy described could happen, but usually did not. The reality was quite different.

Something as simple as a walk on the deck could be truly unpleasant. In the summer, the weather on the lower lakes was often hot and humid. Bugs and birds were a constant problem.[176] Insects could be annoying. If the wind was calm, bugs that swarmed onto the ship in port would simply stay on the ship for the rest of the cruise, treating the vessel as a floating island.[177] The bugs could sometimes become so numerous that the deck became slippery and the crew had to hose down the ship to be rid of them.[178] Birds also treated the ship as a convenient island placed in the lake for their use. Seagulls were disliked because they "bombed" both ship and crew with their droppings, which had to be cleaned off regularly.[179] Birds especially liked to follow closely behind ships equipped with bow thrusters. The thrusters tended to kick up small fish, a fine meal for seagulls.[180]

Life aboard a ship quickly grew monotonous and dull.[181] Off-duty crew members had a limited number of ways to spend their time. Sleeping, talking, card games, and drinking were common activities, with washing clothes or taking a walk always an option. Tobacco was everywhere, with one sailor recalling that his aunt had warned him to take a good supply of cigarettes onboard, because it was not easy to get more.[182] Occasionally, someone might play a small instrument, like an accordion.[183] As technology improved, radio, and later television, became another way to pass the time, although often a day or more could go by without it being possible to pick up a traditional over-the-air signal.[184] Over the long haul, though, there was not much to do.

In the early days, washing clothes was a feat. An old, but not very successful, trick for doing laundry was to tie dirty clothes to a line and heave them overboard, hoping that as they were dragged through the water the clothes would be cleaned. More often, however, they simply bounced on the waves.[185] One sailor recalled that the only "washing machine" onboard the *Amasa Stone* in the 1920s was a home-built device in the engine room. An empty oil drum was filled with hot water, soap, and dirty clothes. The mix was "agitated" by a discarded rod from a pump that was pulled up by a rope tied to a moving rod on a 1,800-horsepower steam engine, then fell back down as the rope went slack. This homebuilt contraption was considered a luxury that was to be shared only with the engine room crew. Everyone else onboard scrubbed their clothes by hand.[186] By the 1930s, conventional washing machines had begun to appear on most ships. Small modifications, however, were necessary. Often the machine was welded to the floor so that it would not tip over in heavy seas.[187]

With only so much laundry to do, off-duty crew most often passed their time talking. The talk most often revolved around bars, sailing, and women.[188] Occasionally, though, a fellow crew member was a gifted storyteller. Fred Dutton recalled Hank Kilfoyle, who was a master of the craft. Kilfoyle's stories drew upon a wide variety of experiences, including prison time served in Alcatraz. Long after they had parted company, Dutton remembered Kilfoyle's tales, which Dutton wrote were wonderful, "even subtracting 20 percent for fiction."[189]

Bars were a regular topic of conversation. The most common reason to go ashore was to drink. The basic goal was to drink as much as they could in the time available. The age of a sailor was often not important. A Merchant Marine card was sufficient to buy a beer. One non-imbibing crewman remembered that he had little interest in these trips because the conversation was so "terribly dull." Having a sober member of the party, however, could be advantageous. A non-drinker became the nautical equivalent of a designated driver. He kept track of the time, got a cab to take everyone back to the ship, and made sure everyone actually got on the boat, even if he had to push or drag them aboard.[190]

Another tale told by a young sailor spoke of an "old-timer" who took him under his wing one night to show him the town. They first visited Molly's Tavern, and then the two moved on to drink at Tommy Burn's Tavern. The youngster explained the itinerary this way: "He introduced me to Tommy Burn's Tavern, the cheapest place to drink in Superior, Wisconsin. Some of Tommy's customers were not well attired and others did not smell very good, so it was important to dull one's senses elsewhere so you could stand to take advantage of the low prices."[191]

Conversation also frequently turned to women. Although the unpredictable schedule and short port stays of most freighters made it difficult for a sailor to have the stereotypical "girl in every port," at least a few managed and were usually happy to brag about it. One sailor reminisced about a chief engineer who, although married, had girlfriends in Duluth and Buffalo. Understandably he was always one of the first off the ship when it pulled into port.[192] In another story about women, a ship arrived in port and a sailor stepped ashore to see both his wife and his girlfriend standing on the dock. Faced with a significant problem, he resolved his dilemma by running back onto the ship.[193] In another account, a newspaper story told a third tale of a captain who died in 1941, willing $500 to "my girlfriend at the time of my death." Twenty-one women in eight different cities claimed she was the rightful recipient. The judge, showing considerable insight into human nature, decided to give the inheritance to the one woman who attended the captain's funeral.[194] Clearly, some sailors did find the time to maintain ongoing relationships during the shipping season.

Card games were another frequent diversion. Generally the games were friendly, but a little cash was often on the table to make the game about something other than bragging rights. On occasion, though, the amount of money on the table was significant, and cheating occurred. One sailor recalled an incident where a fireman used a marked deck in poker when playing with a new crewman. The rest of the crew realized what was going on but decided to "watch the fun" when the "newbie" discovered the scam. In this case the "fun" was a bit anticlimactic. When the man being cheated finally realized what was happening, he suddenly grabbed the cards and threw them overboard.[195]

Cheating at cards was one of several unsavory character traits that sometimes appeared onboard. Theft was a common problem at all levels, and sometimes the making of stories about poetic justice. One sailor recalled an officious mate who suspended a sailor for thirty days without pay for stealing two cans of paint. The same mate was caught coming off the ship with a bag of food he planned to take home, and also received a thirty-day suspension without pay. Captains were also known to take advantage of their position. One ordered ten of the large tarps used to cover hatches delivered to his home for personal use.[196] Another tale is told of a cook who regularly ordered prime rib, but never served it onboard.[197] One crewman told a story about a "sleazy character" who regularly shoplifted items at each port. He would either fence the stolen goods or bring them home for his family in Buffalo.[198]

Crews could extract rough justice for behavior they disliked. One sailor told the story of "Bob," whom the crew found lazy and a whiner. Deciding they wanted to be done with him, they baited him endlessly. Eventually Bob lost his temper and threatened to hit another crew member. Bob, however, quickly realized that picking a fight with one of the largest men onboard was an error in judgment. Despite the loss of face, he backed down. Humiliated, he demanded his pay from the captain and was put off at the next stop.[199]

Crews did sometimes develop innovative ways to spend their off time. One fellow took frayed and thus worthless towlines and reworked them into nylon hammocks, which he sold through a mail-order business. Another fellow made logo caps and T-shirts that featured nautical motifs.[200]

Another developed a habit of going swimming when the ship was docked. He would jump off the ship at one end, let the current carry him down the boat's length, and then climb back aboard on a rope ladder he had previously lowered. This was great fun until the ship was sufficiently unloaded that it rose noticeably and the impact when he hit the water became painful.[201] It should be noted, though, that swimming could also be dangerous. The more fortunate faced jumping into heavily polluted port water.[202] Far more serious was the possibility of death. In 1944 a man drowned when he jumped over the side for a swim while at anchor in Sandusky, Ohio. The death caused the LCA to remind sailors of the *Recommendations for the Prevention of Accidents aboard Ships*, with attention turned specifically to the paragraphs that forbade swimming off the ship or the dock.[203]

And occasionally an entire crew developed ways to pass the time. Empty cargo holds offered unique recreational opportunities. In 1941 the crew of the *Pontiac* set up ping-pong tables in the hold when the ship traveled in ballast.[204] In the 1930s the crew of the *Myron C. Taylor* hosed down the cargo area and used it as a baseball field. A few new rules, of course, had to be agreed upon. For example, if a sailor hit the ball out of the hold it was considered a homer.[205]

Despite the occasionally imaginative ways created to pass the time, in general days aboard ship were most often long and boring. For men with wives and families, separation was often a great burden. There are many stories of well-wishers gathering at various narrow points along the lakes to wave at their loved ones aboard ship and offer a moment's companionship. At the beginning of the twentieth century, James Oliver Curwood wrote with feeling about these brief encounters:

> It may be that for an entire season of seven or eight months the Lake sailor has no opportunity of visiting his family. Yet every week or so he sees his home and his wife and children from the deck of his ship. It is easy for those ashore to learn from the marine officers when a certain vessel is due to pass, and at that hour wives and sweethearts, friends and children, assemble on the shore to bid their loved ones Godspeed. All of the vessels on the Lakes have their private code of signals. Perhaps in the still hours of night, the sleeping wife is aroused by the deep, distant roar of a freighter's voice. For a moment she listens, and it comes again—and from out there in the night she knows that her husband is talking to her; and the husband, his eyes turned longingly ashore, sees a light suddenly flash in the darkness, and

his heart grows lighter and happier in this token of love and faith that has come to him. And in the hours of day it is more beautiful still; and the passengers and crew draw away, leaving the man alone at the rail, while the wife holds up their baby for the father to see, and throws him kisses; and there is the silence of voiceless, breathless suspense on the deck that the faint voice of the woman, or the happy cries of the children, may reach the husband and father, whose words thunder back in megaphone greeting.[206]

Curwood's romanticized description of the scene captures a real suffering felt by many aboard. One crew member described his mixed feelings of pride and homesickness as his parents waved to him on his first trip past their home in Algonac, Michigan. Nor was the shouted news always good. One sailor recalled passing near a bridge where his mother shouted, "Hugh Jackson died yesterday." The news startled the crew member, and a friend aboard said, "I'm sorry. It's tough bein' out here in times like this."[207] A more humorous, but equally poignant, story was told of the young son of a chief engineer who once innocently asked his mother "when that nice guy who brought all the presents was going to come back."[208]

Sometimes this loneliness was resolved through unique, and usually unauthorized, ways. The engineering officers aboard the *Frank Purnell* dealt with the issue by developing the *"Purnell* summer vacation plan." The ship regularly sailed between Detroit and Toledo with coal. The three officers in the Engineering Department, who all lived in the Detroit-Toledo area, realized that if they agreed to cover each other's watch, each of them could spend every third week ashore. There was an obvious problem with the plan—the leave was unauthorized, and if something broke that required the three of them to fix it or even explain the problem, they would all be in trouble. But they rationalized that not only was this unlikely, but also since each of them would only be about fifty miles from the ship, the other two could get in touch with the missing man and he could come running.

Eventually the chief engineer, who winked at the vacation plan, succumbed to temptation and asked for a week off, which, under the circumstances, was something to which his junior officers could not say no. Murphy's Law being always in effect, while the chief engineer was AWOL the ship's engine failed completely, leaving the ship dead in the water. Although the assistant engineers were able to get the ship underway, once docked, the captain refused to sail again until the fleet engineer had come aboard to check the engine. When he arrived at the ship, the fleet engineer demanded to see the ship's chief engineer for an explanation of what had happened. The difficulty in meeting this "request" was that the ship's chief engineer was at that very moment sneaking back onto the ship and had no real knowledge of what had happened. When he finally appeared, the chief engineer pointedly ignored the glaring fleet engineer and "allowed" one of his subordinates to explain the situation.[209]

One captain reminisced about the time when his ship was underway and a second assistant engineer asked for a bit of unplanned leave. As the ship passed through one of the lake's narrow channels, the man's wife pulled alongside the freighter in a small runabout and invited him to join her. Her plan was that after a few hours she would run him back out to the vessel, which would by then be about to move into deeper water. The captain refused permission. The engineer weighed his options, walked to the ship's stern, and jumped overboard.[210]

For all the humorous stories, loneliness and boredom often led crew members to pass the time drinking, and sometimes abusing, alcohol. Alcohol was a frequent distraction and constant problem. Fleet owners tried to limit onboard drinking. In the last years of the nineteenth century, the Bessemer line, owned by John D. Rockefeller, banned alcohol. In the first years of the twentieth century, the Pittsburgh line, the largest group of ships on the lakes when it was formed in 1901, applied the rule to its captains. Harry Coulby, president of the Pittsburgh line, was emphatic when he stated, "It is clearly understood that a captain who takes out one of our vessels in the spring is not to taste liquor on land or water until after the vessel goes out of commission at the end of the season." The line also discouraged, but did not forbid, drinking by the crew.[211]

When Coulby told his captains to not taste liquor, he meant what he said. In 1911 he was criticized because he dismissed an otherwise well-thought-of captain for taking an occasional drink aboard his ship. Speaking directly to the captains at their annual meeting, Coulby explained his action:

> There was a good deal of pressure brought upon me to reinstate McLaughlin, captain of the *Wawatam*. I gave it a good deal of thought and it was with some misgivings that I dropped him out. He was a man whom I had thought was one of our coming men. He made good in every position he had ever been in until he got to be master of the *Wawatam*. Now it does seem pretty hard, I appreciate, to drop a man out of this line for any cause and I don't know of any other thing we are likely to do it for except for drinking. I have been giving the question a great deal

of thought for some time and I have made up my mind that we will not reinstate anybody who is dropped from the employ for drinking.[212]

Coulby's departure as president of the line had no influence on this rule. In 1926 E. F. Harvey, Coulby's successor as president, wrote in a "Confidential Letter to Masters":

> I am very sorry to state that we were compelled to relieve Captain Blessing of the command of his steamer because of intoxication. . . . During the last four or five years I have heard several rumors to the effect that Captain Blessing was drinking. I have had him in the office twice and told him frankly that I had heard these rumors but had been unable to prove them. He arrived at the Soo for Inspection in such a condition that the entire Inspection Committee reported he was more than "half seas over." Under the circumstances there was only one course open to me.[213]

In 1959 the Pittsburgh line, noting that it had the poorest safety record of all United States Steel Corporation divisions, reemphasized safety, in part by telling its captains to get a firm grip on shipboard drinking.[214] The need to do so is found in an almost endless stream of stories about drink and crew that go back to the beginning of the century.

In 1901 a relief captain who boarded one of the Pittsburgh fleet's ships wrote to his wife, "I arrived here last evening at 7 P.M., took a tug and went to the *German* . . . found the old Master had left and about half of the remaining crew drunk."[215] One author recalls a story of a captain during the 1920s going to the galley to get a cup of coffee and discovering four very drunk crew members enjoying a gallon of homemade moonshine. Considering his options, the captain left the galley and returned shortly with a baseball bat, with which he emphatically suggested that the men either go sleep it off or get off the ship immediately.[216] A crewman assigned to the galley told how he was almost fired when, suffering from a terrible hangover from a night "up the street," he mistook a box of dish detergent for spice and used it to liberally season a number of steaks.[217] Another heavy-drinking chief engineer was rumored to be able to smell an open bottle of whiskey through a solid steel bulkhead.[218]

The consequences of drinking often were more serious than the threat of a baseball bat upside the head or a few ruined steaks. The statistics were clear. Although men who died in shipwrecks grabbed both the headlines and the public's imagination, most deaths aboard lake freighters were caused by industrial accidents, and alcohol was frequently a contributing factor.[219]

Alcohol could also lead to fights or violence. On one ship, a watchman, demoted to deckhand, returned from "up the street" after heavy drinking. As the ship prepared to leave port, the demoted deckhand began to set the hatch clamps. Since he was doing the job poorly, another sympathetic deckhand came over to help, but the drunk suddenly turned on him, swearing, waving a wrench, and threatening to take out his frustration on the well-meaning good Samaritan. Fortunately other deckhands intervened, talking the drunk out of a fight.[220] On another ship, a second assistant engineer who had been drinking heavily stabbed a sleeping chief engineer fourteen times in retaliation for a bad performance rating. The assailant was confined to his quarters with his door tied and a guard posted. The ship stopped at the nearest port to turn the attacker over to the state police.[221]

Despite pressure from the home office and occasional obvious problems, captains realized "cracking down" on drinking would be difficult, and took varying attitudes about alcohol. More than one skipper looked the other way if the drinking occurred when the crew was off duty, was discreet, and didn't cause any problems on the next watch.[222] However, practices could vary greatly from ship to ship. One first mate decided drunkenness on his ship had caused too many accidents. He banned alcohol. The test came when a crewman tried to come aboard with a bag full of liquor. The first mate welcomed the crewman, but told him to leave the bag on the dock. When the crewman ignored him and walked aboard with his liquor, the mate threw the bag overboard and fired the man on the spot. Predictably, overt drinking onboard that ship quickly stopped.[223]

If drinking was difficult or banned on a ship, the crew was often tempted by a "bumboat." The prototypical bumboat from the years before World War II until the demise of the business was a 45-foot-long boat with a wide, flat stern, and sides that rose up straight to cabin height. There were usually numerous portholes for light and a small pilothouse on the bow.[224] Bumboats were a floating store selling items similar to those found in a convenience store. Crew could buy clothing, cameras, film, stationery, stamps, toiletries, food, and alcohol.[225] Like any store, the owners sometimes used catchy slogans. "Honest Al, the Sailor's Pal" served sailors at Duluth.[226] A bumboat in a busy port like Cleveland might visit eleven ships in a fifteen-hour day. Many bumboats also included an area where alcohol purchased aboard could be consumed. Since the bumboat would stay alongside the freighter for only an hour or two, drinking was "accelerated."[227]

Legal regulation of onboard drinking began in 1984, when Congress added to the duties of the Coast Guard responsibility for establishing and enforcing rules regarding alcohol for the maritime industry, as well as responsibility for gathering statistics regarding the impact of alcohol use on maritime accidents. Defining the term "intoxication" and developing the required regulations took four years. As part of the process, the LCA and the Coast Guard argued over a draft regulation that would make captains personally responsible for enforcing the Coast Guard's no-alcohol policy aboard freighters.

Argument also took place over what the phrase "intoxicated mariner" actually meant. The Coast Guard drafted regulations that no one aboard ship could be under the influence of alcohol. The shipowners, however, took a less restrictive view and argued that the phrase "intoxicated mariner" meant that no one standing watch could be under the influence of alcohol. What was in dispute was what to do when a crew member who had gone ashore showed up drunk and tried to board the ship. The industry practice was to allow the crew member to board, under the assumption that he or she would sober up by the time they were scheduled to stand watch.[228] Unsurprisingly the Coast Guard considered this assumption quite optimistic.

The regulations eventually put into force by the Coast Guard in January 1988 prohibited the use of alcohol while on duty, or in the four hours preceding duty. Intoxication aboard commercial vessels was defined as .04 percent maximum blood alcohol. The January 1988 regulations also established mandatory testing standards for employers regarding employee alcohol and drug abuse.[229] These rules were not well enforced. Generally the Coast Guard was concerned about alcohol use only when an accident occurred.[230] Nor did the USCG initially collect the congressionally mandated statistics regarding drug and alcohol impact on accidents or overall enforcement. To partly address these issues, in 1991 the Coast Guard equipped its vessels with breathalyzers in order to better enforce rules regarding alcohol.[231]

By the end of the century, some authors claimed that alcohol had been effectively banned from vessels. "There is no drinking aboard the vessel whatsoever," wrote Captain Gary Schmidt, describing the tug-barge combination *Dorothy Ann/ Pathfinder*.[232] Others also described the ships as dry,[233] but the truth is hard to ascertain. Mark Thompson wrote that his first job of the 1996 season came about because "The steward who had been assigned to the boat got drunk the second day he was on the job and got into trouble with the shipyard people."[234] Alcohol was repeatedly mentioned in his book, consumed by captain and crew.[235] Thompson eventually conceded that "drinking is still a problem on the Great Lakes."[236]

However the crew made it through the long shipping season, by the time winter had come the romance of the sea, if there ever had been any, had worn thin. One writer, allegedly paraphrasing Charles Dickens, wrote that being on a Great Lakes ship was like being in jail, with the added possibility of drowning.[237] Perhaps an exaggeration—nevertheless people became crabby and simply hoped the ship would soon tie up for the season. As winter crept up on the lakes, the crew simply tolerated each other, like people on a bus who would go their separate ways at the end of the ride.[238]

In the end, the crew on most ships could be divided into two categories: "steamboaters," who made a life of working on the ships, and those who actually preferred life "on the beach" but needed a job.[239] Steamboaters would be back on the bus when the season began in the spring. The others might not. The men who preferred life on the beach often described steamboaters harshly. Where James Oliver Curwood, at the beginning of the century, saw men of "endurance, enterprise, imagination, [and] patience," a more contemporary author saw men putting in their time, counting the days until vacation or retirement would take them away from a well-paying but boring job.[240] Another felt that they were men who had accepted something less than a full life in return for steady work on the lakes. It was claimed that a steamboater could avoid all sorts of unpleasantness associated with land life by simply sailing up and down the lakes.[241]

Perhaps because of this sort of attitude, the crew of a ship had mixed reactions to those who preferred life on the beach, particularly college students working on the freighters. For much of the century, work on a freighter was a good way to make money to pay college tuition, usually by working as a deckhand or in the galley. College students were outsiders whose plans clearly would lead to life on the beach, but occasionally a steamboater saw something in their future for which they had lost hope. One fresh-faced college student recalled being told that the best thing a wiper could do for him would be to throw him off the ship, lest the student end up like him, with a bunch of stumblebum steamboaters for companions[242]

Over the course of a century, much changed aboard Great Lakes freighters. Crews became smaller, quarters became more comfortable, women found their way on deck, and officers increasingly became college graduates. But in some ways, little changed. The ship and its schedule separated the crew from the companionship and opportunities possible "on the beach." A large ship became a small and often confining community. That confinement, and the separation that came with it, took a terrible toll on many crew members. Life became the boat and little else.

Children barely knew their parents. Inappropriate and sometimes self-destructive habits emerged to deal with the boredom of shipboard life. The ultimate measure of success was not personal, but the delivery of cargo in a timely manner. All told, Patrick Livingston may have summed up the situation well when he wrote, "Since I have begun gazing at Belle Isle from their steel decks, I have discovered that these steamboats have lost much of their allure."[243] For all the changes that had occurred throughout the century, working aboard a Great Lakes freighter remained a difficult job, physically and emotionally. The pay was good, but it was a hard way to make a living or live a life.

CHAPTER 3

THE SHIPS

They are not beautiful. Freighted low down, their steel sides scraped and marred like the hands of a labourer, their huge funnels emitting clouds of bituminous smoke, their barren steel decks glaring in the heat of the summer sun, there seems to be but little about them to attract the pleasure seeker.

—James Oliver Curwood, *The Great Lakes*

G reat Lakes freighters were working boats. Despite the mystique and awe that many felt toward the ships, James Oliver Curwood captured the boats' fundamental character. Another person, a businessman rather than a writer, described a freighter as "an economical and capacious carrying machine."[1] Whether expressed poetically or in the language of business, a lake freighter was an extraordinarily large piece of industrial equipment. Like any piece of industrial equipment, large or small, the boats were designed to do a needed task as efficiently and inexpensively as possible. Occasionally a company might spend a few extra dollars for graceful lines and a pleasing silhouette. But more often a lake freighter's design was based on three simple goals, none of them involving aesthetics: move the maximum amount of cargo, do so for the minimum cost, and get the cargo on and off the ship as quickly as possible. Throughout the twentieth century, appearance was almost always an afterthought.

At the beginning of the century, the Great Lakes enjoyed a boom in shipbuilding never seen before and never again equaled. The rapidly growing American economy had an unending appetite for the ore that was mined in Minnesota and Michigan. Shipowners could hardly keep up with the demand for transportation. As late as 1929 the biggest problem was finding enough hulls to move all the cargo sitting on docks. In 1929 a near record 65 million tons of iron ore moved across the lakes, only a fraction less than the 66 million that had been moved in the peak year of 1916.[2]

With so much ore to move, approximately 420 Great Lakes bulk freighters were constructed between 1899 and 1930.[3] Ships were built so quickly that one draftsman for the American Shipbuilding Company reminisced that he created the plans for the next ship by simply copying the plans from the last ship launched.[4] The result of all this construction was a huge fleet. The Great Lakes commercial fleet was larger than that of the commercial fleet of any nation except two: Britain and Germany. As early as 1910, there were 2,107 steamships sailing the lakes. The vast majority of these ships, approximately 90 percent, flew the American flag.[5]

Although many ships could exemplify the look and feel of a pre-1929 lake freighter, a typical example of the largest ships on the lakes was the freighter *William A. McGonagle*. The ship was launched in 1916, and is described in great detail by Al Miller:

> These were big, brawny ships: 600 feet long overall and 60 feet abeam. From bow to stern, they were the Great Lakes freighter at its zenith.
>
> The McGONAGLE was built by Great Lake Engineering Works in Ecorse, Michigan. Its hull was made of hundreds of the finest inch-thick steel plates, held together by pneumatically driven steel rivets. . . . New ships like the McGONAGLE had portholes, which were stronger than windows and could be secured from inside with watertight steel covers. Atop the deckhouse, the pilothouse was paneled in oak, with windows on all sides offering a 360-degree view. . . .
>
> From outward appearances, the ship's stern was dominated by the white, steel deckhouse that sat on the spar deck aft of the cargo hatches. Inside were the galley, an oak-paneled dining room for the officers, [and] a smaller messroom for the other men. . . . But the stern was really dominated by the boiler room and the adjoining engine room, which housed the 2,200 horsepower triple expansion steam engine—the most powerful of any engine in the fleet.

Engine "room" and boiler "room" were really misnomers, for these spaces were really cathedrals to the latest technology in marine engineering. The engine room was an open compartment extending from the very bottom of the ship up to the spar deck and on through the center of the deckhouse to a set of skylights on the structure's roof. A person standing on the bottom of the hull—in what was called the crank room, where the propeller shaft whirled around seventy times a minute—looked up through the equivalent of a four-story building to the skylights. . . .

Dominating the engine room was the towering triple expansion engine—so named because steam entering the engine passed through three cylinders, driving the massive pistons up and down and expanding in each cylinder as it cooled and lost strength. The engine stood on steel legs, which supported the cylinder chamber at the top. Extending down from each cylinder was a piston rod and then a connecting rod that attached to a crank, which in turn connected to the propeller shaft one level below the main engine room. As the pistons pumped up and down, they worked the piston rods and connecting rods, which spun the crank and turned the shaft. At full speed, the engine was a noisy but smooth-running symphony of moving parts. While an assistant engineer attended to the gauges and throttle on the side of the engine, an oiler walked on a steel grate catwalk among the flashing rods, flicking his hand onto moving parts to feel for heat, and deftly squirting oil from a long-necked oil can. Engine rooms were noisy and hot, and men on watch took every opportunity to stand for a minute or two beneath the ventilators that scooped in air above the stern cabin and funneled it below deck.

Passing through another bulkhead brought the engine room crew into the gloomy recesses of the boiler room. When launched, the MCGONAGLE had three Scotch boilers.[6]

Ships like the *McGonagle* would serve as the backbone of the Great Lakes freighter fleet for the better part of half a century. The *McGonagle* itself would have an extraordinary career, sailing until 1989 (from 1986 to 1989 as the *Henry Steinbrenner*) and finally being scrapped in 1994.[7]

The reason ships like the *McGonagle* were built and continued to sail was profit. Until World War II, the *McGonagle*, and the other 600-foot vessels of the fleet, were the largest ships that could pass through the Soo Locks. And size directly affected profit. Between 1916 and 1920 the average profits, defined by a ship's cargo capacity, were as follows:

CARGO CAPACITY OF VESSEL	AVG. PROFIT PER MILE
10,000 tons or more	$3.08
9,500–9,000	$2.08
8,500–8,000	$1.18
7,500–7,000	$1.06
6,500–6,000	$0.80
5,500–5,000	$0.39[8]

A 600-foot-long ship could carry approximately 11,000 tons of cargo, in contrast to the approximately 4,000 tons of cargo carried by a 400-foot vessel.[9] However, operating costs for a 600-foot vessel were very similar to that of a 400-foot vessel. The crew size was also the same. The larger ship was just as fast, ensuring an equal number of trips per year, and it used only marginally more fuel. Thus a 600-foot-long ship turned a much larger profit than its smaller cousins.

This simple arithmetic of profit, however, needs to be leavened by a surprising observation: during the "golden age" of Great Lakes shipbuilding, more smaller vessels were constructed than larger ships. Between 1906, when the first 600-foot vessel was launched, and 1917, forty-one new 600-foot boats entered the fleet. Ninety 500-foot-long boats were launched. Even though the 600-foot ships could carry more cargo without appreciably adding to operating expenses, smaller ships continued to be built. This occurred because of issues related to navigation within ports and the size of docks. Cleveland exemplifies the first problem. Although it was a major iron port, both the harbor and the winding Cuyahoga River would not be modified to fully accommodate 600-foot vessels until the 1950s. The large 600-foot ships were unloaded lakeside, and their cargo was taken to the upstream mills by train. The smaller 500-foot vessels could sail up the river to unload directly at the steel mill. Unloading ore at a lakeside dock and using railroad cars to carry ore upriver to steel plants represented a substantial increase in transportation cost per ton. Thus smaller ships continued to sail to Cleveland, a practice made economical by the difficult-to-navigate Cuyahoga River. The size of docks represented the other limitation placed on 600-foot vessels. Iron ports, with their frequent and substantial flow of cargo, could invest in the best and latest equipment, and were the usual ports of call for the 600-foot vessels. Small coal ports and other ports used infrequently could not afford to improve the dock to handle the occasional 600-foot vessel. This created an unusual business model. The more efficient 600-foot ships, unable to enter coal ports, usually sailed upbound with no cargo. In contrast, 500-foot ships usually could find a load of coal bound for some port along the way north. A ship that could carry freight both downbound and upbound could make money, even against a ship that could average a much greater profit per mile, but that, because of dock limitations, sailed empty half the time.[10]

The shipbuilding boom of the early twentieth century rested on important decisions that had been made in the last years of the preceding century. In the nineteenth century, shipowners had addressed two fundamental questions: what was the best way to move a ship forward, and of what should a ship be built? The answers to these two questions were far more complex than suggested by the comments of some nineteenth-century observers, who noted that the wind was free but fuel was not, and that wood floated while iron sank.

Everyone realized that steam power cost more, but shipowners soon learned that passengers would pay a premium price to ride a steamship. Steamships were quicker and sailed on a much more predictable schedule than wind-powered vessels. A typical sailing vessel took five to seven days to travel between Buffalo and Detroit. The first steamship in Lake Erie, the *Walk in the Water*, which was launched in 1817, could make the same trip in forty-four hours on a largely predictable schedule.[11] Subsequent steamboats were both faster and even more regular. Pre–Civil War commodity shippers, however, preferred the lower expenses offered by sail, even if the consequence was a longer wait for a vessel and less certainty about when the ship would arrive.[12]

After the Civil War, the economic comparison between shipping commodities by sail or steam changed. Because of numerous improvements to the shipping channels, ships became larger. As steamships grew larger, they could carry more cargo with the same crewing requirements and used only marginally larger amounts of fuel. Bigger steamships cost only a small amount more to operate than small steamships. Thus the ship could carry more cargo without significantly increasing costs, allowing for greater profit while at the same time creating a steady decline in the charges levied to move freight. Larger sailing vessels, particularly as the ships began to exceed a cargo capacity of 300 to 400 tons, required that the vessels add extra sail and rigging. More sail and more rigging required more crew, which represented a major increase in operating cost. The wind was still free, but the hands needed to capture it in sails were not. As sailing vessels grew larger, the cost of transporting a ton of cargo on them generally rose. By the last quarter of the nineteenth century, shippers who compared prices realized that they could pay equal or even lower rates if they switched from sail to steam-powered vessels, while reaping the added advantage of greater predictability regarding the time of arrival. Shippers eventually concluded that steam, not sail, offered them the best buy.

By 1900 no new commercial sailing ships were being constructed. Of those existing sailing ships that remained in cargo service, the fortunate ones made a profit by carrying lumber or potatoes. These were marginal cargoes that usually shipped out of very small ports that did not lend themselves to the new, larger vessels, and were products for which shippers remained largely unconcerned about the timeliness of delivery.[13] Only in these niche markets could a sailing vessel still turn a profit.

The late nineteenth century also saw a second major transition in Great Lakes ships: metal replaced wood as the basic building material. As with the shift from sail to steam, the change was hotly debated. In the 1870s and 1880s wood was cheap and plentiful. Shipbuilders understood the nature and characteristics of wood, and sailors were very familiar with how wooden ships handled. Thus both clung to wood. In 1881 the largest schooner in the world, the five-masted *David Dows*, was launched to serve the coal and grain trade between Chicago and Buffalo. The vessel carried 5,000 to 6,000 yards of sailcloth. It took the crew an average of eight hours to set all the ship's sails.[14]

As the construction of the *Dows* made clear, many people preferred wooden boats.[15] Indeed, in 1882, when the first iron-hulled freighter on the lakes, the *Onoko*, was being constructed, skeptics publicly announced that a metal ship could not float and would sink on launch day. The skeptics were wrong. In 1886 the first steel ship, the *Spokane*, was launched.[16] Although for a brief period "composite ships" of both wood and iron were built, wood soon was completely abandoned.[17]

The transformation from wood to steel construction was driven by the realization that it was easier to build a large ship with metal than with wood. At the beginning of the twentieth century, ships were rapidly growing larger. In 1895 ships reached 400 feet in length and 40 feet in width. This ratio of ten feet long for every foot wide would remain in place for the rest of the century.[18] The 400-foot length however was a temporary accommodation, representing the maximum vessel size capable of passing through the existing Soo Locks. When the new Poe Lock was opened in 1896, shipbuilders took advantage of its much larger size to build much larger ships. In 1900 the first 500-foot-long vessel was launched. In 1906, the first 600-foot-long, 60-foot-wide vessel was seen on the lakes.[19] This was the maximum size ship the Poe Lock could accommodate. For the next half-century the 600-foot vessel became the "standard" size for bulk carriers in the ore trade.[20]

The basic design of a "laker" was also created in the nineteenth century. Well into the twentieth century, the most striking feature about a Great Lakes freighter was the position of the wheelhouse. The template for lake freighters was created in 1869, when the *R.J. Hackett* was launched. Although no one knew it when the ship's wooden hull skidded into the water, the *Hackett* defined the design of a bulk cargo vessel for much of the twentieth century. The *Hackett*'s pilothouse and the officers' quarters were placed in the extreme forward area of the ship. The engine, crew quarters, and fuel storage areas were placed in the ship's extreme aft. In between was an open area allowing for a continuous hold, over which were placed hatches built to match the placement of chutes at docks where freighters loaded iron ore.[21] The last American ship built to this design was the *Roger Blough*, launched in 1972, more than a century after the *Hackett* first sailed. The Canadian vessel *Algosoo*, launched in 1974, was the final Great Lakes bulk carrier to feature this configuration.[22]

During the long service of this design, various divergent ideas were played with and occasionally built, but they remained oddities. At the beginning of the century, the "whaleback" design was advocated. Whalebacks had hulls that looked much like a cigar. The design made the ship slip through the water more efficiently. However, this advantage was lost because the ship's odd design did not work well with the standard loading and unloading equipment of the day, thus delaying both processes. During the late 1940s and early 1950s, a few ships appeared with other variant designs. The *Cliffs Victory*, for example, which entered lake service in 1951, was given the "standard" laker forecastle, but the engine and "aft" quarters were located near the middle of the vessel, with cargo holds placed behind.[23]

The Great Depression vastly reduced commerce on the lakes and brought to a close the golden era of Great Lakes shipbuilding. In 1930, only 46 million tons of iron ore were shipped. In 1932, iron ore shipments fell to a disastrously small 3.5 million tons. Throughout the 1930s, total annual tonnage remained at only one-third to one-half of what had been shipped in the previous decade. War fears in the late 1930s led to increased steel production and thus to increased ore shipments, but as late as 1939 only 45 million tons of iron ore moved from mine to mill across the Great Lakes.[24]

As a result of the Depression, between 1930 and 1936 shipbuilding stopped. In 1937, the second era in Great Lakes shipbuilding began, which would take place in the years just before and during World War II. Optimistic because of a small upturn in shipping, the Pittsburgh fleet ordered four new vessels. The first two were delivered in May 1938. They broke new ground in several areas, but the most significant change was their source of power. The venerable triple expansion engine was replaced with a turbine.

The bulk carriers that sailed into the twentieth century with the most up-to-date power plants featured triple expansion engines. These engines came by their name because they had three increasingly large cylinders through which steam moved. By the time the steam had passed through all three chambers, virtually all of the motive power available was gone. Originally introduced in 1874, triple expansion engines proved superior to other types of nautical steam engines then in existence and became the standard for both military and commercial vessels.[25] In 1895 the first triple expansion engine on the lakes was installed in the *Zenith City*.[26]

Triple expansion engines were large and heavy, often over two stories tall and featuring gleaming brass parts and many moving rods. The engines constantly produced a fine spray of oil that coated everything. Each had its own rhythm. Some sailors claimed they could identify a ship in the fog simply by listening to the sound of its triple expansion engine.[27] However distinctive each engine sounded, at full speed the noise and vibration created by every triple expansion engine was terrific. The engine room became so loud that voice communication with the wheelhouse was difficult or impossible. The noise was such that unique technologies had to be invented to pass orders from the captain in the wheelhouse to the chief engineer.

At first, many ships installed small steam whistles inside the engine room through which the captain could send his commands to the engineer. One blast meant to start or stop the engines. Two blasts meant to reverse the engines. Three blasts meant the engineer should reduce speed and four blasts meant full ahead or "all right."[28] However, in the noisy engine room even counting blasts from a steam whistle was prone to error. The solution was a "telegraph," often called the "chadburn," to communicate between the captain and the engine room. The chadburn was a mechanical device installed both in the pilothouse and the engine room. It was a British invention, first patented in the United Kingdom in 1870 by the father and son team of Charles and William Chadburn, from whom the device took its name. It consisted of a dial on which several engine settings were noted, with "stop" in the middle or 12:00 o'clock position, "ahead" and "astern" to either side, and a pointer that indicated what engine speed and direction were desired. When the pointer was changed in the pilothouse, the order would "ring up" on the duplicate chadburn in the engine room. A loud gong or bell would alert the engineer to look at the chadburn to view the new setting and adjust the engine accordingly. The chadburn was a very successful answer to the problem of noise in the engine room. By 1900, six thousand commercial vessels worldwide had installed the device. The chadburn was also an aesthetic success, placing in a ship's pilothouse an elegant accent piece, with its shining brass stand and dial.[29]

Boats powered by turbines first appeared on the lakes in the 1920s. Two boats owned by the Bradley Transportation line, based in Alpena, Michigan, pioneered the technology. The *T.W. Robinson* in 1925 and *Carl D. Bradley* in 1927 were the first to use turbines.[30] The Pittsburgh fleet's decision in 1937 to incorporate the technology into their new ships made clear that turbines would power the next generation of Great Lakes freighters. These new Pittsburgh ships were the first that linked the turbines directly to the propeller shaft.[31]

Like the triple expansion engines, turbines used a boiler to create steam. However, unlike the gigantic triple expansion engines with their three increasingly large cylinders, turbines generated mechanical power from steam rushing past a single, spinning wheel. Turbines were smaller, lighter, cleaner, and had far fewer moving parts than triple expansion engines.

Like the triple expansion engine, turbines were pioneered by the British navy. The Admiralty, however, did not quickly adopt this steam engine. To persuade it, Charles Parsons, inventor of the nautical turbine, embarrassed the admirals in 1897 by showing up uninvited aboard his privately constructed test ship *Turbinia* at a royal review of the fleet. At speeds up to 40 knots, *Turbinia* literally sailed circles around the assembled battleships and outran the smaller, faster vessels the Royal Navy sent out to enforce "decorum." The unplanned display accomplished its purpose when the Prince of Wales, who was in attendance at the review, indicated his desire to meet personally with Parsons so that they might have a chat about the vessel that had so obviously embarrassed the finest ships in the British navy. The conversation undoubtedly went well, as the Admiralty soon placed turbine engines in a variety of vessels. Commercial shipping interests quickly followed.[32]

In freighter applications, turbines generally used as much fuel as a triple expansion engine, but as the *Turbinia* so ably demonstrated, turbines increased speed. The new engines soon demonstrated that on a Great Lakes freighter, a turbine could increase a ship's speed about two miles per hour compared to a triple expansion engine.[33] Although slight, over the course of the season, this speed advantage translated into more trips completed, more cargo delivered, and thus more profit. A second, albeit less important, advantage of the turbine was that because it had so many fewer parts, in the spring a turbine could be fitted out for the new season in about one-half the time as a triple expansion engine.[34] Similarly, during the season the smaller number of parts simplified daily maintenance and increased reliability.

Although the major changes found in the ships built just before and during World War II occurred in the engine room, other modifications looked toward the future. These were the first lakers to use significant amounts of welding in their construction. Welding was not only lighter than riveting, which was used in older ships, but also offered superior watertightness. When used on the hull, it also reduced resistance as the ship moved through the water. Electricity also began to replace steam in a wide variety of applications. Electrical motors drove the anchor windlass, deck winches, auxiliary pumps, and steering gear. Automatic coal stokers, rather than firemen, placed coal in the firebox and marked another significant change. Crew comfort and safety were also improved. Crew cabins were made entirely of steel, heavily insulated, alleged to be "vermin proof," and given interior doors so that crew did not have to brave the elements to enter or leave their quarters. Perhaps an even more important consideration for the crew was the construction of an interior passageway below decks—quickly dubbed "the tunnel"—that ran between the cargo hold and the hull and made it possible to walk the length of the ship, whatever the weather.[35]

A significant decline in cargo over the next few years proved that the optimism shown by the managers of the Pittsburgh fleet in the late 1930s when they ordered the *Governor Miller*, the *William A. Irvin*, the *John Hulst*, and the *Ralph H. Watson* was premature. What finally created the demand for new ships was the unprecedented quantities of ore manufacturers required to meet the nation's needs during World War II. In 1941 a new record of 80.75 million tons of ore were shipped down the lakes. This led the again-optimistic Pittsburgh line to order construction of five additional boats in March 1941. The first of these ships, the *Benjamin Fairless*, was launched April 25, 1942.[36] The *Fairless*, and all of the boats ordered by the Pittsburgh line in 1941, were called "super dupers." All five ships—the *Fairless*, the *A.H. Ferbert*, the *Leon Fraser*, the *Irving S. Olds*, and the *Enders M. Voorhees*—were the biggest on the lakes, with a length of 639 feet and a width of 67 feet.[37]

In 1941 the United States Maritime Commission, an agency of the federal government, began to meet with the LCA to discuss a private shipbuilding program to launch additional new ships. In addition to the nine ships recently constructed by the Pittsburgh line, the American fleet had already made some significant investments to modernize existing vessels. Thirty-eight new boilers had been installed since 1935. In addition, fourteen steamers had had cargo areas rebuilt to improve efficiency, including new one-piece steel hatches.[38] However, the ship-owners as a group, still acutely concerned about overcapacity, could not agree on a building program. On October 7 the LCA informed the commission that it would not move forward with the construction of additional new vessels. On October 11, 1941, the Maritime Commission announced its plan to contract immediately for the construction of six new steamers. Eventually the Maritime Commission built sixteen Great Lakes bulk carriers.

Unlike the bare-boned Liberty ships built by the commission for saltwater carriage, the sixteen lake freighters were state-of-the-art bulk carriers. Designated the "L-6 design," with one major variation, all of the ships were based on the *Benjamin Fairless*; the difference was the power plant. The *Fairless* had a steam turbine engine, but because of the need for every available turbine for warships, the L-6 boats were constructed with traditional triple expansion steam engines.[39]

At the end of World War II, the opportunity existed to build a third generation of larger vessels. The opening in 1943 of the 800-foot (244 m) long, 80-foot (24 m) wide, and 29.5-foot (9 m) deep MacArthur Lock at the Soo was an enterprise justified as a wartime emergency project, but its potential impact on Great Lakes shipping was obvious. A new, larger class of ships could replace the "standard" 600-footers that had been sailing since the beginning of the century. The economies of scale had not changed for bulk freighters—bigger ships meant larger profits. What delayed construction of a new fleet was uncertainty over the long-term need for new ships.

There were 335 bulk carriers operating on the lakes at war's end. Most of the vessels were old and many were quite small. In normal times, ships built before 1905 and less than 450 feet in length would already have been scrapped as part of a regular cycle of replacement; but the price of scrap metal had declined so much during the Great Depression that there was little if any profit to be made breaking up an existing vessel.[40] The old ships simply rested at anchor. Quite unintentionally, these obsolescent vessels created a reserve fleet that was pressed into service during the war. But with war's end, their days were numbered. Very quickly, boats that were small, old, or most in need of maintenance were retired. The fleet rapidly declined to about 261 U.S. flag vessels, composed mainly of ships launched after 1920.

Shipping companies, still deeply concerned about overcapacity, took a "wait and see" attitude toward new ship construction.[41] This fiscal conservatism was based on a simple observation: iron-ore shipments had peaked in 1943 and declined each year thereafter until mid-1950. Similarly, the coal trade, long the second most important cargo for bulk carriers, and the cargo that had kept many of the ships sailing in the 1930s, was also declining.[42]

Finally, in 1949, the third generation of ship construction on the Great Lakes began, with the launch of the *Wilfred Sykes*. The ship drew 27 feet 7 inches of water and measured a modest 671 feet long by 70 feet wide. Eventually longer ships would be built to take advantage of the larger MacArthur Lock.[43] In addition to size, two other important changes occurred in this cycle of construction. Coal began to be replaced by oil to power the engine, and turbine engines began to give way to diesel power plants.

At the beginning of the century, the choice of coal to fire the boilers was a matter of economics. Coal was the cheapest fuel available.[44] A secondary, but still important, concern was that coal was an important cargo transported by the freighters. The coal companies that paid to ship coal to their customers by water expected the shipowners who hauled that coal to also buy it from them for the ship's boiler.[45]

Oil had become the standard fuel for oceangoing vessels in the 1920s. Oil required less storage space than coal. When looked at in terms of the fuel needed for a long, transoceanic voyage, this translated into a significant increase in cargo capacity. Great Lakes vessels, however, made relatively short trips and thus did not need to take aboard the massive quantity of coal needed for ocean travel. If fuel ran short, coal docks were readily available throughout the lakes. Because of this, Great Lakes freighters gained little in abandoning cheap, bulky coal in favor of more compact but more expensive oil. As a result, after World War II, Great Lakes freighters were the last large cargo ships in the world still using coal.

But the economics of coal were changing. By the early 1950s, the cost of oil had declined, and there was little difference in price between coal and "bunker grade" oil. As cost began to even out, oil's other advantages over coal—requiring less onboard space and being easier and quicker to load—began to become important assets. In 1950 the first oil-fired bulk carrier, the *Wilfred Sykes*, was launched.[46]

Although the crew was never fond of coal, oil also had disadvantages. Unlike coal, which one simply shoveled, the bunker-grade oil used to fuel freighters was too thick to flow in its natural state. It had to be heated to a specific temperature to make it flow. Keeping oil at the right temperature could be difficult. Even if it was heated properly, bunker oil frequently clogged fuel nozzles in the boiler. Crew had long complained that coal was dirty to load. But crews soon learned that coal was easier to clean up than oil. If the thick, tar-like oil spilled during the loading process, it would quickly congeal on the deck. Eventually it could be chipped off, but usually chipping took off the paint as well, requiring repainting of the now cleaned area. Even worse, although coal invariably got the crew loading it covered in black dust, if oil got on a crew member's skin it would burn, then harden. Solvent could take it off the unfortunate crew member, eventually.[47]

Owners were also uncertain about oil. Many of the new ships launched in the first years of the 1950s were designed so that either coal or oil could be used to fuel the boiler.[48] In 1957 the fleet still had 107 hand-fired coal-burning vessels. But their days were numbered. In 1964 only one hand-fired coal-burning ship was left. The last coal-fired steamer on the lakes, the *S.T. Crapo*, was converted to oil in 1995.[49] Although there was an occasional glance backward,[50] such as an article in 1982 suggesting that the decline in coal prices would justify a return to coal-fired vessels, ships never returned to coal-fired propulsion systems.

Once the conversion to oil began in earnest, the possibility of moving from one oil-based product, bunker fuel, to another, diesel, became far more practical. That practicality led shipbuilders in mid-century to replace steam engines with diesel engines. The Ford fleet had pioneered the use of diesel engines in 1924, but diesel engines had not been widely adopted.[51] An experiment by the Pittsburgh fleet in the early 1950s, however, made clear the future. In 1951 the fleet repowered two similar ships that had old triple expansion engines. The *Eugene W. Pargny* was given a diesel engine, while its fleetmate, the *Homer D. Williams*, was given a new steam turbine. Although the transition to the diesel power aboard the *Pargny* proved difficult, once owner and crew became accustomed to the engine, it became clear that the *Pargny* burned only about one-half the fuel of the *Williams*. This fuel savings, added to the fact that diesel engines were cheaper to buy and install, meant the days of steam were numbered.[52] In 1960 the last two U.S.-built steam-powered boats, the *Arthur B. Homer* and the *Edward L. Ryerson*, were launched.[53] The last Canadian steam-powered vessel, the *Feux-Follets*, appeared in 1967.[54] In 1961 the Canadian-built *Canadoc* was the first new-built diesel-powered ship to be launched on the Great Lakes since the two diesel-powered Ford boats had appeared in 1924.[55] By the 1970s diesel engines had become common.[56]

What really propelled new American shipbuilding after World War II was the Korean War, which began in 1950. The government again wanted maximum shipping capacity to move iron ore and other bulk commodities, and this time shipping companies were eager to build new vessels. Eleven ships were quickly ordered.

The problem was that none of these vessels could be delivered before 1952, and most would not become available until 1953. To deal with the immediate crisis in capacity, Great Lakes shipowners struck upon a novel idea: converting easily and cheaply obtained surplus World War II ocean vessels into lakers.[57]

The first conversion began in 1950, when the Cleveland-Cliffs line purchased the 455-foot-long surplus World War II ship *Notre Dame Victory*. The ship was lengthened to 619 feet in a Baltimore shipyard, and in March 1951 renamed *Cliffs Victory*. The vessel was towed up the Mississippi River and began service in June 1951.[58]

Bringing the *Cliffs Victory* into Lake Michigan was a unique challenge since the ship was 20 feet longer than the lock connecting the Chicago River to Lake Michigan. To overcome this seemingly impossible situation, an amazing solution was developed. With the rear gate of the lock open, the ship was nudged up to the closed forward lock gate by two tugs. In violation of all standard safety procedures, the forward gate was then opened, causing water to rush downstream. The ship and the tugs used full power to push against the raging water. Slowly, the *Cliffs Victory* moved forward the necessary distance into Lake Michigan, allowing the lock operator to close the rear gate and end the flood.[59]

After its dramatic passage into the lakes, the *Cliffs Victory* proved an economic success. Conversion of ocean vessels to lakers continued throughout much of the 1950s. What drove the process was cost; it was considerably cheaper to convert an existing, surplus ocean freighter into a lakes' bulk carrier than build a new vessel. Conversion usually involved giving the ocean ships a new, fuller bow to allow for greater cargo capacity, replacing the midship pilothouse and crew quarters with the traditional laker arrangement, and lengthening the ships. These converted vessels tended to have a somewhat smaller cargo capacity than ships built specifically for the lakes, carrying about 3,000 tons less per trip than purpose-built lakers. However, they made up for their smaller size with greater speed. The *Cliffs Victory* was for many years called the "Speed Queen of the Lakes." The converted ocean vessels could make a round trip with iron ore in a little less than five days, while their bigger brothers took at least six.[60]

When fleets began to contract in the 1980s, the converted ocean vessels were among the first ships abandoned. The extra speed that allowed them to average about the same annual carrying capacity as their slower but bigger peers also meant they used somewhat more fuel. As the fleet shrank in the 1980s, the "gas guzzlers" were scrapped. The *Cliffs Victory* made its last voyage in 1981 and was sold for scrap in 1985. The last operating ocean-conversion vessel disappeared from the lakes in

1987, although one refurbished ocean vessel, the *McKee Sons*, was converted to a barge in 1990 and continued to serve for many years in that capacity.[61]

In the 1960s, American ships developed new maneuverability by installing bow and later stern thrusters. Because of the narrow passages Great Lakes ships were required to pass through, navigation was a constant concern of builders and crew alike. Early on, lake freighters employed oversized stern rudders to improve maneuverability.[62] But ships still routinely needed the assistance of tugs in various tight spaces, including many docks. Bow thrusters largely eliminated this need.

A bow thruster is a secondary propulsion device built into, or in some cases mounted to, the bow of a ship. It was not designed to make a ship go faster, but rather to make it more maneuverable. On Great Lakes vessels, bow thrusters were most commonly installed in a 5-foot-wide, watertight tunnel running through the front of the hull and placed beneath the waterline. Within the tunnel were engines capable of turning propellers in either direction. The sudden thrust of water pushed the ship sideways and greatly improved maneuverability.[63]

Bow thrusters first appeared on the lakes in 1961, when one was installed on the aged *J.R. Sensibar*, which was launched in 1906. The freighter *Henry Ford II*, which had to navigate regularly in the narrow Rouge River to deliver cargo to the Ford Rouge Plant in Dearborn, Michigan, was equipped with a bow thruster in 1962.[64] The advantages of bow thrusters both in maneuvering through narrow channels and when docking, as well as the economic benefit gained because the assistance of tugs was less often needed, were quickly appreciated, and the devices were installed as rapidly as possible. By 1970, some 43 percent of the freighters had bow thrusters.[65] Stern thrusters first appeared on the Ford Motor Company's *William Clay Ford* in 1979. They employed the same principles as bow thrusters but were fitted at the rear of the vessel.[66] The massive new ships built in the 1970s sometimes required two sets of bow thrusters: one to use when the ship was fully loaded, and another used when the ship was sailing without cargo. When without cargo, the ship would rise sufficiently that the upper bow thruster was no longer under water.[67]

At the end of the century, bow thrusters were superseded by an even more radical design, a compass drive. Tugboats like the *Dorothy Ann* were outfitted with propellers that could turn 360 degrees. The vessel, in fact, had no rudder. With two compass drives, the *Dorothy Ann* literally could turn in a 360-degree circle.[68]

Increased maneuverability, several converted ocean vessels, and a few new custom-built lakers, however, were hardly enough to revitalize the American fleet. The majority of the U.S. fleet remained both old and obsolescent. If work was done, most shipowners opted for modest changes to upgrade their old boats. The most popular of these was reinforcing the hull and placing single-piece steel hatch covers on the boats. In 1935, Coast Guard regulations allowed ships with reinforced hulls and modified cargo-hatch covers to carry larger loads. This was usually accomplished by installing metal straps and single-piece steel hatch covers.[69]

Modest changes to aging ships, however, had their limits, as shown by the experience of the *W.W. Holloway*.[70] Launched in 1906 as a straight deck freighter, the ship was converted into a self-unloader in the 1950s and repowered with a diesel engine in 1962. Despite these upgrades, the years took a toll on the ship. The most obvious problem was leaks. The small self-unloading ship often visited poorly maintained harbors. The ship frequently pushed its way through mud to reach the dock. Years of this kind of abuse led the rivet heads on the hull plates to shear off. Without a head, water pressure eventually caused the rivet to explode inward, creating a small hole in the hull. As the number of lost rivets accumulated, the *Holloway* began to leak so freely that the pumps were kept constantly running. Eventually an engineer developed an ingenious solution to the problem. He took a broom handle, cut it into pieces about 3/8 inch long, and whittled each piece to more or less fit an open rivet hole. Using a sledge hammer, he drove the wooden piece into the hole; the wood would be stuck in the hole long enough to become wet and swell, creating a watertight seal. The engineer whittled regularly and kept a bucket of the plugs available in the engine room.

In addition to leaking, the aged *Holloway*'s hull was greatly weakened by condensation, and thus prone to unexpected failure. The coal the ship routinely carried and the residue from the coal-fired boiler the ship used from 1906 to 1961 created an acidic condensate that was deposited throughout the vessel. In places where the condensate dripped regularly, it caused the metal to become incredibly thin. In one instance a crew member accidentally pushed a screwdriver through the hull. The hole was below the waterline, but the fully loaded ship was riding low. When the ship was unloaded, the hole rose above the waterline. The crew member who had caused the leak quietly stuffed a rag into the hole and painted it over with quick drying paint, resealing the hull. Amazingly, the *Holloway* sailed until 1981 with these kinds of improvised fixes holding back the water. The vessel was finally scrapped in 1986.[71]

Between 1945 and 1970, the United States fleet declined annually in every year except between 1950 and 1954. At the end of World War II, 335 U.S. flag bulk carriers were in service. In 1950 there were 266 American flag ships. In 1965 there were only

160.[72] This decline in absolute numbers would continue to the end of the century, when about 100 U.S. flag bulk carriers still sailed the lakes.[73] Measured in terms of carrying ability, between 1945 and 1970, about 700,000 long tons of capacity were lost. It was sometimes argued that because newer ships were somewhat faster than older ones, the increased ability to make round trips compensated for this loss in absolute carrying capacity. Increased speed probably only made up for 450,000 tons of lost capacity. Putting all the numbers together, the ships could collectively carry around 15 percent less cargo in 1970 than they could in 1945.[74]

Although on the American side of the lakes the third wave of Great Lakes shipbuilding was a spotty affair that failed to replace the number of ships scrapped or the amount of previously available carrying capacity, the story was completely different in Canada. There, major changes in infrastructure led to new opportunities for shippers. The new infrastructure was the St. Lawrence Seaway. Just as new and larger locks at the Soo created demand for new and larger American ships, the building of the Seaway created the same demand for Canadian vessels.

In 1951 the United States and Canada agreed to construct the St. Lawrence Seaway. Although water from Duluth, Minnesota, flows naturally through the Great Lakes and the St. Lawrence River into the Atlantic Ocean, no ship can sail this passage. The Niagara River, and of course Niagara Falls, includes a 327-foot drop between Lakes Erie and Ontario. Less dramatic but equally problematic, before an oceangoing vessel can reach Niagara Falls, it first has to traverse the 224-foot drop in water level that occurs between Montreal and Lake Ontario. The Canadian government had long maintained a series of locks to allow ships to bypass these obstacles. A way around Niagara Falls, the Welland Canal, first opened in 1829. The Welland Canal was rebuilt several times to increase the cargo capacity of vessels capable of locking through it. The fourth Welland Canal, completed in 1932, made it possible for the largest lakers then sailing to pass from Lake Erie to Lake Ontario. But the Welland Canal was primarily of interest to Canadian shippers. In 1930, of approximately 5,200 transits through the Welland Canal locks, 4,600 were made by Canadian vessels.

If Lake Erie and Lake Ontario were adequately connected for navigation, if generally underused by U.S. flagged vessels, at the other end of Lake Ontario the St. Lawrence River continued to block a ship's navigation to the sea. The Montreal to Lake Ontario section of the river also required locks to navigate. In 1945 the locks available could accommodate a vessel no more than approximately 250 feet in length and requiring about 14 feet of water under the hull.[75] The Canadian and

American governments discussed building new locks several times. A treaty to construct a seaway in this section of the river was signed in 1932. A second executive agreement calling for the construction of a seaway was signed by American president Franklin Roosevelt and Canadian prime minister Mackenzie King in 1941. Despite these agreements, real work was consistently blocked by the American Congress. Finally, a frustrated Canadian government announced that if necessary, it would construct the St. Lawrence Seaway project without American assistance and completely on Canadian soil. This pronouncement led the U.S. Congress to capitulate. In 1954 legislation was signed by President Eisenhower creating a joint Canadian–United States Seaway project. When it opened in 1959, the St. Lawrence Seaway system made it possible for a vessel 730 feet long and drawing 25 feet of water to travel from the Atlantic Ocean to Duluth.[76]

Throughout the 1950s the Seaway created a huge question mark for American shipowners. In the late 1950s a few American vessels were built to Seaway length. The first of the class, and by far the most remembered, the *Edmund Fitzgerald*, was launched in 1958.[77] The *Fitzgerald* was joined in 1960 by the *Arthur B. Homer* and *Edward L. Ryerson*. These three vessels were the last new purpose-built American ships constructed for a decade, although five additional U.S. flag vessels, all saltwater conversions, appeared in the 1960s.[78]

The uncertainty among shipping companies on the American side of the lakes was driven not only by the possible impact of the Seaway, but also by changes in the ore trade. Ore deposits in Minnesota and Michigan had begun to be exhausted. The decline in U.S. ore production opened the possibility for a boom in Canadian iron ore. It had been known for many years that high-quality iron ore existed in Canada near the border between the provinces of Quebec and Labrador. For the first half of the twentieth century, these deposits went undeveloped in favor of the more easily obtained American iron ore. But as the American mines began to play out, by 1949 seven companies, six American and one Canadian, were actively developing mines in Canada. At the same time, a 350-mile railway was under construction to bring this ore to Seven Islands (Sept-Îles), a port on the St. Lawrence River. In 1954 the first shipment of Canadian iron ore reached the United States.[79]

Where American shippers feared a steadily declining ore trade, the Canadian industry saw the kind of possibility that fueled the golden age of American shipbuilding in the early years of the twentieth century. As a result, Canada rebuilt its entire fleet. The Canadian vessels sailing on the lakes in 1945 were small and old. With 153 ships in service, the bulk of the ships, ninety, were sized to transit the existing canals on the St. Lawrence River between Lake Ontario and Montreal. "Canallers" were no more than 261 feet in length and 43.5 feet in width. Only sixty-three Canadian bulk carriers sailed on the Upper Lakes.[80]

With the opening of the St. Lawrence Seaway, 60 percent of the Canadian fleet, mainly the small canallers, became economically unviable and thus obsolete.[81] But Canadian shippers had a vast new opportunity put before them, and by 1970 the Canadian fleet was almost completely rebuilt. Of the 153 Canadian boats in service in 1945, only seven remained sailing. Sixty-two new vessels and thirty-seven rebuilt hulls were on the water, forty-three of them built to the maximum Seaway size. The carrying capacity of the Canadian fleet increased 2.5 times between 1945 and 1970, reaching its peak in 1967. By 1970 the once small fleet of Canadian ships had almost equaled the once much larger U.S. fleet, with 94 percent of the U.S. fleet's carrying capacity.[82]

In addition to building a new fleet of ships, the Canadians revolutionized the basic design of the laker. Questioning the need for, and cost of, building two separate crew structures, one fore and one aft, Canadian naval architects placed all the ship's crew and equipment in one massive structure on the ship's aft. The first vessel of this design, the Canadian ship *Silver Isle*, was launched in 1962 and arrived in the Great Lakes in 1963.[83] The second ship of the design on the lakes was the *Senneville*, another Canadian vessel launched in 1967.[84] The *Silver Isle* and *Senneville* defined a new template for lake cargo vessels. Beginning in 1973 every newly constructed lake freighter placed the superstructure entirely on the stern.[85]

A fourth cycle of shipbuilding on the American side of the lakes began in 1971. U.S. shipyards were the busiest they had been in thirty years. This burst of construction was justified by two factors: resolution of the ore issue in a way that continued large-scale ore movement out of the Lake Superior ports, and the opening of the rebuilt Poe Lock at the Soo. By the late 1960s it had become clear that taconite from Michigan and Minnesota, rather than raw ore from Canada, would be the choice for steel mills around the Midwest. Taconite, a product manufactured from abundant low-grade ore, proved itself a better choice for mills than traditional ore imported from Canada or mined in overseas nations. Opened in 1969, the 1,200-foot-long, 110-foot-wide, and 32-foot-deep rebuilt Poe Lock created a strong reason to rebuild the U.S. fleet. The old economies of scale came into play—bigger ships made bigger profits.[86]

Construction of new American boats continued throughout the 1970s and into the early 1980s. Eventually twenty-eight new American flag ships were launched.

An additional twelve existing vessels were lengthened by 96 to 120 feet.[87] In 1972 the first of the new ships, the *Stewart J. Cort* and the *Roger Blough*, entered service. The *Cort* was the first thousand-foot-long ship on the lakes, with a 105-foot width. The *Roger Blough* was also 105 feet wide, but was only 858 feet long. The *Blough* got its odd dimensions because of fears among United States Steel engineering staff that a thousand-foot vessel could not successfully navigate in the St. Marys River.[88]

Construction in the 1970s and early 1980s also included smaller, 600-foot vessels. The smaller ships were called "river class" vessels and measured around 630 feet in length. They inherited the role played by the 500-foot boats built before the Great Depression. River-class vessels were designed to work in narrow, winding rivers and unimproved ports on the lakes. The river-class vessels were built with a narrow 68-foot width to make navigation easier. Most were rated to carry about 20,000 tons of cargo.[89]

The pride of the fleet, however, was the thirteen vessels that were 105 feet in width and measured between 1,000 and 1,013.5 feet in length. The five largest could each carry 78,850 tons of cargo, almost three times the capacity of the largest ships previously available.[90] Over the course of a shipping season this cumulated to approximately 3 million tons of cargo.[91] The thousand-foot giants that were built in the 1970s meant even more powerful diesel engines on the lakes. The *Stewart J. Cort* was powered by engines adapted from those built by General Motors for diesel railroad locomotives, rather than ones designed specifically for ships. The ships also featured a "boxy" design that maximized cargo capacity. The relatively low speed of lake freighters made it possible to both be boxy and still obtain high fuel efficiency.[92]

Crew working conditions in the engine rooms of the thousand footers were completely different from those of past designs. The engineer on duty sat in a soundproof booth. The time-honored inspection of the engine by an oiler who tickled the bearings and rods to check for problems was replaced by more than 150 sensors and warning lights, reporting to the engineer things like "port engine bearing temperature high" or "oil in bilge water."[93]

The 1970s ship construction boom came to an end in the early 1980s. The last American-built thousand-foot ship, the *Columbia Star* (renamed *American Century* in 2006), set sail in 1981, twenty days after the first voyage of the thousand-foot *William J. DeLancey* (renamed the *Paul R. Tregurtha* in 1990).[94] Also launched in 1981 was the much smaller *American Republic*. These three boats were the last American self-powered bulk cargo vessels launched in the twentieth century on the

Great Lakes.[95] The last new laker of the century, a Canadian vessel, was launched in the mid-1980s.[96]

The *American Republic* was a unique vessel designed to solve the ongoing problems created by Cleveland's Cuyahoga River. In an earlier generation, the winding nature of the river made it impossible for 600-foot-long vessels to sail up the river, thus keeping many 500-foot boats in service before the Great Depression. Improvements to the river eventually made it possible to sail a 700-foot ship to most of the steel mills lining the river, but no captain could possibly navigate a thousand-foot vessel upriver. Despite this, the economies of scale created by thousand-foot ships made using 700-foot vessels from Lake Superior to Cleveland uneconomical. To resolve the problem, a unique solution was developed. The thousand footers unloaded their taconite just outside of the river. Even for the short distance involved, water transportation was preferred to trains, and thus the taconite was reloaded into the purpose-built *American Republic*, which took the pellets upriver for the final few miles of their journey.[97]

At the end of the twentieth century, Great Lakes ship designers began to reconsider a very old idea: using barges. Steamers pulling old sailing vessels had been a common sight at the beginning of the twentieth century. Called "consorts," they came about because of the glut of unprofitable sailing vessels on the lakes. By the late nineteenth century, most sailing vessels were losing money, and their owners would often part with the ship cheaply. The *David Dows*, the largest sailing ship ever built on the lakes, began serving as an occasional consort in 1883, only two years after the ship had been launched.[98] Given the ready availability of cheap but still seaworthy hulls, the owners of steam-powered vessels experimented with increasing their cargo capacity by pulling one or more fully loaded sailing vessels. The hope was that a steamship could not only carry its own cargo but, with only a modest additional expense and with little loss in speed, pull the consorts, which sometimes still carried minimal crews and a limited number of sails to assist.

The practice of towing consorts went on for many years, and in some cases steel barges eventually replaced older wooden hulls. However as the twentieth century moved forward, consorts and barges fell out of favor. Many steamboats lacked sufficient power to pull consorts. Larger ships that could tow consorts or barges discovered that delays caused by waiting for a string of additional hulls to be loaded lessened the number of trips made by the steamship. When all the numbers were added together, even with the added cargo capacity consorts and barges offered, fewer trips could actually reduce the overall profit obtained by simply sailing a large ship more frequently. Barges slowly disappeared from the bulk cargo trade. The last barge hauling iron ore was taken out of service in 1956.[99]

Although many thought the use of barges to move cargo long distances had ended, in reality barges were transitioning into a new configuration. In 1950 the first "new" tug-barge combination, the *Carport*, was introduced. It was built to move cargo from the Great Lakes through the Erie Canal to the East Coast without any unloading and reloading. A little over a decade later, in 1963, the *Horace S. Wilkinson*, an aged steamer, was converted into a barge that was moved by the tug *Wiltranco I*. The *Wiltranco I* used an innovative notched hull that allowed the tug to be linked directly to the stern of the converted *Wilkinson*, pushing it forward in a way similar to how river boats on the Mississippi River pushed barges. The *Wiltranco I* experienced problems with this linkage. Under certain weather conditions, the tug was required to pull the barge rather than push it. The *Wiltranco I* also proved slow because the vessel was underpowered. Nevertheless when designers returned to the concept a decade later, the *Wiltranco I* became the prototype for a new group of Great Lakes cargo carriers.[100]

What led shipping companies back to tugs and barges was cost: specifically crew costs. As early as 1963, the Lake Carriers' Association noted that a tug pushing a barge could operate with a crew of sixteen, compared to a crew of thirty-six on a typical freighter.[101] By the end of the century the difference in crew size had become less dramatic. Tug-barge vessels operated with a crew of fourteen, while self-propelled vessels required a crew of nineteen to twenty-three.[102] Nevertheless, because crew costs made up about one-third of a ship's annual operating budget, a reduction in crew size meant that significant annual operating savings could be realized.[103]

In 1971 a newly constructed thousand-foot barge-tug combination was launched, directly competing with the thousand-foot bulk cargo ships then being constructed. Learning from the problems experienced by the *Wiltranco I*, the *Presque Isle* could push the uncrewed barge under any weather conditions and, because it was the most powerful tug on the lakes, was competitive in speed with traditional bulk carriers. However, because of an unanticipated issue with the coupling mechanism between the barge and the tug, the real reason for building the *Presque Isle*, the anticipated dramatic reduction in crew size, did not happen. Although the *Presque Isle* was designed to operate with a crew of fourteen, the Coast Guard would not license it to do so. In 1981 the Coast Guard determined that because the barge was connected to the tug by a unique locking system that made the tug unseaworthy when it operated independently, the vessel was an "integrated unit" and as such required the traditional number of crew called for on a freighter.[104] Although the *Presque Isle* continued to operate on a regular basis, because of this ruling it did not become a model for other thousand-foot vessels.[105]

The idea of tugs pushing barges, however, continued to have appeal, but with changes in the linkage design so that both the tug and the barge were independently seaworthy. An Articulated Tug and Barge (ATB) unit, successor to the *Presque Isle*'s Integrated Tug and Barge unit (ITB), connected the barge and tug by a pin system that allowed the two hulls to operate independently. In 1981 the USCG adopted regulations that recognized a distinction between ITB and ATB units and allowed smaller crews on an ATB unit than were required on a traditional laker. This ruling led to a series of conversions of old hulls into barges equipped with an ATB linkage system, and a few newly constructed ATB units.[106]

In 1982 Amoco launched two barge-tug combinations to move petroleum products on the lakes. Together the barges and their tugs replaced an aged steamer.[107] Other conversions included the *Buckeye* in 1979, the *Joseph H. Thompson* in 1985, the *McKee Sons* in 1992, the *Adam E. Cornelius* in 1989 (a Canadian flag vessel), and the *St. Marys Conquest* (the *Amoco Indiana* before conversion) in 1987.[108]

In 1996, two old cement carriers, the *E.M. Ford* and the *S.T. Crapo*, were replaced by the tug *Jacklyn M* and barge *Integrity*. The *Jacklyn M* was operated by a crew of nine.[109] In 1998 the *J.L. Mauthe* was converted into the barge *Pathfinder* and linked to the tug *Joyce L. Van Enkevort*. In 1999 the *Pathfinder* was given over to a newly constructed tug, the *Dorothy Ann*.[110] The *Van Enkevort* was in turn assigned to move the newly constructed barge *Great Lakes Trader*, which was put into service in 2000.[111] The *Great Lakes Trader/Joyce L. Van Enkevort* combination was built to maximum Seaway length.[112]

Although the tug-barge combinations remained slower than conventional ships, they consumed only about one-half the fuel used by a conventional vessel. Captains also considered these new vessels more maneuverable, giving them an additional advantage in some situations.[113] The *Pathfinder/Dorothy Ann* was so maneuverable that it could navigate up the Cuyahoga River in Cleveland, even though it was 80 feet longer than any other vessel on the river.[114] At the end of the twentieth century, naval architects believed barges with a capacity of up to 50,000 tons were economically viable on the lakes, although it was unlikely that barges would eliminate the need for traditional self-powered ships.[115]

Over the course of a century, change in the appearance of the freighters frequently drew criticism. The ships built in the 1970s, for example, were very different in appearance from those that had preceded them. As Raymond A. Bawal Jr. noted, "These vessels represented a new era in U.S. flagged Great Lakes shipping which had witnessed a class of ships being built for maximum efficiency with little attention being paid to traditional freshwater ship design. The days of building ships with stylish curves and cabins placed both forward and aft had passed by and were replaced by the building of ships with square lines and cabins placed only at the stern."[116] Less charitable authors described the new vessels as "shoebox ships" and "six decks of ugly."[117]

Engineers were equally unhappy with the change in power plants. As one chief engineer who had worked with steam put it, "Then there was an economic downturn. I had to go on the hellish big diesel ships to keep a job. . . . Several times, the god awful pounding of the main engines and the relentless noise of the ship service generators seemed to scream, 'Get the hell off of here while you can still hear the birds sing.'"[118] Some suggested the real reason engineers objected to diesels was that they required more labor than the older steam engines. As one chief engineer in the early twenty-first century put it, "The guys that have been on the steamships for a long time don't like going to diesel because, well, it's more work."[119]

These, however, were hardly the first complaints about changes in ships. Despite their noise, vibration, and spraying oil, many sailors found in the triple expansion engine's movement a vision of mechanical beauty, something lacking in their successor engines. One old-timer wrote in the 1950s at the end of his career:

> I shipped out one fall on one of the "super dupers"—which were the largest and most modern vessels on the lakes. . . . driven by turbines. . . . The engine room was a disappointment to me. I always liked to go down and watch the engines work. Turbines had no visible moving parts. They look for all the world like great tanks. The only thing that seems to be moving is the tail shaft. The pumps are driven by turbines that are enclosed, as are all the dynamos. An interesting place in the eyes of the young men aboard, but I found it boring.[120]

Men serving in the early twentieth century on the surviving sailboats held steamboats in contempt. "With the introduction of steam came a new condition for the sailor. To him the steam engine was a mystery he neither understood nor liked. It threw soot, steam and oil on the deck, and was a dirty affair."[121] Past experience and nostalgia shaped one's opinion. A shoreside observer who likely never served on a sailing vessel described the sight of the tug *Champion*, towing behind it eight three-masted vessels with their sails unfurled, this way: "Every sail set beautifully rounded out with the gentle following wind flattening every bit of bunting, as a painted banner—it was truly a vision of loveliness and grace."[122]

No crew member of a sailing vessel ever penned such words about what was in their mind a beautiful craft chained behind an ugly, smoke-spewing tug. As James Oliver Curwood had noted at the beginning of the century, lake freighters "are not beautiful. Freighted low down, their steel sides [are] scraped and marred like the hands of a labourer, their huge funnels emitting clouds of bituminous smoke, their barren steel decks glaring in the heat of the summer sun."[123]

Freighters existed to turn a profit, not display grace or loveliness. As George Ryan, president of the LCA, would write in another era, "sentimentality cannot take precedence over economic realities." In a world where the reason why a freighter was built was economic, the ship's beauty was not to be found in how it looked, but in what it accomplished. Great Lakes freighters were waterborne laborers, whose beauty was found not in appearance, but rather, similar to the measure of the ship's crew, in the swift and safe completion of a job.

CHAPTER 4

CHANGES ABOARD

In all these decades of steamboating, strangely (or maybe everybody's that way), I continued thinking of myself as a young man on the way up. Always looking ahead, not behind me. I apparently never noticed the gradual influx of young seamen coming aboard behind me. Didn't notice that now there were more men aboard who were younger than men who were older. . . .

One day, I casually asked one of the new men to give me a hand at the ladder with my duffel. Usually a fellow would answer, "Sure." But this young fellow, in all sincerity and with much alacrity, said, "Sure, sir!"

It gave me pause.

—Fred Dutton, *Life on the Great Lakes*

Over the course of a century, the casual observer saw many changes to lake freighters. The ships grew longer and wider. The classic freighter look, with superstructure fore and aft, was replaced by superstructure found only on the stern. Heavy black smoke from coal-fired boilers was replaced by pounding diesel engines. Besides these obvious differences that anyone could see or hear, there were a series of equally significant, but far less visible, changes. Some of the most important occurred in navigation. At the beginning of the twentieth century, the basic tools for navigation were not substantially different from those known in antiquity. A chart, knowledge of landmarks visible when near the shore, and a magnetic compass served as the sailor's way of knowing the ship's position. By the end of the century, huge changes in technology had made these traditional tools all but obsolete.

Communication was also revolutionized. As the twentieth century dawned, crew on one ship "spoke" to those on another vessel by whistle signal and lights. By century's end, satellite communication technology was a common denominator among freighters. Significant changes also occurred regarding the length of the sailing season. Crew safety was significantly improved, sometimes through lessons learned tragically.

The story of change aboard the ships is also about the reaction of owners and crews to change. Some changes, such as year-round navigation, were laid aside. Other changes, such as satellite communication, were quickly adopted. Some changes, such as the gyrocompass and radio communication, while beneficial in retrospect, were resisted for a variety of reasons. Aboard Great Lakes freighters throughout the twentieth century, there was a constant tension between tradition and change, between the promise of new technologies and the consequences of their implementation.

One of the fundamental changes aboard Great Lakes freighters was in navigation. At the beginning of the century, sailors plotted their course and knew their location by chart, compass, landmark, and other purpose-built aids to navigation. Charting the entire Great Lakes system had not been accomplished quickly. In 1841 Congress created the United States Lake Survey to create navigation charts and gather information useful to lake navigation. The only available charts at the time were those created by the British Admiralty, which described the Canadian shoreline and "common passages" like the St. Marys and Detroit Rivers. In addition to leaving uncharted the American side of Lake Huron, Lake Erie, and Lake Superior, as well as leaving Lake Michigan totally undescribed, the British charts had minimal information about water depth and frequently did not locate offshore reefs and shoals.[1]

In 1845 the Lake Survey's office was located in Detroit, where it remained until 1970. The Survey faced the daunting task of developing charts for 95,000 square miles of open water and 8,300 miles of shoreline. The first charts, of Lake Erie, were published in 1852. By 1882 seventy-six charts covering all of the Great Lakes had been published, completing the survey. These charts were designed for vessels drawing approximately 11 feet of water, the basic size of a pre–Civil War ship, and measured water depth to approximately 18 feet. In 1882 the federal government declared the job accomplished and disbanded the Lake Survey. The decision ignored the consequences created by the growing size of Great Lakes freighters and the ongoing "improvements to navigation" that the government itself was funding.[2]

By 1900, it was obvious to virtually everyone involved in the freighter industry that the charts created before 1882 were inadequate. What finally brought about the new survey was a vessel striking a shoal where old charts indicated 22 feet of water.[3] The making of charts, especially in an area of rapidly expanding commerce using vastly larger ships, was not a "once and done" project. The Lake Survey resumed chart making, routinely recording depths of 25 feet in rivers and 30 feet in the open lake. By 1936 the Survey had created and was maintaining 129 separate charts.[4]

Open-water charts at first seemed less necessary. However, dangerous surprises could lurk in what was usually deep water. In 1929 a Canadian survey vessel discovered the Superior Shoal fifty miles off Copper Harbor, Michigan. A volcanic hump in an otherwise deep area of the lake, the shoal lay only 21 feet beneath the surface.[5] As late as 1959 the U.S. Lake Survey was looking for similar uncharted underwater pinnacles near Lake Michigan's Boulder Reef, which is located to the west of Beaver Island.[6] In all, about two hundred Great Lakes charts were created and maintained by the federal government.[7]

One of the most important notations on any chart was the water's depth. Although early charts routinely included this information, sailors quickly realized that the charts' numbers were more guideline than guarantee. Seasonal fluctuations as well as long-term patterns affected the actual water depth at any given moment. During the shipping season of 1859–60, the Lake Survey took on the responsibility of observing and reporting on actual, current lake levels rather than simply pointing to the past measurements taken by a survey crew and printed on a chart. In 1898 the Survey's mission was formally enlarged to include monitoring and studying causes of fluctuation in water levels, as well as to monitor the flow of water in the lakes, including the effects of engineered improvements.

Determining fluctuations in water level created a unique problem: what was the point of comparison? To answer that question, the Lake Survey established a "base" elevation from which future annual comparisons could be made. In 1875 the first "base" determination of Great Lakes water level compared the water in the Great Lakes to the mean tide at New York City. A second, more accurate study was undertaken between 1898 and 1901. This work was incredibly thorough, but in 1920 it appeared that mistakes had been made. Some water-level meters began to show peculiar readings, and by 1935 the inconsistencies had become sufficiently large to affect dredging and other harbor improvements. Eventually the Lake Survey staff demonstrated that over time the earth's crust had literally changed, and this cumulative movement of the earth's crust altered water depth.[8]

At the beginning of the twentieth century, a ship's crew had reasonably complete charts and current knowledge of water depth. This information was supplemented by landmarks, lighthouses, and other aids to navigation. These visual indicators were committed to memory by many, but inexperienced navigators and old hands alike also frequently turned to *Thompson's Coast Pilot*. First published in 1858, *Thompson's* was the navigator's bible and almanac, carefully describing what the captain and crew saw from the pilothouse.

Like any almanac, the book printed a great deal of useful information. Besides expected descriptions of coastline features and lighthouses, compass headings, and the distance between ports, there was also detailed information about shelter harbors: noncommercial harbors where a ship could take refuge during a storm. In addition, *Thompson's* was full of random but useful information, such as ways to estimate distance. The novice navigator was informed that one could distinguish clearly a horse at a distance of 4,000 feet. The movement of a person, whether ashore or aboard another ship, could be determined at 2,600 feet.[9]

What even experienced sailors frequently needed from their *Thompson's* were descriptions of the "aids to navigation" maintained by the U.S. Government. Changes to the shoreline were often slow and incremental, but in the late nineteenth and early twentieth centuries, the number of aids to navigation maintained by the government dramatically increased. At the beginning of the twentieth century, an already extensive network of navigational aids dotted the Great Lakes. The Lighthouse Board operated 334 major lights, 67 fog horns, and 563 buoys.[10] But in the first decades of the twentieth century, the Lighthouse Board and its successor agency, the Lighthouse Service, continued to expand the network of navigational aids on the Great Lakes. In 1925, the board operated 433 major lights, 10 lightships, 129 fog signals, and about 1,000 buoys.[11]

Of all the purpose-built aids to navigation, lighthouses were the grandest. The first lighthouse on the Great Lakes was erected in Canada to mark Toronto Harbor. In 1828 Buffalo received the first light on the American side of the lakes, and by 1860 Congress had funded the construction of forty-seven lighthouses in Michigan alone.[12] The first purpose of lighthouses was to mark harbors and guide ships into port. Port lights were supplemented by range lights, two illuminated beacons set several hundred feet apart or at different elevations, and located either behind or above each other. While entering a harbor or navigating a narrow passage, the ship's crew, if on proper course, would see both lights either as a single point of light or in a vertical line. If the two lights diverged in any way from this pattern, the ship was off course and action was necessary to avoid an accident. The first range lights were installed at Saginaw, Michigan, in 1860 and involved little more than two very carefully placed lanterns.[13]

Lighthouses and their more easily placed cousins, light ships, were also used as warning beacons. Warning lights helped a ship's crew avoid dangerous waters. They marked the location of shoals and other hazards to navigation. In dangerous areas where construction of a lighthouse was difficult, a light ship would be anchored. In particularly dangerous water, the government preferred a lighthouse over a lightship, and a lightship over any other form of warning buoy. The history of Lake Michigan's Grays Reef tells one such story of navigational warning.

Grays Reef Passage is the only opening for deep-draft vessels between the Straits of Mackinac and the waters east of Beaver Island and the Manitou Islands. In its 1869 annual report, the Lighthouse Board noted:

> These reefs are situated in the northern end of Lake Michigan, 6 miles due west from Waugoshance light-house, and consist of several rocky patches upon which there are but 5 feet of water. They are much dreaded, and probably have been the cause of a greater number of disasters than any other of the many dangers in this locality. It is proposed to mark these reefs by a first-class iron buoy, placed on the eastern side, in 16 feet [of] water.

An iron buoy was placed to mark the site, but many found it insufficient. In 1889, Congress appropriated funds to establish a light and fog signal in several places, including Grays Reef, but the amount of money was insufficient to construct all of the projects on the list. The Lighthouse Board asked, and was given permission, to reallocate some of the money to construct three less expensive lightships. Beginning in October 1891, one of those lightships was stationed at Grays Reef. A lightship marked the reef's location for more than forty years. In 1934, work began on replacing the lightship with a lighthouse. When the Grays Reef Lighthouse was commissioned on April 1, 1937, the Grays Reef lightship was decommissioned.[14]

In addition to marking harbors and warning ships away from danger, lighthouses served as navigational beacons, alerting sailors to points where course changes were typically made. The Point Betsie light at Point Betsie, Michigan, alerted a ship's crew to set course to enter the Manitou Passage or to depart from the Michigan shoreline and begin a new course for ports on Lake Michigan's western shore.

To avoid misidentification, lighthouses had distinctive features. During daylight hours, architectural features or unique paint schemes made it clear to a ship's crew which light they were seeing. At night each light displayed a unique signal, a combination of long and short flashes of light that again left no uncertainty about the light's identity, in the same way that telegraph operators of the day keyed communications.[15]

Crewing remote lighthouses, or for that matter placing lightships, was a challenge. As early as possible each season, tenders took the crew out to the light. However, because many lights marked dangerous shoals and similarly treacherous locations, the tender often could not directly sail to the lighthouse. Instead the ship had to anchor near the light and transfer the crew and the supplies needed for the season by small boat. In rough weather this could be impossible. It was not uncommon for a tender to have to wait by a light for several days until weather conditions allowed for the safe use of a small boat.[16] The Light House Service and its successor agency, the Coast Guard, both sought to automate lighthouses whenever possible. Although the process of finding suitable equipment to replace a crew was a long one, the Coast Guard persisted in developing and deploying ever more reliable technologies. The last crewed lighthouse, at Grays Reef, was automated in September 1976.[17]

Buoys also played a critical role in aiding navigation. These uncrewed aids to navigation ranged from "tiny" 800-pound signal lamps to massive devices weighing up to 12.5 tons. The first illuminated buoy on the Great Lakes was lit off Cleveland Harbor on July 6, 1895.[18] To extend their useful life, buoys were customarily removed from the water in November and December to protect them from ice. In the spring they were placed back into the water, with the captain of the ship placing the buoys personally responsible for the accurate placement of each device. Placing and removing the buoys was hard work in any circumstance, but the rough weather of the spring and fall often made the challenge daunting.[19] Nevertheless the challenge had to be met, as a missing buoy could cause serious problems. In November 1976 the *John Sherwin* ran aground near Escanaba because of a buoy gone astray.[20]

Improved charts and better aids to navigation were components of nine-teenth-century navigation welcomed deep into the twentieth century. Another change, one that was less welcomed by some captains, was a slowly growing body of "rules of the road." For the first half of the nineteenth century, a captain on the lakes followed whatever course he pleased. When two ships approached one another, the good sense of the captains was relied upon to avoid accidents. Sadly, on more than one occasion good sense was noticeably lacking.

The problem of strong-willed captains stubbornly sailing their ships into harm's way was not unique to the Great Lakes. To create a safer, more predictable situation when two ships met, British insurance companies in 1840 pioneered the world's first set of navigation rules. These voluntary rules evolved into an international treaty created by the British in 1863. By 1866 thirty other nations had signed the treaty. Although the United States was not among the treaty's signatories, in 1864 Congress enacted legislation that essentially incorporated the treaty into American law. The U.S. law covered treaty-related matters such as lights and steering practices to be used when two ships met.

The British treaty and the American law of 1864 were largely designed for ships at sea or near port, and proved insufficient for the heavily traveled, but often very narrow, Great Lakes shipping lanes. To remedy the situation, in 1871 Congress created a "Board of Supervising Inspectors," which was granted the authority to issue additional regulations regarding navigation on the Great Lakes. Among the first acts of the board was to adopt uniform whistle signals.

The first whistle had appeared on a Great Lakes steamboat in 1831.[21] Captains of the era, however, used the whistle as simply a loud noise calling attention to their ship. The Board of Inspectors took what was essentially steam-powered shouting and regularized it into agreed-upon signals. When two steamships approached one another, the first to sight the other was required to use a standardized signal to indicate the course it would follow. The second boat was obliged to whistle an acknowledgment that the signal had been heard. If confusion occurred, both ships were to reduce their speed to the minimum needed to be able to maneuver and continue at this very slow rate until the confusion was resolved. In the era before radio communication, whistle signals grew ever more complicated. By World War I, when ships of the Pittsburgh fleet approached port, they identified themselves first by a fleet whistle signal, then after five seconds by a second whistle signal that indicated their size, and after an additional five seconds a third and final whistle blast assigned to the ship.[22] Although whistles and horns would eventually be supplemented by other communication devices, at the end of the century a ship's horn continued to be used as a communication tool.[23] In another example of supplemental regulations on the Great Lakes, in 1885 the board required Great Lakes vessels to display unique lights, different from those specified for other U.S. flag vessels in the law of 1864.

Although a congressionally approved board ensuring uniform practices was an improvement over relying on common sense, it left unresolved problems caused by the international nature of the lakes. Both American and Canadian ships sailed in the Great Lakes. In the lakes' many narrow passages, ships weaved in and out between the two nations' territorial waters. Despite this functional integration, the two nations adopted different navigational rules. To resolve the problem, Congress passed the "White Law" in 1895, which was drafted with Canadian concerns in mind and established separate navigation rules for the Great Lakes from those found on other American waters. In 1896 Canada reciprocated by establishing navigation laws for Canadian vessels on the lakes essentially identical to the American "White Law." The result was the first common set of U.S.-Canadian navigation rules, and thereafter a common set of navigational rules governed commercial ships on the lakes.[24] By the beginning of the twentieth century, Great Lakes ship crews spoke a common whistle language, and Canadian and American ships followed a certain number of common practices; but the master of the ship was still the master. Captains may have acquiesced to common whistle signals and a few other shared practices, but a successful captain was measured by how quickly he delivered his cargo, and to be a success, a captain routinely traveled the shortest possible route. In the narrow waters of the Great Lakes, this practice led, on a good day, to upbound and downbound vessels coming dangerously close. In fog or bad weather, the practice was a disaster waiting to happen. The solution was to require captains to use distinct upbound and downbound courses that created two "channels" for ships going in opposite directions. The first courses were established in 1911 on Lake Huron and Lake Michigan in the busy area around the St. Marys River and the Straits of Mackinac. These routes were voluntary, but had been adopted by the two major shipowners groups, the Lake Carriers' Association in the United States and the Dominion Marine Association in Canada. If a captain chose he could still set his own course, but a captain who did not voluntarily follow the prescribed course would likely find himself in significant trouble with the ship's owner, particularly if his actions led to an accident.

Despite their obvious value, defined courses seem to have been resisted. They were created only when there was a clear consensus to do so. In 1911 separate courses were charted in Lakes Huron and Superior. In 1926 channels were created in Lake Michigan. In 1947 eastern Lake Erie was given separate channels. Lake Ontario received channels in 1948.[25] It was not until the 1951 shipping season that permanent separate courses were agreed upon for the western end of Lake Erie, where ships entered and exited from the busy Detroit River.[26]

If the slow adoption of defined courses suggests a tendency to keep to the old ways, technological improvements to the compass made this point clear. For centuries, the magnetic compass had helped navigators around the world find their way. But an experienced navigator knew that magnetic compasses did not point to true north and, furthermore, were unpredictably inaccurate. Although he might not be able to explain why this was so, the navigator who did not adjust for the fluctuations of a magnetic compass could send a ship off its course. Scientists eventually determined that magnetic compasses erred for two reasons: a natural phenomenon known as declination, and a human-created problem, deviation.

Magnetic declination recognized the earth's own inexactness between true north and magnetic north. A ship's compass points to magnetic north, which is close to but not exactly "true north," defined as the location of the North Pole. Declination is the difference, measured in degrees, between magnetic north and true north. What complicates the navigator's task is that not only does a magnetic compass not point to true north, but the angle of declination is not constant. The earth's magnetic field is dynamic, causing it to change from location to location on the globe, and also change over time at the same location.

Since the first magnetic compass was brought aboard a ship, sailors have had to adjust for declination. The historic solution in the Northern Hemisphere was to compare the location of Polaris, the North Star, to the compass reading. The difference between where Polaris appeared in the night sky and the compass when the ship was heading north was the magnetic declination at a given point on the Earth's surface. Obviously "shooting Polaris" had limitations. In 1701 a navigation chart first appeared that included lines connecting points where the magnetic declination was the same, called isogenic lines. This pioneering effort was regularly updated, and the resulting charts were available to navigators in the Great Lakes and around the world. Because the earth's magnetic force lines are unstable over time, the work of drawing isogenic maps was unending. In 1600 declination in the western and southern parts of the Atlantic Ocean was east. By 1905 it had changed to west. Localized conditions could change far more swiftly.[27]

Magnetic deviation was caused by placing a magnetic compass in a metal vessel. Even small amounts of nearby metal could disturb a magnetic compass. One sailor recalled visiting a wheelsman who suddenly asked, "Have you got a knife?" Assuming the wheelsman wanted a knife to cut something, the visitor began to pull it out of his pocket. The sailor was more than a little surprised when, after the wheelsman saw the knife, he said, "Well, take it out of your pocket would you, and put it over there on the chart table because it's interfering with the compass."[28]

Sophisticated nineteenth-century compasses adjusted for magnetic deviation by placing two large iron balls on either side of the compass. Patented in the 1880s, the device was called "Kelvin's Balls" in England, in honor of their inventor, Lord Kelvin, but "navigator's balls" in the United States. Whatever a sailor called them, when properly adjusted, the spheres eliminated the predictable deviation created by metal in the ship, although the heading was still subject to error when unexpected metal objects came near the compass.[29]

In the early twentieth century, scientists developed a new and far more accurate way to determine true north. Gyroscopic compasses, or more commonly gyrocompasses, pointed to true north by relying on principles of physics and the interaction of the earth's rotation with the rotation of an electrically powered gyroscope. The first gyrocompass appeared in 1906 in Germany, and in 1909 the German navy placed them on its ships. In the United States, Elmer Sperry patented a workable gyrocompass in 1908 and founded the Sperry Gyroscope Company. In 1911 Sperry's gyrocompass was adopted by the U.S. Navy.[30]

A device that reliably pointed to true north would seem to answer the prayers of every navigator. But on the Great Lakes, neither captains nor shipowners warmed to the new invention. The first commercial gyrocompass on a Great Lakes freighter was installed by the Sperry Company in 1919 on the *Daniel J. Morrell*. The device proved too fragile and was removed. In 1922 Sperry tested an improved model, again on the *Morrell* since it already had all the necessary electrical connections. The new device worked well, but despite its success, gyrocompasses were not quickly installed on lake freighters.

Partly it was a matter of cost. A gyrocompass cost thousands rather than hundreds of dollars to buy and required a constant flow of electricity to work. By the 1920s electricity was common aboard the ships. The first ship with electric lights, the *Yakima*, was launched in 1887.[31] But vessels of the era usually carried only one electrical generator, and an electrical failure would stop the gyrocompass and leave the ship without any way to determine its heading. Even if the generator was in fine condition, standard practice called for it to be shut off during daylight hours as a cost-saving measure. Something that cost more, that would likely require a backup electrical generator, and that increased operating costs was not welcome by owners. And captains had their own concerns: they understood the magnetic compass and had long lived with its quirks, but the gyrocompass was something untested. It might work, but a cautious captain would likely still demand a magnetic compass to supplement the gyrocompass. Finally, even if the shipowner and the ship captain decided that a gyrocompass was a good idea, it was still novel technology. Shipowners hesitated to adopt it too quickly, lest they have to reinvest in "improved" models. All this slowed the adoption of a clearly useful and effective technology. It took a generation before gyrocompasses were standard equipment on lake freighters. It was only after World War II that most bulk carriers relied on gyrocompasses to plot their course.[32] The Ford fleet may have been the last to adopt gyrocompasses. They were installed aboard their vessels in 1953.[33]

The invention of the gyrocompass also made possible a nautical autopilot. The idea of developing a mechanical system to steer a ship was an old one. However, to make this dream a reality, two devices were needed—a mechanical steering system that could control the rudder, and a way for the mechanical steering system to know the ship's heading. By the 1860s the British navy had placed into service the necessary mechanical steering system, equipping various ships with "steering engines." The impetus for steering engines was that as ships grew bigger, it became increasingly impractical for the helmsman to physically move hundreds of feet of chain connected to a massive rudder. It was too much weight for a person to move. As a result, steering engines, steam or electrically powered motors that actually moved the rudder, became common on large military and commercial ships.[34]

Although steering engines created a mechanical means for rudder control, a ship's autopilot also needed a way to determine the heading. Magnetic compasses, with their incredible sensitivity to local magnetic fields, defied the development of an instrument that could read the compass without affecting the compass's accuracy. Electrically operated gyrocompasses had no such limitation. Developers of the gyrocompass began to work on devices that could monitor the heading reported by a gyrocompass and send that information to the steering engine.[35]

In 1911 Elmer Sperry tested his first automatic pilot, though the needs of World War I led Sperry to put aside work on the autopilot. However, in 1921 Sperry again began to work on the device because the number of gyrocompasses in use made an autopilot a likely additional sale, and secondly and perhaps more importantly,

Sperry's major competitor, the German firm Anschütz, was also working on the idea. Sperry feared that if Anschütz was successful, they would have a sales package that would give them firm control of the market for both autopilots and gyrocompasses.[36]

In April 1922, Sperry's first autopilot prototype was tested successfully on a ship sailing in the Atlantic Ocean. During the second ocean test, the officers aboard the vessel nicknamed the device "Metal Mike," a name that stuck. As a captain explained, the virtue of Metal Mike was that it "doesn't drink, smoke or kick about working overtime." Metal Mike became something of a national celebrity when, in addition to its exemplary personal habits and accommodating attitude toward management, it was described by the president of the Massachusetts Institute of Technology as a most exciting robot and thus caught the public's imagination.[37]

By 1932 Metal Mikes had found their way onto about four hundred commercial ships, including some Great Lakes freighters.[38] On the lakes they worked well on open waters, but they were never trusted on the narrow confines of the St. Marys or other rivers. Even after years of use on the open lakes, a Metal Mike could still cause problems. One incident occurred on the *Edmund Fitzgerald*. On a routine downbound trip, the captain ordered a course correction as the ship was passing from Lake Huron into the St. Clair River. The wheelsman attempted to make the change, but the rudder would not respond. For the next several minutes a controlled panic seized the ship. The captain ordered the engines to full reverse, making the ship shudder violently. The engineer on duty was ordered to immediately inspect the steering apparatus and rudder to determine what the problem was. A few minutes later the chief engineer ran into the wheelhouse. Before the startled captain could utter a word, he reached for the Metal Mike and turned a switch from "auto" to "hand." For the remaining tenure of that captain, the ship never again used its autopilot.[39]

Gyrocompasses and Metal Mikes show that the adoption of technology on lake freighters was a complex interaction between new technology, shipowners, and the crew of the ship. The story of how electronic location systems and wireless communication came to the lakes tells a similar tale. Electric systems that made it possible for a ship's crew to determine the location of their own or other vessels were quickly adopted. But in the first half of the century, communication tools, such as ship-to-ship and ship-to-shore radio, were resisted both by shipowners on shore and the crew aboard the ships.

The old ways of location had clear limitations. For all the work undertaken to place, maintain, and keep lights bright and other navigational aids afloat and in their proper place, a captain and crew had to be able to see them in order to benefit from the effort. When conditions were worst, virtually all of these systems failed, and captains were left to fend for themselves. During the proverbial dark and stormy night, some captains proved amazingly resourceful. During the Great Storm of 1913, a blinding snowstorm that reduced visibility to zero, Captain S. A. Lyons resorted to regularly measuring the depth of the water. His knowledge of Lake Huron's bottom was such that knowing the depth of the water was sufficient information for him to navigate safely and eventually bring his vessel to port.[40] Lyons's act of seamanship, however, was not matched by many. The storm destroyed nineteen ships and stranded nineteen other vessels.

The Great Storm of 1913 demonstrated what most sailors already knew: that in an emergency, a compass, a chart, and visible aids to navigation were insufficient to ensure a boat reaching safety. Because of this, the twentieth century saw an array of electronic means developed to help a crew determine a vessel's location. The first electronic technology deployed for this purpose was radio direction finding (RDF). After World War I, the U.S. Navy set up a series of radio beacons around the lakes. The beacons broadcast a continuous signal, usually a letter of the alphabet in Morse code. A radio direction finder aboard ship had a sensitive antenna that could be turned by hand to detect from where a signal was coming. Charts quickly denoted the location of each transmitter, making it possible to draw a line between the source of the signal and the ship. By doing this for two or more transmitters and noting where the lines crossed, the crew could determine the ship's location. RDF technology came aboard ships relatively quickly. In 1926 the Pittsburgh fleet began installing RDF, equipping all their ships within a year. RDF's impact was most obvious in the dramatic decline in the number of groundings. Regardless of light and weather, RDF gave a ship's crew a good idea of where they were.[41]

After World War II, RDF was supplanted by radar.[42] Radar used radio waves to detect both the distance and the direction of either stationary or moving objects. The basic technology was developed secretly and independently by the military in a number of nations during the 1930s and was used by those nations exclusively for military purposes throughout World War II. The English word "radar" came from a U.S. Naval acronym coined in 1939 that originally stood for "Radio Detection and Ranging." Although radar was an American military secret, its widespread use during World War II in all parts of the U.S. armed forces led to its existence becoming fairly well known. When peace came, the civilian applications for the technology were many, including use aboard freighters.[43]

Like with RDF, shipowners and crews quickly accepted radar. Not only did radar help ships locate themselves, but it warned them of nearby vessels, making it possible to navigate when it would be otherwise impossible. Prior to the installation of radar, when a ship in narrow channels encountered heavy fog, a prudent captain anchored the vessel until the weather improved. Radar changed this. In October 1946, as every other ship near the Soo went to anchor because of fog, the radar-equipped *A.H. Ferbert* steamed through the St. Marys River and into the Soo locks.[44] It did not take many such demonstrations to prove how useful radar could be.

On April 24, 1946, the first commercial radar unit on the lakes was installed on the freighter *John T. Hutchinson*. During the shipping season, several units made by different manufacturers were tested. Based on the compiled tests' results, in May 1947 the LCA issued recommendations for radar units to be used on all ships, with a minimum range of between one to two miles and a maximum range of forty miles.[45]

Radar's acceptance on the freighters was almost too rapid. In 1947 captains were warned that radar was no silver bullet. No system tested could see a close object; thus radar was not an electronic replacement for a watchman posted at the ship's bow, and in a tight spot, the presence of the captain in the wheelhouse.[46] Work on charts that could be used in conjunction with radar began in 1948.[47] By 1950, about 93 percent of the ships affiliated with the LCA were equipped with radar.[48]

In the 1970s new technology dramatically improved radar's accuracy. In 1974 a Loran C radar system was installed along the St. Marys River. Loran (Long Range Navigation) was in some ways similar to the pre–World War II RDF system; it allowed ships equipped with special receivers to automatically triangulate the ship's position and speed from low-frequency radio signals transmitted by fixed radio beacons.[49] Accurate to approximately 25 feet, this system dramatically improved safety as ships navigated the narrow passages to and from the Soo Locks.[50] The system was so successful that by 1980, Loran C radar covered the entire Great Lakes. All freighters larger than 10,000 tons were required to have Loran C radar operating by 1981, though it became far less important in the closing days of the century.[51]

In the early 1990s, electronic navigation systems used satellite-based Global Positioning Systems (GPS) to locate a ship's position and display it on a computer-generated navigation chart.[52] Two additional advanced technologies made an even greater impact. ECPINS (Electronic Chart Precise Integrated Navigation System), when coupled with AIS (Automatic Identification System), showed the location of each vessel by name, shared each vessel's direction and speed, and plotted the information instantly either on a satellite view of the area or an electronic lake chart. ECPINs also allowed captains to enter detailed sailing plans into the ship's computer. The sailing plan could include as many checkpoints as he or she felt was needed. A checkpoint might include things like where changes in the ship's heading were required, or reminders of at what point the mate on duty should call harbor traffic control to arrange for docking. Each captain developed a personal set of checkpoints, and because they could be stored in the computer, the sailing plans were reusable.[53]

If location technology was adopted quickly, the implementation of direct communication technology (ship-to-ship and ship-to-shore) had a more checkered history. The first years of the twentieth century offered a dramatic new possibility in communication: radio. In 1899, ship-to-shore radio communication first took place in the United States, and on the coasts the technology was accepted fairly rapidly. In 1910 Congress mandated that all vessels sailing more than two hundred miles off the U.S. mainland and carrying fifty or more passengers be equipped with radios. In 1912, the first international agreement was signed establishing an emergency radio frequency, 500 kilohertz (kHz). The agreement included provisions for regular radio silence on the frequency to ensure that an emergency signal would be heard.[54]

The railroad ferries crossing Lake Michigan pioneered radio communication on the lakes. In 1906 the Ann Arbor Railroad ferries were the first cargo vessels on the lakes equipped with wireless. They were followed in 1909 by the Pere Marquette Railroad's ferries. Though railroad ferries accepted them, owners of the bulk carrier fleets were categorical in their refusal to install radios. In 1907 the president of the Pittsburgh Steamship Company stated that his line was not considering installing wireless and never would. Though wireless communication seemingly proved its worth when, in September 1910, the sinking railroad ferry *Pere Marquette 18* communicated its plight by radio to the *Pere Marquette 17*, thus saving many lives, the following month a similar rescue was accomplished by a Pittsburgh vessel, summoned to help by means of signal flares. Pittsburgh officials used the incident to restate their belief that radio equipment was unnecessary.[55]

Among the many consequences of the *Titanic*'s sinking in 1912 were calls to require the installation of wireless equipment on all large ships. Reflecting the opinion of the Pittsburgh fleet, the Lake Carriers' Association opposed the idea, but several Great Lakes passenger lines announced that, for safety reasons, they supported placing radios on all ships. In response, the General Counsel of the LCA said that if the passenger-ship owners were truly concerned with safety, then rather than asking freighters to carry wireless equipment, they should replace their old, fire-prone wooden passenger vessels with ones built of steel, similar to "modern" freighters.[56] When, in 1915, the legislation first proposed in 1912 to regulate a variety of concerns aboard ships became law, it did not include a requirement for the mandatory installation of wireless equipment.[57]

Although legal requirements for wireless equipment were beaten back by the LCA, the owners of some freighters did voluntarily follow the example of the railroad ferries and installed the devices. The *Col. James M. Schoonmaker*, flagship of the Shenango line, in 1911 became the first bulk carrier on the lakes to have wireless aboard.[58] By 1913 the Shenango line had become the first shipping company on the lakes to systematically use wireless on all its vessels. The value of the decision was demonstrated during the Great Storm of 1913. Warned in advance by radio, the entire Shenango fleet rode out the violent event in safe harbors. Even more telling, other lines contacted the Shenango home office to inquire if the Shenango ships at anchor had any news about their vessels. Slowly shipping lines decided to voluntarily equip their ships with wireless, although as late as 1929, bulk carriers without any electronic means of communication were still sailing the lakes.[59]

What likely drove this change of heart regarding radio communication were weather bulletins. Information about the weather was vital to ships. To obtain it, in 1870 Congress created the United States Weather Bureau. One of the new agency's responsibilities was "giving notice on the northern lakes and on the seacoast, by magnetic telegraph and marine signals, of the approach and force of storms."[60] In November 1870 the Weather Bureau issued its first Great Lakes storm warning.[61] In the early years of the twentieth century, the bureau attempted to signal weather reports to crews on the water by a system of land-based warning flags during daylight hours and lights at night.[62] The 1913 storm convinced the Weather Bureau that flags and lights were not enough, and it began issuing weather broadcasts via radio in 1914.[63]

Many captains, despite the 1913 storm experience, continued resisting ship-to-shore communication. For them, safety took a back seat to the concern that radio communication would allow the home office to micromanage the ship. For almost a decade these captains blocked any systematic decision about radio communication, but finally, in 1924, they accepted telegraphy aboard ships, rather than voice communication. Likely their thinking was that the limited data-transmission ability of Morse code would keep the home office from being overly intrusive. Efforts to establish voice communication were abandoned.[64]

Federal law eventually forced voice communication aboard Great Lakes freighters. In 1934 radio telephones were introduced on lake freighters, most likely in response to the Federal Communications Act of that year finally requiring that ships carry and use voice-equipped radio receivers to monitor the 500 kHz emergency frequency.[65] Although the law was enacted for safety reasons, it obviously opened the vessels to all types of voice messages. The typical radio communication configuration of the era was installed on the Steamer *William C. Atwater*. It employed two channels broadcasting on AM radio frequencies. In 1938 about fifty ships had radio telephones, and by the beginning of World War II virtually the entire fleet was equipped with them.[66]

Three radio stations around the lakes provided full coverage, and switchboard operators could connect the ship-based telephones to telephone landlines, thus making communication between the ship and the home office possible on a routine basis. Because the system was run by the Ohio-based Lorain County Radio Corporation, crews almost universally referred to the communications system as the "Lorain."[67] The radio telephone was quickly used to share weather forecasts. By the 1950s regular weather reports were radioed to commercial ships every six hours, with warnings issued on an as-needed basis. Onboard resistance to the system had disappeared.[68]

For a brief moment in the 1950s, it looked like telegraphy might return to the Great Lakes. With the opening of the St. Lawrence Seaway, a number of saltwater ships began to enter the Great Lakes. Although the Great Lakes ships had universally adopted telephones for ship-to-ship and ship-to-shore communication, relevant international treaties allowed commercial freighters to communicate using either telephone or telegraph. In a flurry of activity, shipping interests across the lakes worked to eliminate the option of telegraphy. If "salties" wished to sail on the lakes, they needed the communication equipment used "here" rather than insisting that the Great Lakes shipping industry accommodate communication equipment used "there."[69]

The matter was resolved when the Canadian government announced in 1960 that effective January 1, 1962, all ships locking through the St. Lawrence Seaway must communicate with the Seaway authorities exclusively by radiophone.[70] There was only one way for oceangoing vessels to enter the lakes, and the locks would not be opened for them if they did not use a radiophone to communicate with the lock operators.

Although the continued operation of the radiophone for ship-to-ship and ship-to-shore communication was assured by this decision, the AM radio system adopted in the 1930s had already reached the end of its useful life. Traffic on the system was overwhelming its capacity despite additional channels being added. After World War II, five were available for use. But the volume of calls, over 120,000 in 1953, was too large even for five channels. The problem became worse in the evening when, because of a fluke in AM radio communication, marine communications from different parts of the nation and the hemisphere could routinely be heard on the Lorains aboard Great Lakes ships. Three channels regularly picked up traffic from Central and South America, while another received signals from Florida.

In 1951 the Lorain Company began to experiment with FM frequencies and eight communication channels.[71] As a practical matter the transformation from AM to FM communication was relatively quick on lake freighters, but adopting a legal requirement to move from the older AM system to the newer FM system proved slow. Only in 1974 did Coast Guard regulations require all ships to employ a lakewide FM system. The new system did not become fully operational until 1977, when fourteen FM land stations finally replaced the three AM land stations established during the 1930s. The system automated ship-to-shore communication, eliminated the operators necessary in the AM system, and added regular weather updates and automatic positioning information.[72]

From a business standpoint, the FM Lorain system had one major shortcoming. The many land-based transmitters needed to make it work were more expensive than the smaller number of transmitters needed to run the AM system. These costs were passed on to the system's users. Because the system was expensive, Great Lakes cargo carriers became early adopters of satellite and cellular communication systems. In 1982 the *Indiana Harbor* became the first freighter capable of satellite communication.[73] By the mid-1980s, satellite communication systems were coming into widespread use.[74] The adoption of satellite technology became mandatory under a series of subsequent international agreements. In 1988 the International Maritime Organization required ships to install a satellite-based Global Maritime Distress and Safety System (GMDSS) no later than 1999. Although it, like the radiophones of the 1930s, was mandated for reasons of safety, GMDSS quickly proved a useful channel for routine communication.[75]

Safety is a good area to demonstrate the complex interplay of considerations that affected ship operations. The Lake Carriers' Association routinely emphasized safety in publications distributed to the crews. Similarly the Lake Carriers' Association's annual report routinely included information about safety aboard the freighters, with a strong emphasis on reducing accidents. Safety, however, was not simply a question of humanitarian goodwill. Bundled into safety considerations were good intentions, as well as sound business reasons for supporting safe operations, and, should an injured worker take a ship owner to court, an unusual legal environment that heavily favored sailors over shipowners.

Safety on ships directly affected owners' insurance rates. According to the federal government, the shipping industry had one of the highest rates of accident claim experience of all occupations. When accidents happened, shipowners were unusually vulnerable to lawsuits filed by an injured sailor or his family. The admiralty law concept of unseaworthiness was tantamount to absolute liability. If something went wrong and a crew member was injured, generally speaking the law held the shipowner liable. Under the Jones Act of 1920, the survivors of a deceased crew member could also file a suit under the unseaworthiness doctrine. Up to 50 percent of the industry's protection and indemnity insurance costs resulted from protection for personal injury accidents. Fewer accidents meant lower premiums.[76]

In matters of navigation, safety of the crew and the efficient business operation of a vessel were also often intertwined. Radar, for example, added to the safety of the crew by helping to avoid collisions. At the same time, radar allowed a ship to operate under conditions that previously would have forced the vessel to anchor, thus helping maximize the vessel's utilization.[77] In some cases, safety improvements resulted from lessons learned through tragedy. In November 1966 the *Daniel J. Morrell* sank without issuing a distress call. All but one crew member died. The Coast Guard concluded that the most likely reason for no distress call was that the wheelhouse in the boat's bow had been suddenly separated from the ship's electrical generators housed aft in the ship's engine section. As the ship literally tore into two pieces, electrical lines broke and the wheelhouse was left without power, making the radio useless. The Coast Guard also concluded that the loss of life was caused in part by an inadequate supply of self-inflating rafts. As a result of these findings, in 1967 battery-powered emergency radiophones and additional self-inflating life rafts were voluntarily installed on most freighters. Eventually the Coast Guard made these changes mandatory.[78] A year after the November 1975 wreck of the *Edmund Fitzgerald*, the Coast Guard required individual emergency survival suits on all freighters.[79] The lack of survival suits had been a sore point between the crews' union and the Coast Guard for years. The union angrily noted that survival suits in some form had existed since World War II, yet the Coast Guard repeatedly delayed requiring the suits on lake freighters though they were placed on Coast Guard vessels.[80]

Safety sometimes took a back seat to delivery schedules. Although no shipping company would ever admit to winking at safety violations, much less publicly approve them, shipowners routinely rated captains on the speed of delivery. This criteria encouraged captains to improve their statistics by cutting corners. Reports of such behavior rarely occurred in official records, unless in an accident report, but when captains sat down to write their reminiscences, they often mentioned themselves or other captains engaging in questionable or dangerous practices to gain a competitive advantage.

One retired captain, recalling his career at the beginning of the twentieth century, remembered that the "rules of the road" were regularly ignored in order to shave time off a trip. In a comment that made it unclear whether he was referring to himself or to others, he also recalled that some captains went so far as to run at night without lights, in the hope of slipping into port ahead of another boat.[81]

If the anecdotal data in published accounts are to be believed, things only improved marginally as the century progressed. During World War II, the *Eugene J. Buffington* ran aground and broke its hull on Lake Michigan's Boulder Reef when the captain deviated from the prescribed course "to cut corners to make good time."[82] Another retired captain reminisced that one day, in a race with another ship to an Ohio port, he saved time by calling for full steam and pumping ballast to lighten the ship. The speed was not the safety concern—pumping of the ballast was. He altered course and sailed the lightened ship over a dangerous shoal. Such adventures made a good tale, assuming the captain got away with it. The same captain who risked grounding his ship on a shoal told another story of a ship's captain who, in a rush to beat a lineup of ships at the Soo Locks, came in too fast, could not check his speed, and collided with the lock gate.[83] Captains concerned about their company rating were still making interesting decisions late into the century. A reminiscing crew member recalled the day his captain, hoping to dock before another vessel, called for full speed and maintained radio silence all day, hoping that the other ship would not speed up.[84]

For all the tools and improvements, in the end the safety of the ship often depended on the skill of the crew and the ability of the captain. When systems failed, quick thinking and unexpected answers made the difference between making harbor and foundering amidst the waves. One of the most remarkable examples of a ship's survival occurred on Lake Superior in November 1926. The *Peter A.B. Widener* was on a routine run bound for Duluth. About 120 miles from port, in heavy seas and bad weather, the captain suddenly discovered the rudder had been torn away from the vessel. Distress signals summoned several nearby freighters, but the weather and seas were such that a towline could not be attached to the *Widener*. Eventually the *William K. Field*, the first ship to arrive equipped with a radio, asked that tugboats be dispatched from the nearest available point: Duluth. The *Field* was soon advised that the weather made it impossible for tugs to leave port.

Most people on the scene thought the *Widener* was doomed. The ship's captain, however, noticed something helpful: the direction of the wind. He ordered the ship's ballast pumped aft so that the bow was raised high to catch the wind, and then asked the engineer to slow the propeller to an absolute minimum. As the wind caught the bow, the ship was pushed like a giant weathervane, a weathervane slowly being put on a course for Duluth. With the correct heading established, the propeller sped up and the ship began to make headway toward port. The rudderless ship inevitably fell off course, but again and again the captain repeated the process of using the wind to point his ship in the right direction and then using all power to make additional progress toward safety. After thirty-six long, frightening hours, the rudderless ship arrived at the entrance to Duluth harbor. With the weather still too severe to send out tugs, the ship dropped anchor and waited out the storm until tugboats could finally tow it into a dock. When he was later interviewed by newspaper reporters, the captain proved a modest man. Rather than take credit for the ship's survival, he paid tribute to a good ship, a good crew, and the good Lord. But more than a few observers thought he might also have mentioned how he himself, the captain, through an extraordinary act of resourceful seamanship, had brought his ship and crew safely to port.[85]

Another story tells the tale of a captain whose split-second decision saved his ship and his crew. In a heavy fog, the prudent captain had dropped anchor in a narrow passageway, waiting for the fog to lift. A less wise master, running in the fog, rammed the anchored vessel. The anchored ship was clearly sinking, but rather than accept his fate, the quick-thinking captain raised anchor, called for full speed, and ran toward the beach. With water literally coming over the side of the ship, he successfully beached the ship, ensuring the safety of the crew and making subsequent repair far easier. Like the captain of the *Widener*, he took little credit for his quick thinking. Instead he said of the experience, "I wouldn't have minded so much, but they fined me a hundred dollars for landing in a foreign port without a clearance."[86]

A third captain also demonstrated how skill could help a ship. On a stormy night, a self-unloader was forced to run into Charlevoix's harbor too fast to undertake the necessary maneuvers to reach the dock. The captain's only choice seemed to be deciding what the ship would ram: a closed highway drawbridge the ship would normally pass through, a pier, or a waterside restaurant. The quick-thinking captain, however, ordered the engine to full reverse. As the propeller sucked water out from under the fully loaded ship, the hull struck the shallow harbor bottom and friction dragged the ship to a rapid stop. By reversing the propeller, the captain navigated his refloated vessel through the now open drawbridge.[87]

YEAR-ROUND OPERATION

Since the beginning of the twentieth century, as winter ice thickened, the shipping season ended. Everyone accepted that the Great Lakes were a seasonal waterway. To make the point, stories about the great freezes of 1926 and 1927 were frequently told. In 1926 a harsh and early winter stranded 150 ships at the Soo. Frantic icebreaking began. A freighter breaking ice would usually empty its forward ballast tanks and fill the aft tanks. With the bow now far higher in the air than the stern, the ship was run forward, forcing 50 to 100 feet of the bow over the frozen water until the ice cracked with a tremendous roar. Despite strategies like these, twenty-six ships were trapped in the St. Marys River until spring. The winter of 1927 saw even more ships stranded with another early freeze locking 247 ships in ice at or near the Soo. Although the weather relented sufficiently to free all the ships, the experiences of the two years were long remembered.[88] The common wisdom became that although Great Lakes freighters could break through solid ice, when thick ice was pushed toward a vessel by the wind, moving forward was almost impossible.[89] The wind could blow fresh ice in the ship's path at a rate about as fast as the ship could break through.

Although not as dramatic, stories were also told about ice in the spring. The shipping season usually began around April 1, but the weather could play odd tricks. In 1952, April ice jams in the St. Marys River idled over fifty boats, which could not travel through the river.[90] The 1984 season opened normally, but strong and consistent northerly winds in early April pushed large masses of floating ice out of Lake Huron and down the St. Clair River. The ice filled the river and in some places extended from the surface to the river bottom. At its worst, twenty ships were stuck in the ice while another seventy waited for the ice to clear. Although several icebreakers tried to break the ice, favorable winds and warm spring weather probably had the greatest responsibility for reopening the river to navigation.[91]

Despite these often-told tales, shipowners had always pressed to sail in the marginal days of early spring or late autumn. Tugboat companies actually bragged about their ability to continue working into the cold months, as an ad for the Great Lakes Towing Company published in 1917 made clear: "Thirty-four New Steel Tugs, built by us during the past ten years, were constructed with special reference to the requirements of Winter Navigation."[92]

Shipowners became truly serious about attempting year-round navigation in the late 1960s. A booming economy and prodigious demand for bulk cargo justified the idea. Taconite made the idea workable. The real limitation on year-round sailing, despite the tales of icebound vessels, was the cargo. Traditional ore froze in the winter. Regardless of how strong the ship was or how advanced its electronics, frozen masses of raw ore could not be loaded or unloaded. Taconite pellets, however, contained virtually no moisture and did not freeze; thus it could be shipped year-round.[93] If the cargo could be shipped, steel producers wanted to do it. As Christian Beukema, U.S. Steel's vice president for Ore, Limestone, and Lake Shipping, expressed it:

> One thing has become abundantly clear to U.S. Steel—it must maximize utilization of its most efficient facilities to attain optimum costs. The transportation of iron units from Lake Superior became a likely area for increased performance when U.S. Steel commenced operating its first taconite pellet plan in Minnesota late in 1967. For the first time in history we had tonnage of iron ore to move that was of sufficiently low moisture content that frozen cargo was no threat.[94]

Year-round navigation was also made possible by the increasing automation of navigation aids. By the 1960s automated, rather than crewed, systems had been installed throughout the lakes. Once-crewed lighthouses that were traditionally abandoned during the winter months now could operate year-round, requiring only an occasional "maintenance" visit by Coast Guard personnel, which was often done by helicopter. In addition, regular weather reports and frequent communication made it possible for ships at sea to avoid the worst nature might offer.

The 1967 shipping season was extended to January 3, 1968—about two weeks longer than normal. This modest beginning marked a decade-long effort to establish year-round navigation. In 1968 and 1969 the end of the season was again extended, respectively to January 7 and January 14. And in 1970 Congress appropriated funds for a three-year experiment to test both the technical feasibility and economic viability of extending the season even further. "Operation Taconite" commenced in 1970.[95] Congress was clear, however, that Operation Taconite was not an open-ended subsidy. The project would have to pay for itself in improved productivity: in return for a $5 million appropriation, Congress required $18 million in benefits.[96]

The demonstration project was eventually extended through the winter of 1978–79. For four seasons the project attempted to keep the lakes open for the entire year, beginning in 1974–75 and continuing through 1978–79. Three out of the four seasons this was accomplished, with only the harsh winter of 1976–77 closing shipping in February. The project demonstrated that it was feasible to operate year round. Operating in the winter months, however, proved expensive, slow, and hard on the crew and the vessels. Delays were common. The point is well documented by the log of the *Philip R. Clarke* in January 1976:

January 20

1130 hours . . . Beset 16 miles west of Mackinac Bridge. Awaiting [Coast Guard] cutter assistance. Very hard heavy ice.

1230 . . . Under way with [Coast Guard] cutter *Westwind*.

January 23

0435 hours Encountered hard, heavy ice a few miles east of Whitehall [Michigan] Light. Difficult progress between Garden Island and two miles west of Lansing Shoal. Cutter *Westwind* was assisting steamers *Ferbert* and *Fraser* eastbound.

January 30

0440 . . . Johnson's Point [in the St. Marys River] . . . Snow

0612 . . . Beset—Assistance required.

1040 . . . Cutter Woodrush arrived.

1225 . . . Freed—Under way.[97]

January 1976 was a particularly bad month. The St. Clair River and the Port of Buffalo were closed by ice.[98] At the Soo, ice in the lock narrowed the waterway such that the *Roger Blough* simply would not fit. It took over a day to break enough ice to make it possible for the *Blough* to enter the lock.[99] Even when movement was possible, days might be needed to cover water sailed in hours during the regular season. Hull damage was also common, even to the Coast Guard's ships.[100] Some of this was caused by the ice itself, but ships confined to relatively narrow lanes and often traveling in close companionship collided with some regularity, particularly when a lead ship hit a pocket of ice that suddenly slowed or stopped it, causing a trailing ship to run into its stern.[101]

Even when ships avoided one another, ice damage could be severe. The first voyage of the thousand-foot *Edwin H. Gott*, which like many of the newly constructed thousand footers had been reinforced to deal with ice, is instructive. Beginning on February 16, 1979, the *Gott* was in a convoy with three other ships, all going to Two Harbors, Minnesota, for a load of taconite. Aboard were senior officers of the Pittsburgh line, to observe, and likely celebrate, the success of their new all-weather ship. The trip, however, resulted in an experience that was hardly celebratory. The convoy encountered 16-inch ice, some of the heaviest ice of the demonstration project. Three of the four ships were damaged. The *Gott*'s bow was punctured and the ship took on water. One of the ship's twin rudders was lost completely, and the second rudder was damaged. Frozen ballast tanks buckled cargo-hold plates. The *Gott* reached port, but repairs took until late April to complete.[102] Cold-weather operation also created additional dangers for crew. In February 1976 two men died when the frozen cargo they were trying to remove from the side of their ship suddenly gave way.[103] Tragedies of this magnitude were fortunately rare, but winter sailing was hard on both the crew and the boat.

By the late 1970s it was clear that although ships could operate year-round, it was difficult and expensive to do so, and not profitable unless there was a substantial demand for taconite. As the national economy collapsed, the economic reason for year-round navigation ceased. Although U.S. Steel, which had led the charge for year-round operation, never conceded that the experiment had failed, it also never publicly disagreed with the Lake Carriers' Association's assessment that endorsed permanently extending the shipping season only until approximately January 8 as they concluded that the costs of operating ships in February and March, particularly in the St. Marys River, were simply too high to justify the practice.[104]

Over the course of a century much had changed. Satellite-based positioning systems located ships and facilitated communication in almost any situation; gyrocompasses and Metal Mikes, supplemented by GPS data, could steer a ship almost anywhere. Change had not always been welcome and in some cases, such as the desire for winter navigation, had proved possible but not economical. But the changes in how ships sailed safely from port to port had been both dramatic and dramatically effective. Technology could not completely replace seamanship, as Captain S. A. Lyons proved during the Great Storm of 1913, the captain of the *Peter*

A.B. Widener demonstrated after he lost his rudder, and the captain who avoided a catastrophe in Charlevoix by bringing his ship under control using the shallow harbor bottom showed. But increasingly such acts of seamanship were more the exception than the rule. Over the course of the twentieth century, captains and crews sailed their ships less and less, while more and more of the day was spent monitoring the highly technical systems that kept the vessel afloat, and engaging in the kind of cost analysis that made operating economically successful.

Fred Dutton, a wheelsman whose career began in 1916 and concluded in the 1950s, ended his published reminiscences by noting that he found boring the steam turbine engines that had replaced the older triple expansion steam engines.[105] Dutton had similar thoughts about the new electronic navigation tools in the pilothouse.

> There was a time this new gadgetry would have made me marvel. . . . But I found myself instead marveling at mates I'd known who had to do with pencil what some of these gadgets did—had to know down to a point as fine as frog's hair their wind and drift and whether she's loaded by the head or stern and how much water she's got in her, and be able to do everything by hand or they'd lose their tickets.[106]

Casting a knowing eye about the ship, Dutton concluded his final voyage, and his book, with the simple words "It was time to go ashore."[107]

CHAPTER 5

LOADING AND UNLOADING

The thing which in my judgment most influenced the change in type and size of the bulk freighters on the lakes came about through the invention of the Hulett unloader.

—William Livingstone, president, Lake Carriers' Association, 1902–1925, quoted in Eric Hirsimaki, "The Hulett Story"

Although many people watched freighters as they made their way up and down the lakes, boat watchers rarely observed the docks where the boats called. A freighter on the water might be romanticized, but the dirty, hardscrabble docks that the ships visited, near steel mills, quarries, huge piles of coal, and other industrial settings, were much harder to cast in a romantic light. The ports were working sites, not very different from the nearby factories. As in the work in those factories, speed mattered. The relatively short trips made by the ships, usually a week or less, made speedy loading and unloading a priority. The boats made money moving cargo—not while the cargo was being loaded or unloaded. The longer a boat was tied to a dock, the less profit it made. As a result, the loading and unloading facilities at commercial harbors on the Great Lakes, and eventually on the boats themselves, became models of mechanical efficiency.

In the final years of the nineteenth century and the first half of the twentieth century, this dedication to efficient cargo handling led to a series of devices designed to load and unload iron, coal, and stone at speeds far surpassing those achieved at the nation's saltwater ports. In the second half of the twentieth century, the goal to load and unload quickly led to a radical transformation of the ships themselves, eliminating the need for portside assistance when unloading.[1]

Despite these fundamental changes, there were pieces of continuity that linked loading and unloading operations throughout the twentieth century. The most notable example of continuity was the design of the ship's hold. Nineteenth-century Great Lakes freighters used beam and stanchion construction in the holds: horizontal beams spanned the cargo hold, while vertical stanchions placed at regular intervals held the beams in place. The design was strong and sensible, but the large number of beams and stanchions in the cargo hold got in the way of loading and unloading. To simplify this, the cargo hold was redesigned. Stanchions and beams were replaced by arched girders and heavy steel plating placed on the deck between cargo hatches. The result was one long, continuous hold that required no internal support. In 1904, the *Augustus B. Wolvin* was the first ship to have this kind of hold, and this unobstructed design continued to serve as the model for all Great Lakes freighters throughout the twentieth century.[2]

Having created a vast, open space for cargo, engineers turned to the question of how best to fill this cavern. In 1888 iron ore became the leading commodity shipped on the lakes, and it would remain the largest cargo into the twenty-first century.[3] Because moving iron ore was the largest part of the ship's work, loading and unloading techniques were designed first and foremost with iron ore in mind. Existing loading technology worked well for iron ore. It was placed into ships by a system used for loading vessels on the East Coast. An elevated railroad trestle was extended out over the water, creating a dock that towered above the waterline. Unlike a typical trestle, the space underneath the track was closed off into a series of "pockets," huge containers that could hold cargo waiting to be loaded into a ship. Tracks on the top of the trestle were carefully positioned so that railroad cars filled with ore could be located over the pockets built into the dock. Gravity emptied the ore from the railroad cars into the pockets beneath the car. Then the docking ship was carefully positioned under the raised chutes at the bottom of each pocket. With the open hatches and chute in alignment, the chutes were lowered, and gravity caused the ore to flow down, this time from the dock pocket into the ship below.[4]

Ore docks were massive. The Duluth, Missabe & Northern Dock number 4, built in 1906 in Duluth, was 2,304 feet long and had 384 pockets (192 a side). It was 57 feet wide and stood 72.6 feet above the water, and 13,782,263 board feet of lumber had been used to build the dock, with an additional 317,473 board feet used in constructing the approaching trestle. Completely filled, the dock's pockets could hold 119,274 tons of ore. A typical 600-foot-long, pre–World War II freighter, carrying about 12,000 tons of ore, could be fully loaded in four to six hours.[5]

Because of their cost, only a few major ports had ore docks. The first ore dock opened in Marquette in 1857, with others following at Escanaba, Michigan; Ashland, Wisconsin; Duluth and Two Harbors, Minnesota; and Superior, Wisconsin. Eventually the twin ports of Duluth/Two Harbors dominated the trade. The last ore dock constructed in the United States, built of concrete, was put into service in 1932 to improve loading facilities at Marquette. The last Great Lakes dock opened in 1945 at Port Arthur, Ontario.[6]

Ore docks required specialized railroad cars, as the hopper and gondola freight cars developed to carry bulk commodities by rail would not work. Hoppers had flat bottoms with "hatches" that allowed cargo to fall out, while gondolas improved upon the hopper by adding a slanted bottom that would facilitate the flow of cargo once the hatch was opened. These standard cars, however, were too large to easily carry the heavy ore and did not line up properly with the pockets on the ore docks. So in the 1870s, "ore jennies," shorter than the regular gondola cars and specifically designed so that hatches and dock chutes lined up, began to appear.[7] By the 1920s the design was standardized and would remain essentially unchanged for over a half-century. The key features of the system were a uniform car length of 24 feet, uniform distance between pockets, and uniform hatch openings on the ships.[8] To load a single ship required about forty jennies of ore.

When loading, care had to be taken, since raw iron ore was not all of a single type but came in several varieties. Ore was subdivided by its content of iron, phosphorus, silica, manganese, alumina, and moisture. The two main classifications were "Bessemer," ore destined for the Bessemer steel-making process, and "non-Bessemer," ore for open-hearth furnaces. Ore could be further subdivided—Minnesota's Mesabi Range had grades 1, 2 and 5 for the Bessemer steelmaking process, and 3 and 7 for non-Bessemer mills. Other major mining areas had their own nomenclature: Minnesota's Vermilion range offered Pioneer, a Bessemer grade ore; Frontier, a non-Bessemer grade; and Vermilion, while Michigan's Marquette range shipped non-Bessemer "Bedford" ore. Ships often carried multiple ore types, but mixing was not allowed.[9]

Loading also had to be done in stages, since the force generated by thousands of tons of ore simultaneously emptied into a ship would literally sink the vessel. To avoid this, only a few pockets, each holding about 350 tons of ore, were simultaneously emptied into the hold. The process, although safe, still sounded as if it was tearing the bottom out of the vessel.[10]

In addition to the noise, there was considerable danger to the crew created by stray pieces of falling ore and the frequent use of winches and cables to reposition the ship under the appropriate pockets. Hardhats and other protective gear minimized the danger from falling ore.[11] From the crew's perspective, repositioning the vessel, in order to place the open hatches under chutes still holding ore, was usually the greater risk. The simplest way to accomplish these small moves was for the crew to manipulate the cables linking the ship to the dock and literally drag the ship back and forth.[12] A crew member (often the wheelsman or boatswain) would simultaneously run two winches from a single control station, one aft and one forward. By pulling with one and letting off on the other, the ship was "gently" nudged along, placing the ship's empty hatches under still-loaded chutes.[13] In Marquette a ship was typically repositioned three times in order to load the cargo holds.[14] If a cable pulled free from the bollard, it could fly off, injuring or killing a deckhand.[15] Therefore, deckhands gave cables generous clearance. Moving the ship was demanding and required a surprising amount of artistry.[16]

Loading ore posed many other challenges. If rain or some other cause made the ore wet, it became very sticky and often refused to flow down the chutes. In cold weather, ore routinely froze into a solid mass.[17] Ore docks were built so dock workers could climb down ladders to various platforms from where they could poke at the stuck or frozen ore with long steel poles. Fire hoses connected to steam engines were sometimes used to direct hot steam at frozen ore. Care needed to be taken, however, because whether wet or frozen, the ore could fall with a sudden rush.[18]

Because time was so important, loading activity began before a boat arrived at the dock and sometimes continued after it had set sail. Whenever a port drew near, the deck crew began to remove the hatch covers. Deckhands were expected to have all the hatch covers removed when the ship tied up at the dock, making the vessel ready to immediately take on or discharge cargo. In good weather, ships would often leave port while the deckhands continued to put hatch covers in place.

At the beginning of the twentieth century, ships had wooden hatch covers, built in sections with each resting on a "coaming." The coaming was simply a metal edge that extended vertically from the deck and completely surrounded the hatch opening. The coaming's purpose was to keep water that came onto the deck from washing into the hatch opening. To open or close a hatch with a wooden cover, two men worked together, one on each side of the hatch. Using a "carrying club," which looked much like a baseball bat, the men slid the club through iron rings, lifted each hatch-cover section off the coaming, and then carried each section away from the hold. A typical wooden hatch-cover section weighed two hundred pounds.[19]

In bad weather, working the hatches was even harder because tarps would have been placed over them, as wooden hatch covers leaked. To keep water out, crews covered each hatch with very large waterproof tarpaulins. A tarp was first draped over the hatch and down the coaming. Battens, thin pieces of board pushed up against the edge of the coaming and fastened in place using clamps, held the tarp in place.[20] Removing or setting tarps as the ship approached a port or set off on a voyage was additional work for the deckhands.

When the wind picked up, tarps could work loose in mid-voyage, allowing water to enter the hold. The safety of the crew and the ship required that the tarps be refastened or replaced. But the job often required working on a pitching deck that was wet or icy, with waves crashing over the ship's side. Deckhands had to rely on a keen eye for waves, their sense of balance, and their wits to avoid being washed overboard. Because of where and how the work was done, lifelines were impossible to use. Usually the crew first tried to tighten the tarps. But if the tarps began to shred, the crew replaced them. This meant taking off the old tarp and hauling up and installing new ones from below. A used tarp was extremely difficult to handle as it was always wet and often ice-encrusted. The dry tarps brought up from below had their own challenges. If one was caught by the wind, it acted like a giant sail. It could take five to eight men two hours to remove a tarp off a hatch and then replace it with a new one.[21]

The limitations of wooden hatch covers, whether in port or at sea, were obvious. In the first decade of the twentieth century, new ships were equipped with metal "telescoping" hatch covers that folded onto themselves. Telescoping hatches were first installed in 1904 on the *Wolvin*, and in 1910 the *Emperor* became the first Canadian ship to use them. Cables were attached to the telescoping covers, and a winch was used to pull the overlapping pieces of metal to either open or close the hatch.[22] This process was much faster than deckhands using clubs, and the speed with which telescoping hatch covers could be opened or closed made them the standard in new freighter construction.[23]

When they were introduced, telescoping hatches were also said to be waterproof and thus designed so that a tarp could not be battened over them. Tragedy put the lie to the claim that telescoping hatches were waterproof. In 1907 the ship *Cyprus*, equipped with telescoping hatches, sank in heavy seas. The ship took on water during the storm, and local newspapers quickly identified the lack of tarps as the cause of the sinking. "It would seem that on somebody rests the responsibility of sending the lost steamer *Cyprus* to sea in unsafe condition—with her hatches still uncovered." Although the individual on whom "rests the responsibility" for the sinking was never identified, after the loss of the *Cyprus* the coamings that supported telescoping hatches were redesigned to allow for tarps, and the use of tarps over the hatch covers in heavy weather or late-season sailing remained standard practice, insisted upon both by government agencies and insurance companies.[24]

In 1925 a hatch-cover design employing a single piece of metal placed on a gasket was used on the *William C. Atwater*. This design replaced telescoping hatch covers in new construction and was used for the remainder of the century. Using a crane, often called the "iron deckhand," a single piece of metal weighing about a thousand pounds could be placed over or removed from a hatch opening in about twenty minutes, more quickly than either wooden or telescoping hatch covers could be manipulated. The new design was genuinely weathertight, meaning it would keep out rainwater but would leak if submerged. Weathertightness was achieved by welding a continuous round bar to the coaming that fitted snugly into a channel equipped with a watertight gasket located on the bottom of the metal hatch cover. When the hatch cover was lowered into place, the bar fit into the channel and compressed the gasket, creating a weathertight seal. The design eliminated the need for tarps. The advantages of this type of hatch cover were obvious to both shipowners and ship crews, and by 1938 all new vessels used this design, while many older vessels were retrofitted with them.[25]

Deckhands, however, continued to perform a great deal of labor to open or close even the single-piece metal hatch cover. Despite its weight, each solid-metal hatch cover was fastened to the coaming by clamps, usually placed at 2-foot intervals. The exact number of clamps would vary by ship and cargo, but the number was always large and the work of setting or removing them was always hard. One deckhand reminisced about entering port and looking with little joy at the fifty-six clamps placed on each of the ship's eighteen cargo hatches.[26] After several hours working with the clamps, his back and arms always ached.[27]

If removing clamps was the bane of deckhands aboard more modern ships, many crews continued to wrestle with tarps long after the introduction of single-piece hatch covers. Because of the long life of lake vessels, old boats often featured outdated hatch covers, and even in the 1960s wooden hatch covers could still be found on some ships.[28] In 2008 a ship using telescoping hatch covers was still in service. Thus, although technologically outdated, on some ships tarps continued to be used for the rest of the century.[29]

Although Great Lakes ship designers were free to use different types of hatch covers, the height of coamings was eventually regulated. Coamings were first standardized by the International Freeboard Convention of 1930, which set the height of coamings for ocean ships at a minimum of 24 inches in the bow of the vessel and 18 inches for the rest of the ship. Although this accord did not immediately apply to Great Lakes vessels, in 1935 the USCG made the 1930 coaming rules mandatory on the lakes. Eventually regulations on the lakes were modified so that coamings on the forward one-fourth of a ship were required to be 18 inches or taller, while those on the remaining parts of the ship need only be 12 inches tall.[30]

The nature of coamings and hatches, although constantly improved, fit a relatively standardized template throughout the twentieth century. The way ships were loaded, although it changed in the last half of the twentieth century, was not significantly different than what a person might see at any seaport. What was impressive about loading was more the scale of the operation than the technology. Where the Great Lakes shipping industry made its greatest portside innovations was in unloading. In the words of William Livingstone, longtime president of the Lake Carriers' Association, "The thing which in my judgment most influenced the change in type and size of the bulk freighters on the lakes came about through the invention of the Hulett unloader."[31]

Gravity, used so efficiently to load vessels, was no friend when it came time to unload a lake freighter. For most of the nineteenth century, the only way to get the cargo back on the dock was by men using shovels. The earliest method of unloading ore placed men with shovels and wheelbarrows in the ship's hold. The ore was shoveled into wheelbarrows, and the wheelbarrows were pushed up scaffolding to move the ore upwards from the ever-lowering pile, eventually rolling from the boat to the dock. Under the best of conditions, this method took about a week to unload a typical three-hundred-ton cargo carried by a pre–Civil War vessel. The best of conditions overlooked choking clouds of red dust that rose when the ore was dry, as well as the way wet ore clumped together and became almost impossible to shovel.[32]

Shortly after the Civil War, wheelbarrows and scaffolding were replaced by mechanical systems to raise ore out of the hold. Using block, tackle, and horses, three thousand pounds of ore could be shoveled into a huge bucket and lifted out of the ship's hold. In 1867 a steam engine, called a "steam donkey," first replaced the horses to raise and lower the bucket. Capable of lifting nine thousand pounds at a time, the steam donkey quickly replaced horses at dockside. The process was simple. A ship's hatch was positioned under the "donkey" and a bucket lowered into the hold. Workers in the hold shoveled ore into the bucket, which was, when filled, raised to the dock. The ship was then repositioned to put the next hatch underneath the donkey and the process was repeated. Using a steam donkey, a typical freighter of the era could be unloaded in about a day.[33]

In the 1880s a variety of innovations speeded the lifting of ore from hold to dock. The most frequently seen was the Brown hoist. The hoist was introduced in Cleveland in 1882 and employed a tramway to first pick a bucket of ore out of the hold and then move it to where it was desired on the dock. By 1890, over 150 Brown hoists were in operation around the lakes. The growth in use of Brown hoists reflected the phenomenal growth in the amount of ore being shipped. In 1884, roughly 2.5 million tons of ore moved across the lakes. By 1888, that number had grown to more than 5 million tons. A decade later, in 1898, 13.6 million tons of ore were shipped. Despite a variety of small improvements, the Brown hoists simply could not keep pace with the growing size of ships or the growing volume of trade.[34] As ships grew larger, they spent more and more time in port, losing money.[35] The fundamental problem was that unloading still relied on men in the hold shoveling. A good man, working a fourteen-hour day, could move at most about one hundred tons of ore, and there was only so much room in a hold for men with shovels.[36] As long as holds were emptied by shovelers, there was no way to make the process faster.

The solution was to replace men with machinery. The machine needed was developed in 1898 by George H. Hulett. A specialist in loading bulk cargo, Hulett envisioned a huge scoop pulling iron ore out of a ship's hold, then moving it back to the dock. Others had considered the idea of using a scoop but failed to develop a workable model. To make his idea work, Hulett developed three innovations. First, the bucket he imagined was ten times more massive than those previously used, the extra weight giving it more "bite" than its predecessors. Second, the bucket was hinged at the bottom, with hinges designed to close inward, thus scooping ore inside. Finally, hydraulic rods powered by steam pressure created enough force to close the bucket, regardless of the weight of the ore. The bucket was attached via a steel leg to a crane-like apparatus. The operator stood on the steel leg directly over the bucket, allowing him to position the bucket over the ore in the hold, drop the bucket, then retract the bucket and swivel it about to unload the ore on the dock. The thing Hulett envisioned was like nothing ever seen before.[37]

The first Hulett unloader was constructed at Conneaut, Ohio, on the dock owned by steel magnate Andrew Carnegie. Carnegie agreed to buy the contraption only after obtaining two extraordinary concessions: the machine would be built at the expense of Webster, Camp & Lane Co., for whom Hulett worked, and there would be no "upfront" charges. If the machine did not work as promised, Webster, Camp & Lane would not only absorb all the construction costs but would also pay to have it removed from Carnegie's dock. In 1899, when the machine was ready to be demonstrated, the final challenge proved to be finding someone to operate it. Common wisdom among the workers who had watched the machine being constructed was that only a crazy person would try to unload an ore boat standing on top of an iron leg, operating a giant ten-ton bucket, all while dangling high above a freighter on what appeared to be an impossibly weak crane. Eventually an operator was found.[38]

Once it began working, the Hulett quickly proved it was faster than anything that had preceded it and everything that had been promised. The first Hulett could unload 275 tons per hour. A more efficiently designed cargo hold could lead to even greater speed. Thus, beginning in 1904, the cargo holds of all newly constructed ships were redesigned to eliminate stanchions and beams. This change allowed the machine to reach 98 percent of the cargo. Prior to the Hulett, the least expensive way to unload a ship full of ore cost about nineteen cents per ton. Early Hulett machines lowered that cost to about six cents per ton. By 1908 various improvements drove unloading costs down even further.[39] The machines were usually constructed in groups of from two to seven. Eventually about seventy-five Hulett machines were built.[40] They became the standard unloading device for Great Lakes iron-ore boats for the first seventy years of the twentieth century.[41]

Hulett unloaders, however, had limitations. One of the early modifications to the machine was to change the energy source from steam to electricity. The amount of electricity needed to operate a Hulett was so large that turning on the machine literally dimmed the lights in many port towns. Several docks had to build independent power plants until a city or a public utility could sufficiently increase its electrical generating capacity to meet the Hulett's demand for power.[42] Given the massive size of the bucket, which quickly grew from a scoop capable of grabbing ten tons of ore to one capable of bringing up fifteen tons, a careless operator could seriously damage a ship.[43] Huletts were also somewhat top-heavy, and over the years a few Huletts were actually tipped over when a boat's bow fouled one of them.[44] A far more common problem was that the size of the bucket also meant that at some point the Hulett would be unable to pick up "small" amounts of ore in obscure corners or simply scattered across the hold's bottom. Because of this, there were times when the crew had to work in the hold while the Hulett was operating. Men with shovels, sometimes aided with a bulldozer that was lowered into the hold, would pile the last of the cargo in places where the Hulett could reach it.[45] This was dangerous work. One sailor recalled how an accident with a Hulett's bucket slammed him from one side of the hold to the other.[46]

Although Hulett machines represented a huge increase in unloading capacity, the most impressive achievement of the pre–World War II shipping industry was not the Hulett itself but rather the construction of custom-built harbors full of the machines. An early example of this undertaking was at Conneaut, Ohio. A port town through the first half of the nineteenth century, by the late nineteenth century Conneaut had fallen into commercial disuse. The port was revitalized in 1892 when a railroad company selected it to serve as its major depot on Lake Erie. In 1896 Andrew Carnegie bought control of the railroad and, incidentally, the Conneaut dock. He decided to make Conneaut a focal point of his vast steel empire. Symbolic of its newfound importance, the largest battery of Hulett unloaders were installed in Conneaut between 1911 and 1914. Although Conneaut was an extreme example, at the beginning of the twentieth century customized facilities to maximize the efficient handling of iron ore were constructed and then enlarged.[47] Custom harbors continued to be constructed well after World War II. For example, in 1957 Taconite Harbor was built in Minnesota to make it possible to load taconite pellets from the Erie Mine.[48]

For all the mechanization, unloading ore remained hard work. For good reason, the ballad "Red Iron Ore" long remained a sailor's favorite:

Come listen young fellows who follow the Lakes,
In iron ore vessels your living to make.
I shipped in Chicago, bid adieu to the shore,
Bound away to Escanaba for red iron ore.

Some Sailors got shovels and others got spades
And more got wheelbarrows, every man to his trade:
We looked like red devils; our fingers got sore
And we cursed Escanaba and her red iron ore.[49]

If iron ore was the most frequently shipped commodity on the lakes, coal represented an always welcome secondary cargo. Through World War II, coal fueled America. It was the most common product shipped by railroads and was also a frequent cargo on the lakes. Coal, however, was a very different cargo from ore. Unlike iron ore, which could be dropped into a ship's hold with no concern over how the ore's size or shape would be affected, for the first half of the twentieth century, coal was shipped in lumps already sized to be shoveled by hand. Any loading process that broke the lumps into smaller pieces made the product less useful. Thus coal, which was surprisingly fragile, needed to be loaded with unexpected delicacy. For most of the nineteenth century the only solution was to load and unload coal by hand.[50]

However just as the volume of iron ore being shipped required new ways to load and unload the product, so too the volume of coal required a way to load and unload that was faster than could be achieved by men using shovels. The first step toward this occurred in 1893 when "whirlies," first used for iron ore, were modified to load coal. Whirlies were swiveling derrick cranes that moved on railroad-like tracks. Whirlies were modified to move large metal tubs loaded by hand with coal and then lowered into or raised out of a ship's hold. This however, remained a slow process, akin to the way iron ore was unloaded using steam donkeys, and various individuals began to experiment with ways to directly transfer coal from railroad cars into the ship.[51]

The idea that several people came upon was to run fully loaded railroad coal cars up an incline that positioned them next to, but above, a docked ship, and then use chutes and gravity to transfer the coal to the ship. The challenge was to invent a gravity feed process that was sufficiently gentle to avoid pulverizing the coal. Several techniques were attempted, but the one that was perfected in 1907, and eventually gained widespread acceptance, combined features of various predecessors. The fully loaded coal hopper car was pushed up an incline and then literally turned sideways. The sideways dumping minimized the amount of crushing. As the car slowly turned, the coal fell into a large, funnel-shaped pan. Gravity pulled the coal down the pan into an articulated spout that could deliver the coal into the bottom of the ship's hold gently enough so that breakage was minimal. By 1917, thirty-two such machines were on the lakes, modified only in that the car to be unloaded "bumped" the empty car down the other side of the incline, and gravity rolled the empty car into the appropriate holding track, where a switching engine would eventually claim it for another load.[52]

Like iron ore, coal could be difficult to ship. It took from two to three hundred railroad cars of coal to fill a Great Lakes freighter. Simply amassing this quantity of coal and moving it from dock to ship took considerable planning. Coal, like iron ore, was graded into types, usually three, which could not be mixed. Ships could carry more than one grade, but this meant taking care that the grades were divided. Coal generated methane gas, and the hold had to be carefully vented to avoid possible explosions.[53] A final complication was that, like iron ore, wet coal tended to be difficult to move. Wet or fine coal tended to stick. The crew usually had to enter the hold to push wet coal into or onto whatever was being used to unload it, a dangerous job that was eventually eliminated by improved technology in the 1970s. Finally, coal, like iron ore, froze together into a solid mass both in the railroad cars during transport and in the hold of the ship, making it very difficult or impossible to move in the winter.[54]

Changes in the form of iron ore and coal shipped after World War II changed the docks and the ships. By the 1950s, high-grade "raw" iron ore from Michigan and Minnesota was becoming scarce. It was replaced by taconite, an enriched ore product that was manufactured at the mine from various low-grade ores and produced as small, uniform pellets.[55] Raw ore, because of its high water content and sticky nature, defied all efforts to use conveyor-belt systems for loading. Taconite, with low water content and a standardized shape, worked well on conveyors. Taking advantage of this, the first conveyor system to load taconite became operational in the spring of 1957 at the appropriately named Taconite Harbor on Lake Superior.[56]

Taconite revolutionized ore transport, eventually allowing for the creation of conveyor-belt systems for both loading and unloading. But a few echoes of the past remained, as loading taconite by conveyor was just as noisy as loading ore from an ore dock. And, like raw ore, taconite had to be loaded carefully lest its weight literally sink the ship.[57] But the gravity docks and Hulett machines that had dominated major ore ports became a thing of the past.[58] The last Hulett unloader was built in 1960, and the last working Huletts, found in Cleveland, went silent in 1992.[59]

How coal was loaded and unloaded was also transformed. This change came about because of changes in the coal market. The adoption of automatic stoking machines in most industrial applications meant that commercial users pulverized coal prior to its use. Size no longer mattered to them. At the same time, the home-heating market, a primary destination for coal, was rapidly moving to oil or natural gas. Homeowners preferred allowing a thermostat to automatically "fire up" a gas- or oil-operated heating unit instead of starting a new fire in a cold house or getting up in the middle of the night to shovel extra coal into the furnace. Maintaining lumps of coal sized for hand shoveling no longer mattered, and conveyors were vastly more efficient at loading and unloading than the older coal-dumping apparatus. The last coal-dumping apparatus was constructed in 1924. After World War II it, and all of its earlier predecessors, were quickly replaced by conveyor belts.[60]

Even when they were the marvels of modern technology, the size, complexity, and expense of Hulett unloaders and coal-dumping platforms created a niche market for self-unloading Great Lakes freighters at smaller, less frequently visited ports. Self-unloading vessels discharged bulk cargo without assistance from any shoreside equipment or shoreside personnel. The cargo was unloaded using a system of conveyors built into the ship. The cargo holds were "hopper-sloped," or slanted on their sides, so that the cargo flowed down through gates located at the bottom of the holds. The cargo dropped onto a tunnel conveyor belt that carried the cargo to one end of the ship. There it was transferred onto a second belt system that carried the cargo up to the main deck of the ship. Once on the main deck, the cargo was again transferred onto a third and final conveyor belt, this one built into a long, movable metal boom. Just as a crane moves both vertically and horizontally, the boom could be raised over the deck and then swung in either direction. This ability allowed the crew to position the boom, and the final belt running inside it, over the side of the ship and above the dock, where the cargo being brought out of the hold would fall off the final belt.

The *Wyandotte*, which began service in 1908, is often listed as the first self-unloading freighter on the Great Lakes. It was certainly the first purpose-built self-unloader. However, the prototype ship employing the technology was the *Hennepin*. Launched in 1888 as a small, steam-powered wooden freighter, the ship was severely damaged by a fire in 1901. In 1902 the ship was rebuilt in a radical new way and became the first self-unloading ship on the Great Lakes.[61] Coal became a regular cargo for the self-unloaders because most power plants or factories located along the water fired their boilers with coal, and coal was shipped to them more cheaply by water than by rail.[62] That it might not arrive in as nice a shape as might be desired took a back seat to the cost savings water transport offered over railroads. Coal moved on self-unloaders, particularly when it was being sent to smaller ports.

By the 1920s, stone, which also often went to small ports, frequently moved on self-unloading vessels. Of the many cargoes carried by bulk ships, limestone was among the easiest with which to deal. It was relatively clean. It rarely froze, and it was easy to unload via onboard self-unloading systems. Because quantities of limestone were necessary in the steelmaking process, and were also used in the construction, cement, and agricultural industries, stone made up a significant quantity of the cargo carried on the lakes. Most stone came from the Alpena area.[63] Limestone from Alpena, also called dolomite, was useful in blast furnaces because of its purity and the nearness of the quarries to lakeside docking facilities.[64]

Self-unloaders tended to be smaller than the big ore boats. The less frequently used ports they called upon were already shallow and had often silted up, a combination of factors that made it difficult or impossible for even a small boat to reach the dock. The story of one self-unloader attempting to deliver stone to a dock along the Saginaw River documents both the problem and the crew's ingenuity in getting the job done. When he realized that the fully loaded ship could not come anywhere near the dock assigned for unloading, the captain ordered the self-unloading apparatus started and used it to move as much stone as possible from the front of the ship to the aft, raising the bow. When that idea proved insufficient to allow the ship to reach the dock, the captain repeatedly ran the ship full speed ahead and then full speed back—to carve his own channel. Eventually this process left the ship stuck in the mud but still a few feet short of the reach of its unloading boom. As a last resort, the captain ordered unloading to begin anyway, with the conveyor on the boom running at maximum speed. Stone was literally thrown over the remaining water and onto the shore. After unloading as much stone as possible this way, the captain ordered the engine to full speed and push the lightened ship the last few feet needed to completely unload.[65]

Even when well maintained, some docks were so miserably located that it was always a challenge to make a delivery. One of the worst docks on the lakes was Indiana's U.S. Gypsum facility, located about two miles upriver from Lake Michigan's Indiana Harbor. The "easy" part of the trip involved traveling through a narrow canal and past seven bridges, to reach a small turning basin. At the basin, the captain ran the bow of the ship into a mud bank and used the engine to swing the ship 180 degrees. The captain then backed the ship, stern first, for another one-third of a mile towards the dock. The dock was such that to unload the material in the desired location, the ship had to be positioned perpendicular to the dock rather than next to it. To accomplish this feat, while the ship was still moving, six crew members were put over the side. Four went onto the U.S. Gypsum dock, two assigned to each end, while the remaining two were dropped off at the Texaco dock on the opposite side of the canal. With crew ready, lines were thrown to all three sites and, using the ship's winches, the vessel was tied broadside across the canal, the stern pointed at the U.S. Gypsum facility. If some other vessel wanted to pass through the canal, unloading stopped, the line to the Texaco dock was allowed to go slack and sink, and the unloading ship was pulled parallel to the gypsum dock. Once the unloading ship was parallel to the gypsum dock, the passing vessel could proceed, sailing over the sunken line still attached to the Texaco dock. When the other ship had passed by, the line to the Texaco dock was again pulled tight, the unloading ship was put back into its position across the canal, and unloading resumed. This maneuver took from an hour to an hour and a half to accomplish, and it was common to have to do it two or three times while unloading.[66]

So long as raw iron ore and coal sized for shoveling were the most common bulk cargo carried by the freighters, self-unloaders remained a subset of the Great Lakes fleet. This can be seen by how early self-unloaders came into service. Rather than being purpose-built, new vessels, most pre–World War II self-unloading ships were obsolescent straight deck boats given a new lease on life by being converted to self-unloaders.[67] During World War II there were only fifty-four self-unloaders on the lakes.[68] Until the 1960s the self-unloaders remained "specialty" vessels primarily hauling stone throughout the lakes, or coal into small ports that lacked unloading equipment.[69]

Within the self-unloading category there were even more specialized boats: cement ships and crane vessels. Crane vessels were usually old, small straight deckers that were refitted with two cranes for unloading, rather than a conveyor belt. To increase their versatility, the crane ships could mount different types of devices on the end of their crane. Clamshell buckets were used to unload coal, slag, slate, or sulfur. An electromagnet could be attached to move pig iron or scrap iron. A sling-like device could be used on the odd occasion that finished products, such as new automobiles, were being transported.[70]

Because of the ready availability of basic ingredients in several Great Lakes port cities, cement was made in many places and became a frequent cargo on Great Lakes ships.[71] In the nineteenth century, cement was bagged and loaded into ships. However, in 1915 Huron Cement of Alpena revolutionized waterborne cement transportation. The company's first bulk freighter, the *Samuel Mitchell*, enjoyed an economy of scale previously unrealized. Size, however, was the lesser reason for the *Mitchell*'s success. Innovative technology made it possible to load the *Mitchell* and its successors in approximately 3.5 hours.

The cement put on board the *Mitchell* was not bagged. Instead the *Mitchell* employed a unique loading system that took powdered cement stored in silos and used a combination of conveyor belts, gravity, and air pressure to blow the powder directly into the ship's hold. Because cement was sensitive to moisture, cement carriers had hatch covers unlike those found on other Great Lakes freighters. In place of the massive single piece of metal that usually covered each hatch on a bulk carrier, cement carriers had small circular openings over the hold. These openings could be fitted with hoses to blow cement in or out of the ship. Because of their small size, the openings were also much easier to seal against moisture.[72] The cement trade proved to be the last posting of many venerable Great Lakes ships. The old boats that carried cement were well suited to the many small ports where cement was made and delivered. Also the capacity of these small ships was well matched to the storage capacity of the terminals they served.[73]

Two changes made self-unloading vessels the backbone of the fleet: taconite and the new Poe Lock, opened at the Soo in 1969. The thousand-foot vessels made possible by the new lock and built in the 1970s and early 1980s were so large they required a complete rethinking of the existing ore transportation system. These vast ships could not be accommodated at existing chute-style loading docks, nor could they be easily unloaded at existing port facilities. To accommodate the new ships, shippers would have to either rebuild old port facilities or rethink the traditional straight-deck ore carrier. Redesigning the ships proved cheaper than rebuilding the ports. The first thousand-foot ship, the *Stewart J. Cort*, was designed to be loaded with taconite brought on board by a conveyor, and it used an onboard, self-unloading system to deliver its cargo to the dock.

The self-unloading system on the *Cort*, however, was not the one that later thousand-foot ships employed. The conveyor system that eventually became standard on the thousand footers was pioneered on Canadian ships. The traditional limitation on conveyor systems was that if the belt was tipped at too high an angle, the cargo would fall off. This limitation led most pre–World War II self-unloaders to use a bucket system to lift cargo vertically. The more or less flat conveyor in the hold would empty into a series of buckets attached to a rotating belt that ran vertically from the hold up to the third conveyor, which ran in the boom. The speed of the conveyor in the hold was synchronized with the speed of the belt holding the buckets such that as one bucket was filled with cargo it was lifted up by the belt and, without an interruption, a new, empty bucket appeared. Eventually, the full bucket reached the conveyor on the boom, emptied onto it, and then made its way back into the hold for another load. Synchronizing the operation of the three belts, two using belts running horizontally and the other buckets running vertically, was always a challenge. Most often the problem occurred in the hold. If the horizontal belt moved too slowly, the buckets moving upward were not completely filled and the unloading took extra time. But if the horizontal belt in the hold moved too quickly, too much cargo arrived and the bucket overflowed.

In 1969 the Canadians installed a newly designed belt system on the *Quetico*. One belt carried the cargo while a second belt running nearly on top of the first belt held the cargo onto the first belt. A simpler variant on this idea, installed on the *J.W. McGiffin* in 1972, became the industry standard. In this version the horizontal belt running underneath the cargo hold deposited the cargo onto a second, semi-circular-shaped belt that would eventually rise vertically from the hold. Before the now full semicircular belt began its vertical assent, another "holding" belt literally began to run on top of it. The holding belt formed a seal with the semicircular belt that held the cargo in place as it began to rise vertically. Eventually the two belts reached the boom, where the holding belt peeled away and the cargo was deposited onto the boom belt, which then carried it to the shore.[74]

The belts were almost an inch thick and made of multiple plies. They were amazingly durable but not indestructible. The most likely cause of serious trouble was a piece of stray metal falling onto the belt. A piece of steel that landed in the center of a belt might cut a 200- to 300-foot gash before the belt could be stopped and the steel removed. Even this seemingly extreme damage would usually be repaired rather than installing a new belt. One way or another, a typical belt would remain in service for about ten years.[75]

Self-unloading systems not only eliminated the need to rebuild shoreside facilities; they were also much faster at both loading and unloading ships than ore docks equipped with Hulett machines. In 1981 when the 767-foot-long straight decker *Philip R. Clarke* was modified to become a self-unloader, unloading time for the vessel was reduced from seventeen hours to six hours.[76] A thousand-foot self-unloading vessel was typically unloaded in about seven to ten hours.[77] The speed with which a conveyor system could both load and unload a vessel led to the decision to make all the thousand-foot-long vessels self-unloading.[78]

The new smaller ships built in the 1970s were also built as self-unloading vessels. As was traditional, most of the new, small self-unloaders earned their keep by calling on infrequently visited ports to deliver products such as coal or stone. But a few of the last generation of self-unloaders constructed in the 1970s served a very specialized purpose. Cleveland's winding Cuyahoga River proved an impossible navigation challenge for the thousand-foot ships that could not travel up the river to reach several steel mills. But the cost of shipping taconite from Duluth to Cleveland on a thousand-foot vessel was so low that it made using a six-hundred-foot vessel uneconomical, even if the smaller boat could sail upriver to the mill. The solution was a transshipment point built at Lorain, Ohio. Ore was taken off the thousand-foot cargo ships and placed on smaller six-hundred-foot vessels to be moved up the Cuyahoga. The *American Republic*, launched in 1981, was built especially for this purpose.[79]

Although iron ore, coal, and stone were the basic cargoes of the American fleet, other "minor" cargoes were also carried in bulk freighters. Salt, oil, lumber, and potatoes in particular deserve mention. Salt was an unwelcome cargo. Because it corroded the cargo hold, salt was usually carried only by older ships that the owner planned to soon withdraw from service.[80] Many once-proud vessels ended their days as salt carriers. For example the *Henry Ford II*, the pride of the Ford fleet when it was launched in 1924, was chartered by International Salt at the end of its career. Renamed *Akzo*, the vessel hauled salt for several seasons until, in 1989, the ship was towed to Toledo and scrapped.[81]

Although infrequently discussed, both crude oil and refined petroleum products were also carried on the Great Lakes. Crude oil was most commonly carried on Canadian oil tankers. These ships took on oil that had been piped from Canada's western provinces to Lake Superior's shore, and carried the crude eastward to refineries near Canada's population centers. In 1909 the first oil tanker on the lakes, the *Imperial*, was placed in service. When it was launched in 1951, the Canadian ship *Imperial Le Duc*, with a cargo capacity of 125,000 barrels, was the largest freshwater tanker in the world.[82] Crude-oil tankers generally disappeared from the lakes in the mid-1950s when the Canadian pipeline that ended at Lake Superior was extended across the two peninsulas of Michigan, as well as underneath the Straits of Mackinac, to Sarnia, Ontario, where it connected with an existing pipeline network serving eastern Canada. Although crude oil largely disappeared as a cargo, in the large industrial cities along the lakes, small tankers as well as barges were used frequently throughout the twentieth century to move refined petroleum products from their point of creation to distribution centers located along the waterfront.

In the nineteenth century, lumber had been an important cargo. Chicago at the western end of the lakes and the ports of Buffalo and Oswego in New York had been key lumber ports.[83] At the beginning of the twentieth century, production from the region's once seemingly endless forests had declined dramatically. By 1910 both the South and the Pacific Northwest exceeded the lake states in lumber production.[84] But in the 1890s, lumber schooners and substantial "floats" of lumber were still seen in Lake Huron. A float could be made up of over ninety thousand logs, towed by tugs at an average speed of one mile per hour. Floats were disliked by other commercial shippers who sought to regulate these large, slow-moving hazards to navigation. Significant floats, as well as schooners carrying lumber, continued into the early years of the twentieth century, and the odd float was seen as late as 1987. Occasionally even a "modern" steamer would carry a load of lumber on the deck, as did both the *Henry Ford II* and *Benson Ford* on their last downbound trips of 1924. But the onshore lumber industry in the Great Lakes region was failing, and as it declined, so too did the need for waterborne transportation of lumber.[85]

The same ships that carried lumber in the nineteenth century sometimes also carried potatoes. As the lumber began to decline, settlers arrived, purchased the land where the lumbermen had removed trees, and began to farm. The lumberjacks, however, left behind stumps. These were a huge impediment to growing field crops. Farmers could neither plough around them nor easily remove them. Although stumps were eventually eliminated, in the short run farmers found two solutions. One was to plant fruit orchards, which could be placed between the stumps. While the fruit trees slowly matured, the stumps slowly rotted. The quicker solution was to plant potatoes, which did not require plowing and turned into an immediate cash crop. Lumber hookers, repurposed as "potato hookers," would obtain a load of the staple, particularly on their last trip home. While tied up for the winter months, the ship would become a retail store and commodity storage facility. In cities like Chicago, potatoes could be bought dockside as late as March.[86]

Salt, lumber, oil, and potatoes, however, all collectively were only a small portion of the cargo carried on lake freighters. The real business for American ships was in iron, coal, and stone. To limit port time for vessels carrying these commodities, no detail was too small to catch the attention of the shipping industry. The Great Lakes bulk carrier industry devised not only the most efficient means possible to load and unload cargo but also the quickest way to move ship stores to the freighters. Throughout the Great Lakes, major port cities had chandlery operations, or suppliers who could bring needed items to the ship while it was in port loading or unloading cargo. The most important chandlery, however, was run at the Soo and loaded vessels on the move. Begun in 1901 by the Pittsburgh line, the store was located about three-quarters of a mile below the Soo Locks. It stocked over six thousand items, including over five hundred grocery items, two hundred types of packing and gasket material, a few nine-thousand-pound anchors, fifty tons of anchor chain, and over fifty different types of propellers, weighing as much as three thousand pounds each. During the busy years, the Soo Warehouse distributed twenty thousand pounds of meat each week, and over the course of a busy season, fifty thousand pounds of both coffee and butter moved through the store and onto the ships. In the 1950s the warehouse supplied twenty-five vessels a day.[87] Not only did the warehouse stock supplies, it also maintained repair facilities. Various small items, such as fire tools used in the boiler room or damaged tarps, could be dropped off for repair. Blacksmiths, sewing machine operators, and other skilled individuals fixed the items and had them taken back out to the ship when it next passed through the locks.[88]

These supplies and repaired items were moved aboard a small vessel, which met the freighter and transferred the cargo.[89] Operating on a twenty-four-hour schedule during the shipping season, three different ships located at the Soo served this purpose. The *Superior* sailed until 1917 and was replaced in 1918 by the *Frontier*, which was in turn replaced in 1947 by the *Ojibway*. These ships were built solely to supply other vessels and were designed to function primarily in the St. Marys River. The ungainly vessels won no awards for either appearance or handling on open water. When the *Ojibway* made its maiden voyage from Ashtabula, Ohio, where it was constructed, to the Soo, it ran into heavy weather. The vessel was never designed for sailing on the open lakes, and the trip came to be known as "the cruise of the Pitching Pickle."[90] The Pitching Pickle, and its predecessors, used an onboard crane to load pallets of supplies. It then sailed out, tied onto the moving freighter, and in about five minutes used its crane to lift the pallets full of supplies onto the freighter's deck and, if needed, unload items in need of repair, which also were usually on pallets. The work done, it cast off and returned to the dock for the next group of pallets to be delivered to the next passing ship.[91]

Prior to ship-to-shore radio, the custom was to leave an order or items in need of repair while passing upbound through the locks, and receive supplies or repaired items while passing downbound. The system depended on the Coast Guard's lookout towers, which sighted ships entering the St. Marys River and informed the lockmaster of their arrival.[92] The Coast Guard lookouts first informed the lockmaster of the approaching ship, then helpfully shared the same information with the Soo Warehouse. By the late 1990s the warehouse was serving a total of less than twenty-five ships, but it remained an important part of the overall operation of the fleet.[93]

The United States Postal Service (USPS) also accommodated the need to keep freighters moving with specialized service. The USPS established and maintained marine post offices, the most important at the Soo and Detroit. Movement of mail at the Soo was quite simple. During the time the ship was in the lock, mail was transferred to and from the ship in a bucket. Mail for the ship was placed in a bucket by postal workers, who brought the bucket to the lock's edge; there a rope was used to bring the bucket aboard the ship. Outgoing mail from the crew was placed in the now empty bucket and returned by rope to the postal worker on the dock. The mail service in Detroit was far more interesting. Since the ships did not stop in the Detroit River, in the nineteenth century a private service would row out to meet passing boats. Small items could be delivered, and of equal importance, "mail in a pail" could be raised up to or down from the passing freighter. This practice became so expected in Detroit that in 1948 the Postal Service recognized the *J.W. Westcott* as a floating post office, serving in the Detroit River. In its first year of service as a post office, the small vessel ran almost a million pieces of mail to and from passing freighters. The service continued throughout the twentieth century, with mail being sent to "Vessel Name," Marine Post Office, Detroit, MI 48822.[94]

The *Ojibway* and the *Westcott* were two small examples of the lengths taken to keep the freighters moving. But the real concern was not mail or supplies, but the time spent in port loading or unloading cargo. Throughout the century there was a constant emphasis on finding and using the quickest, most efficient way to accomplish these two tasks. Port visits became shorter and shorter as faster means were employed to first fill the hold and then empty it of cargo. Massive ore docks and Hulett machines eventually gave way to even quicker conveyor-belt systems, but the portside goal throughout the twentieth century was to use whatever device minimized port time and allowed the vessels to do what made money—sail.

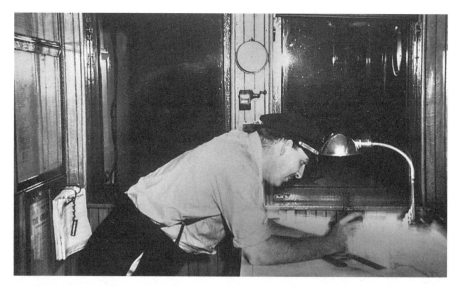

Fred Schaufele, third mate, at chart table in the wheelhouse, aboard the Steamer *Pontiac* (1941).

Frank Walters, watchman, setting clamps on a hatch cover on the Steamer *Pontiac* (1941).

Stanley Yonkers, deckhand, painting aboard the Steamer *Pontiac* (1941).

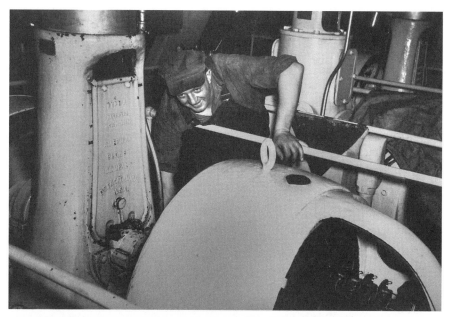

Clarence Hanger, oiler, "tickling rods" aboard the Steamer *Pontiac* (1941).

Gale McCanna, fireman, shoveling coal into firebox aboard the Steamer *Pontiac* (1941).

Arnold Branstrom, wheelsman, at ship's wheel aboard the Steamer *Pontiac* (1941).

Frank Glowacki, porter, smoking cigarette on the stern of the Steamer *Pontiac* while watching another ship pass (1941).

Steve Dellerba, watchman, and Phillip Bergeron, watchman, washing down the deck of the Steamer *Pontiac* after taking on cargo (1941).

"Junior" (Albert A. Bartlett) in the galley of the Steamer *Pontiac* (1941).

Unidentified crew removing a tarp from a hatch cover on the Steamer *Pontiac* in preparation for unloading (1941).

Crew in mess at Thanksgiving dinner aboard the Steamer *Pontiac* (1941).

Ray Morin, steward, demonstrates his cooking skill to Frank Glowacki, porter, aboard the Steamer *Pontiac* (1941).

Bernard Fisher, oiler, tickling gears aboard the *Peter White* (1942).

U.S. Marine Postal Service, Detroit River, delivering mail, ca. 1911.

Poe Lock Construction, photo by U.S. Army Corps of Engineers.

Hulett #1, Pennsylvania Railroad Dock, Cleveland, Ohio, constructed 1911–12.

Ice blockade at Sault Ste. Marie, Michigan, December 8, 1926.

U.S. Marine Postal Service on the Detroit River approaching a freighter, ca. 1901.
DETROIT PUBLISHING CO. COLLECTION, LIBRARY OF CONGRESS PRINTS AND PHOTOGRAPHIC DIVISION, WASHINGTON, DC.

Cargo hold, looking forward, SS *J.H. Sheadle*, 1906.
DETROIT PUBLISHING CO. COLLECTION, LIBRARY OF CONGRESS PRINTS AND PHOTOGRAPHIC DIVISION, WASHINGTON, DC.

Steamer *R.W. England* on the ways, Great Lakes Eng. Co. (aka Engineering Works), May 5, 1904.

DETROIT PUBLISHING CO. COLLECTION, LIBRARY OF CONGRESS PRINTS AND PHOTOGRAPHIC DIVISION, WASHINGTON, DC.

Steamer *James Watt* loading at the South Shore Railway docks, Marquette, Michigan, ca. 1905.

A triple expansion engine made by Detroit Shipbuilding Co., 1901.

Loading coal into a lake freighter at the Pennsylvania Railroad docks, Sandusky, Ohio, May 1943.

CHAPTER 6

ASHORE

One thing has become abundantly clear to U.S. Steel—it must maximize utilization of its most efficient facilities to attain optimum costs.

—Christian Beukema, U.S. Steel vice president for Ore, Limestone, and Lake Shipping, quoted in Mark L. Thompson, *Steamboats and Sailors of the Great Lakes*

The lakes made commerce possible. The crew and their ships carried the cargo from port to port, where machines helped load and unload the boats in what would be anywhere else a seeming blink of the eye. But for all the rough beauty of the ships, the red color of the iron ore in the hold, and the legends told about the crew, some of the story about Great Lakes freighters took place far away from the water. Economics, management, unions, and government all played a role in determining the size, scope, and character of Great Lakes shipping.

What would most shape the Great Lakes shipping business in the twentieth century was the interaction of three nineteenth-century titans of the U.S. economy: Andrew Carnegie, John D. Rockefeller, and J. P. Morgan. Andrew Carnegie founded Carnegie Steel in 1873, and by 1900 his company was the largest steel manufacturer in the United States. But Carnegie was slow to move into mining, preferring to let others run those businesses. John D. Rockefeller had made his money in oil, but in the 1890s he entered the iron business, somewhat by accident. In 1892 he had invested $500,000 in railroads in Minnesota's Mesabi Iron Range, only to see his investment placed in peril by the Panic of 1893. To save his initial investment, he put another two million dollars directly into mines and docks, and in 1894 he bought the business in which he had invested.[1]

Once he entered the business, Rockefeller followed the practices he almost always used, seeking to vertically integrate his holdings into a monopoly. As part of this goal, he obtained his own fleet of fifty-six ships and also chartered other ships. Rockefeller's efforts to establish a monopoly made the possibility of conflict between Carnegie and Rockefeller very real. In an effort to avoid an economic war, the two men struck a deal. Rockefeller would stay out of steel manufacturing while Carnegie would rely on Rockefeller for ore and transportation. But when Rockefeller's ships proved insufficient to move all of the ore Carnegie needed, and independent shippers began to charge Carnegie exorbitant shipping fees, Carnegie decided to acquire his own ships, founding the Pittsburgh Steamship Company. Now lacking trust in Rockefeller, Carnegie also began to buy his own mines in the Mesabi Range. These moves led Rockefeller to retaliate, with his most effective weapon being the enlargement of his already substantial control over ships moving ore. By 1899 the two industrial giants were at war. Both were making plans for an extended battle, one part of which would be carried out by their Great Lake fleets.[2]

Unlike Carnegie and Rockefeller, who had made fortunes making things, J. P. Morgan was a financier who made money through money. Morgan had entered the steel market in 1898 when he helped pay for the consolidation of several firms into Federal Steel, which included mines, mills, and the twenty-two-ship Minnesota Steamship Company.[3] Morgan saw nothing but lost profit in the looming battle between Carnegie and Rockefeller. Instead of industrial warfare, Morgan hoped to maximize profit by forming a cartel or some other form of overarching structure that could regulate prices.

Carnegie and Rockefeller, however, had no interest in peace, or in Morgan. Carnegie dismissed Federal Steel with the comment "I think Federal is the greatest concern the world ever saw for manufacturing stock certificates." Carnegie planned to crush Federal, as well as Rockefeller. But Morgan was aware that Carnegie was interested in retiring. Knowing this, Morgan became intrigued when Charles Schwaab, Carnegie's right-hand man, first publicly and then in a private meeting with Morgan laid out the financial advantages of a merger between Federal and

Carnegie Steel. Morgan eventually agreed to buy out Carnegie if "Andy" were willing to sell and retire. Schwaab knew the subject was a delicate one, but one day after a round of golf, Schwaab asked Carnegie how much money it would take to buy the company. The next morning Carnegie gave Schwaab a handwritten note with an asking price of $480 million. The note was delivered to Morgan, who, after reading it, said simply, "I accept this price."

With Carnegie's empire now under his control, Morgan turned his attention to Rockefeller. The two men disliked each other, and both pointedly snubbed the other during negotiations. However, the long-term profit Morgan envisioned and the 50 million dollar windfall Rockefeller would receive led both men to eventually put aside personal matters. In 1901 Rockefeller sold his iron assets to Morgan, who in turn combined them with his other holdings and created United States Steel (USS). Included in the sale was Rockefeller's Bessemer Steamship Company.[4] United States Steel came into being with a fleet of ships of almost unimagined size. As one contemporary newspaper gushed:

> Greater than the number of vessels in commission in the combined fleets of the United States Navy, larger than the invincible armada sent against England by Philip of Spain, is the colossal force of vessels gathered together on the Great Lakes to carry iron ore for the United States Steel Corporation, generally known as the Steel Trust.[5]

U.S. Steel actually consolidated six separate fleets into a new Pittsburgh Steamship Company with an eventual fleet of 112 ships and barges. By its very size, the "Steel Trust" fleet set the tone for lake shipping for most of the twentieth century, and thus it is worthy of special attention. At the beginning of the century, other vessel owners feared that the new Pittsburgh fleet might monopolize lake commerce and attempt to eliminate the independent ships. But Morgan had no interest in creating a monopoly, and the Pittsburgh line's senior management realized that there could be a use for independent vessels. While Pittsburgh owned many ships, the haphazard way they had been assembled did not create an integrated fleet.[6] Creating such a fleet would take time. Nor did the 112 vessels have sufficient capacity to haul all the iron ore needed by the new steel company. When the Pittsburgh line was formed, the fleet could move about 10 million tons of ore a year, but Morgan's new company needed about 13 million tons of ore to operate at full capacity, thus creating considerable opportunities for the independent shipping lines to obtain business.[7]

U.S. Steel decided that the Pittsburgh fleet would be run as an independent company, operating as a "cost" subsidiary. By this, USS meant that the fleet was not expected to make a profit but rather to haul ore and other needed commodities exclusively for USS at the lowest possible cost. Money to pay the operating costs of the Pittsburgh fleet came from USS, taken from revenue received from the sale of steel. With a single, guaranteed customer, the fleet had no sales department and created no advertising. In meeting its parent company's directive to operate at the lowest possible cost, the Pittsburgh fleet developed a culture of—some said an obsession with—identifying and controlling costs. That obsession soon became commonplace across the industry.[8] At the same time, the decision that the Pittsburgh fleet would exclusively carry goods for USS meant that independent shippers would not have to compete with the Pittsburgh fleet for contracts hauling ore for other steel companies, and, incidentally, the independents could also make money from USS if the Pittsburgh ships could not fully supply all the ore USS needed.

When Harry Coulby became the Pittsburgh fleet's general manager in 1904, he made it his business to drive down operating costs, giving teeth to the claim that the Pittsburgh fleet was obsessed with the subject. Coulby stressed modern management techniques and cost management. He also took an interest in safety, partly for humanitarian reasons but also because insurance played such an important part in operating costs.[9] Coulby went out of his way to make clear who was boss. He imposed standardized rules on his captains, and through these rules made it clear that the company, not the captain, was in charge. In case a captain somehow missed the point, in his first year as general manager Coulby required each captain to reapply for his job. Coulby was equally quick to pick battles with various unions that in the past had tried to organize sailors or officers. His goal was again to ensure that the company had full control over costs. Because bigger ships could operate more efficiently, Coulby aggressively built new vessels. By 1913 he had built eighteen ships longer than 600 feet for his fleet. When the capacity of shipyards to construct additional ships slowed his plans for fleet expansion, Coulby bought three existing 600-footers from other shipping firms.[10]

Coulby's drive for efficiency, likely combined with a genuine sense of managerial cooperation, led him to institute annual meetings for the company's captains and the chief engineers to discuss problems and seek fleet-wide solutions. Coulby usually followed a self-imposed rule that a new regulation would be instituted only if a majority of the relevant officers favored the change. Although Coulby did not invent such meetings—they had happened as early as the 1890s, in the Minnesota Steamship Company—Coulby's adoption of the practice was widely publicized and led to it becoming a common practice among most fleets.[11]

If Coulby used the annual meeting as a way to listen to a variety of opinions and obtain consensus, the meetings also gave him a platform to preach the gospel of efficiency, an opportunity he rarely failed to take.[12] In 1924 when Coulby retired from the Pittsburgh Steamship Company, his legacy was clear: large, efficient ships, low costs, and significantly improved onboard safety records.[13] Coulby's retirement changed the fleet's leader but not its philosophy. His successor, A. F. Harvey, used a series of communications entitled "Confidential Letter to Masters" to let his captains know who was boss and exactly what he thought. When the *Francis E. House* grounded near Lake Michigan's Grays Reef, Harvey wrote a long Confidential Letter to Masters criticizing the captain's handling of the ship in the specific instance of the grounding, as well as his overall performance. Harvey ended the long, semipublic letter by saying, "I feel compelled to hold Captain Parke solely to blame for this accident and to criticize his navigation severely." Although Captain Parke kept his command, he and his fellow masters were given a clear directive about what was expected of them.[14]

During the shipping season, Pittsburgh's home office in Cleveland employed more than a hundred people to coordinate activity. Key to the operation was the Traffic Department. The traffic manager coordinated with various other U.S. Steel operations to determine the mills' immediate needs. The goal was to have the right cargo, loaded on the correct ship, and delivered in a timely manner to the right dock. The entire staff met weekly, determining operations for the next few days by considering all of the information each person brought to the table, as well as intangibles, like the week's weather.[15]

As the season drew to a close, the home office in Cleveland determined where each ship would be berthed for the winter and drew up maintenance and repair schedules for the ship. In January, preparation for the next season began at the office. The fleet's administrators worked closely with all of U.S. Steel's component organizations—mines, railroads, and steel mills—to determine the overall need for ore, coal, and limestone. By early April, estimates were firmed up, ships assigned to duty, and a schedule drawn up for bringing ships out in the spring. Because of the size of the fleet, Pittsburgh staggered the entry of the ships into service to avoid delays caused by too many ships simultaneously arriving at docks or trying to transit the Soo Locks.[16]

The home office also maintained an Engineering office, divided into departments that dealt with machinery, hull, and design. Design was staffed by individuals who usually were hired from shipyards and had experience in naval architecture. The Machinery Department was made up of staff who had served as fleet engineers. They faced significant challenges because of the widely varying age of—and thus equipment on—the line's many ships. They routinely rode on ships to "check the plant" and also served as an emergency pool of chief engineers. One of their major responsibilities was determining repairs to be done over the winter months. A list of jobs was kept and broken down into three priorities: "must jobs," "desirable," and "improvements." The first category, as the name implied, simply had to be done. The second category depended on time and money, while the third was the department's wish list.[17]

At the end of World War II, the Pittsburgh line still dominated the lakes. Although reduced to sixty-two vessels, those ships could carry 776,064 gross tons. The fleet in 1905, although it had far more hulls, could carry only 513,651 gross tons. Pittsburgh's nearest competitor, Interlake Steamship Company, had thirty-six ships, while Cleveland-Cliffs Steamship Company had twenty-two vessels and the Hutchinson & Co. fleet numbered twenty-one.[18]

The 1940s represented a high point for the company, as changes over the next half-century would lead to decline in the steel industry and the Pittsburgh line. In 1953 the long-independent subsidiary was folded into the U.S. Steel Corporation as the Pittsburgh Steamship Division. By 1959 it was clear that the corporation was unhappy with the economic performance of the division. At the annual meeting of the line's captains and engineers, the division's head bluntly criticized the assembled officers for poor performance. The fleet had overspent its budget by over a million dollars, and the blame was placed squarely on the ship's senior officers. Eleven thousand hours had been lost due to various inefficiencies, such as underloading, excessive time in port, accidents, and other problems. But the harshest words were yet to come: "Lake Superior iron ore is in a life-and-death struggle to retain the ever-shrinking markets in which it can successfully compete. . . . To my mind, the only way to meet this challenge during 1960 is to establish the most practical yardsticks of optimum or maximum performance for our facilities and peel off every possible element of waste and excessive costs in our operations." To accomplish this, performance standards would be established for each ship, and each captain would be responsible for seeing that they were met.[19]

The new performance standards were extraordinarily comprehensive, even for a fleet that had long considered cost an important issue. Average times required to sail from port to port, time from harbor entry to dock, and the time needed to unload various types of cargo were all to be measured. Fuel consumption, lubricant consumption, food costs per meal, safety, and much more were also matters the captain was to track, compare to standards, and if not meeting goals, correct. The masters were told, "Train your subordinates in cost control just as you would train them in navigation and maintenance."

The fleet's marine superintendent made clear to the captains that the company was not simply talking about a fad:

> The program is new to Pittsburgh Steamship but it is not new to the Corporation. You may pass it off as just another one of management's gadgets for cutting costs. Gentlemen, I can assure you the program is not just a passing fancy. It is a proven method of evaluating management's effectiveness, and it will be used in the division to evaluate your contribution and effectiveness to the division's overall objectives.

The superintendent added, "I can assure you that in addition to myself, there will be others looking over your shoulder and following your course very closely." This was a message to redouble previous efforts to cut costs.[20]

Despite an emphasis on efficiency, the Pittsburgh fleet, as well as many others, continued to maintain one tradition: allowing the occasional passenger onboard for a voyage. Although they were working boats, some of the ships were built with a small number of passenger cabins. This was initially a business decision that gave senior fleet managers a way to personally watch ships in operation while resting in a comfortable berth. As it turned out, passenger quarters also created a unique way to recognize important clients. Guests only traveled during the summer months—June, July, and August—and normally one or two extra crew members were added to take care of their needs, most often a porter and a steward/cook. Launched in 1905 as the flagship of the Pittsburgh fleet, the *William E. Corey* typified the quarters built for guests on otherwise working boats. The *Corey* featured five staterooms decorated in birch and enameled white, each with its own bath, and guests were provided with a private dining room and private observation lounge.[21] The number of ships with guest quarters can only be estimated, but at least forty such ships were in service in 1940–1941.

A typical vacation trip lasted seven to ten days, beginning at a port in the lower lakes, then heading north to Lake Superior, where cargo was loaded, and then back south to the port where the cargo was unloaded. Because working freighters lacked amenities to entertain the guests, various special accommodations were made. Usually an awning and deck chairs were placed forward for the guests' enjoyment. Shuffleboard courts were painted onto the deck. Passengers occasionally enjoyed skeet shooting, and at least on one occasion an empty hold was flooded to be used as a swimming pool. Usually passengers just took in the sights and toured the ship. The crew enjoyed the visitors. If nothing else, visitors asked questions, and the crew, often doing relatively boring work, found answering questions a pleasant pause from daily chores and one for which they would not receive a reprimand from a deck officer.[22] Guests, in turn, usually loved the trips. As one wrote in the guest logbook of the *William A. Irvin*, which served as the flagship of the USS fleet from 1938 until 1975:

> This wonderful trip we shall never forget
> The beautiful ship and the feed we et [*sic*]
> While flying is great and sometimes unnervin'
> It can't top sailing on the *William A. Irvin.*

A slightly more practical person wrote in the same logbook:

> Happy those few who may enjoy
> A trip that so delights the senses.
> One can no week the better employ
> Especially with the company paying all the expenses.[23]

Among the most legendary of guest quarters were found aboard the *Henry Ford II*. Put into service in 1924, the *Henry Ford II* was, in part, the industrialist Henry Ford's personal yacht. Ford had enjoyed sailing for years. In 1913, for example, he took a summer cruise on the *James A. Farrell*, where he would wander onto the deck early each morning in his bathrobe and bare feet, admire the sunrise, and chat with the crew. An inveterate tinkerer, he liked to look at the mechanical apparatus. During the same trip on the *Farrell*, he was invited by the chief engineer to inspect the ship's failed steering engine. Ford took delight in being the person who discovered the sheared pin that had disabled the rudder.[24]

When Ford built the *Henry Ford II*, named after his grandson, it was well appointed for visitors. The wood-paneled guest quarters were done in a manner resembling Ford's home, Fairlane Mansion. As coming aboard could be a bit inconvenient, an "elevator" was carried on the ship and was placed on the dock to lift Mr. Ford and his guests from the dock to the deck. Ford often traveled north to Marquette, from where he could motor to a summer retreat he had built in Michigan's Upper Peninsula. Ford was known to be particular about the appearance of the dock, and the captain usually planned the *Henry Ford II*'s arrival at Marquette to be at night. As Mr. Ford slept, the elevator was placed over the side, and the crew cleaned the dock so it would be to Mr. Ford's liking when morning came and he departed from the ship.[25]

Adjusting speed to arrive at Marquette at a "convenient" time was typical of the unusual practices the boat followed when Mr. Ford was aboard. The ship traveled at a pace designed to please him and his guests. Speed was modified to ensure that the ship would pass through the St. Clair River and the Soo Locks during daylight hours. Should it suit his fancy, and apparently it often did, Ford ordered unplanned excursions, such as a trip into Georgian Bay or the upper reaches of Lake Michigan. Such diversions often made a two-day trip stretch to five. It might be poor business practice, but since Ford was the sole owner of the boat and the company, both operated to his liking. Ford was also particular about the captain. While on board the *Henry Ford II*, he once summarily relieved Sidney Inch of his duties as master when he was outraged that Inch had caused the ship to collide with a coal dock. At the time of the accident, the ship was attempting to dock in hurricane-force winds with the assistance of a tug. However, insofar as Mr. Ford was concerned, the inclement weather was no excuse for Captain Inch's poor seamanship.[26]

Having guests aboard sometimes led to unexpected problems. As Captain Inch's experience suggests, master and crew were expected to perform well, regardless of the circumstances. Manners not always observed aboard a working boat were also to be maintained. Out of deference for the guests, cursing was at least to become less common. The crew never knew who the guest they were speaking with might be. William A. Irvin, president of U.S. Steel, was fond of riding on his namesake vessel and was equally fond of wandering about the ship chatting. It is understandable that captain and crew alike did not want to make the mistake of giving a guest like Mr. Irvin an uncensored piece of their mind.[27]

The *William A. Irvin* carried so many guests it was referred to by some as a "passenger boat." For the convenience of these many guests, the ship's captain had more or less permanently installed a tarp over the bow for shade. One day when a tug was pulling the *Irvin* into port, it blew a shower of hot coals out of its smokestack. The coals landed on the *Irvin*'s bow and set fire to the guests' tarp. When the captain of the *Irvin* demanded the tug stop venting hot coals, he was told, "These tugs don't run on love, Cap."[28] Perhaps, but the "Cap" probably had a bit of explaining to do if any guests were aboard.

Guests, however, were always a minor matter in overall fleet operations. Although guests came and went, the goal of efficiency remained. In 1967, U.S. Steel achieved additional efficiencies by merging the Bradley fleet with the Pittsburgh line. The Bradley fleet had long been a subsidiary of USS, but because it consisted of self-unloaders that largely carried stone, it had been operated separately from the Pittsburgh line. The fleet's origin began in 1920 when USS acquired the Michigan Limestone and Chemical Company and the three self-unloading vessels it owned. In 1923 a decision was made not to include these ships in the Pittsburgh line but rather to form them into the Bradley Transportation Company.[29] But forty-four years later, maintaining two fleets with two separate offices simply could no longer be afforded.

The move also may have come about because of a growing concern within U.S. Steel about the Bradley management. The sinking of the *Carl D. Bradley* in 1958 had brought unfavorable attention to the line and its parent company, USS. Captain Roland Bryan, who died along with most of the crew, had written about the ship, "This boat is getting pretty ripe for too much weather. I'll be glad when they get her fixed up." The investigation into the sinking not only revealed the captain's concerns about the *Bradley*'s seaworthiness but also discovered that the ship had run aground twice during the 1958 season, with neither accident being reported. U.S. Steel consistently claimed that even if the ship was in need of some work, it was seaworthy. Critics, however, remained unconvinced. Additional questions about the line's management occurred when another Bradley boat, the *Cedarville*, sank in 1965. The ship was rammed by a Norwegian freighter and sank with the loss of ten crew members. The Coast Guard investigation into the tragedy revealed that the *Cedarville* was running at near full speed, although visibility was severely limited. As a result of the investigation, the *Cedarville*'s master, who survived the accident, lost his license for a year.[30]

The merger of the Bradley line into the Pittsburgh fleet may have helped efficiency, but nothing could change the fact that the American steel industry was in serious decline. In 1981 U.S. Steel turned the ships it owned into a wholly owned subsidiary company, the USS Great Lakes Fleet.[31] The fleet, although it had a special relationship with U.S. Steel, was legally listed as a "common carrier" and thus was free to take paying cargo from any source. For the first time in eighty years, the "tin stackers," as sailors often called the Pittsburgh ships, would compete with other fleets on the open market. Suddenly the Great Lakes Fleet needed a marketing plan and a sales force, although it also clearly benefited from a special relationship with USS and a long-standing culture of cost containment.[32]

The timing for this change was terrible. The poor economy of the 1980s was brutal on the USS Great Lakes Fleet. Older straight deckers were sold or scrapped, and U.S. Steel, looking for cash, began seeking a buyer in order to divest itself completely from the still profitable but clearly economically vulnerable shipping line. In 1988 majority interest in the fleet, along with the other transportation properties owned by USX Corporation (as USS had then become) were sold to Blackstone Capital Partners, a Wall Street investment firm. Blackstone made only minimal changes to personnel and operations. The fleet was making money, and Blackstone, which was interested primarily in short-term profit, left well enough alone. By the 1990s the fleet had declined in size to only twelve ships.[33] With a slightly changed name, these ships were sold to CN Rail (the Canadian National Railway Co.) in 2004.[34]

Although the Pittsburgh fleet was always the largest, several other shipping lines existed. The interests of the various fleets were represented and protected by the Lake Carriers' Association (LCA). The association had its roots in the nineteenth century, when in 1880 shipowners in Cleveland formed the Cleveland Vessel Owners' Association. In 1885 owners in Buffalo formed a similar regional organization under the more sweeping title of the Lake Carriers' Association. In 1889 the two groups merged, retaining the name Lake Carriers' Association, and added owners from other port cities. By the end of the century most, although not all, shipowners had become members of the LCA. In 1903 the LCA was reorganized and incorporated to accomplish several broad goals. These included establishing and maintaining shipping offices, which largely served as hiring halls for seafarers; establishing and maintaining aids to navigation; improving channels and harbors, and in other ways promoting efficient and safe navigation; and assuming responsibility for industry-wide employer-employee relations. The LCA worked as the shipowners' lobbyist in Washington. One of its greatest accomplishments, and that of the U.S. merchant marine industry overall, was passage of the Merchant Marine Act of 1920 (sometimes called the Jones Act) requiring that all cargo transported between ports within the United States be carried on U.S. flag vessels built in American shipyards. Although repeatedly amended, throughout the twentieth century the basic principle that goods shipped between United States ports should be carried on American built and owned bottoms guaranteed that a large portion of the Great Lakes trade would travel on American flag vessels, regardless of cost advantages that might exist on Canadian vessels, or after the opening of the St. Lawrence Seaway, on vessels flying an international flag of convenience.[35]

During wartime (World War I, World War II, and the Korean War), the Jones Act was temporarily suspended to allow Canadian ships to haul desperately needed iron ore to American steel-manufacturing plants.[36] Except during emergencies, the Lake Carriers' Association sought to protect the legal monopoly the Jones Act created on intercoastal trade. In 1987, when free trade was high on the political agenda, the LCA protested vigorously when the Reagan administration agreed in principle to allow Canadian ships to haul cargo between U.S. ports. The proposal was eventually dropped by the administration.[37]

Occasionally the LCA found itself lobbying the government in unusual ways. For example, although the LCA usually worked for passage of government-funded improvements to navigation, for the first fifty years of the twentieth century, Great Lakes shippers consistently lobbied Congress against improvements that would allow large ocean ships to enter the lakes. This included opposition to agreements signed by the United States and Canada in 1932 and 1941 to undertake major improvements to the St. Lawrence River that would create a navigable path for ocean-sized vessels between Duluth and the Atlantic Ocean.[38] It was only in 1948, facing a growing shortage of high-grade domestic ore and considering the possibility of importing ore from eastern Canada, that Hanna Co., which had acquired iron mines in Quebec and Labrador, broke LCA ranks and endorsed the construction of a seaway capable of accommodating deep-draft vessels.[39]

One of the LCA's most critical functions was labor relations. Before World War II, crewing a ship was largely taken care of by the captain and the chief engineer, working within a framework of hiring halls, pay, and labor rules established by the Lake Carriers' Association. Officially hiring was done through the halls maintained by the LCA.[40] However, if a captain or chief engineer had a preference for someone, the hall manager usually assigned the person they desired to their ship. William Wallace, for example, recalled that in 1936 a chief engineer took a liking to him, and a job on a boat was quickly made available. That Wallace was only fourteen years old at the time, and legally a sailor had to be at least eighteen, did not cause a problem. Wallace observed that while he knew of only one other sailor who began his career at fourteen, sixteen-year-olds were commonly found aboard ships.[41] It was also fairly common for the captain and the engineer to hire men from their hometowns, men who had sailed with them in the past, or individuals recommended to them by friends.[42] Hiring locals sometimes had unintended consequences, such as when the need for workers back home to harvest crops caused many men to leave the ship.[43] But the practice was common.

All firms officially gave preference to hiring and promoting past workers, with promotions to a licensed rank being contingent on an individual passing the necessary government tests. Seniority was also important and was considered, after ability, both for promotions and layoffs.[44] During the mid-1930s, some fleets, such as Cleveland-Cliffs, began to truly concentrate hiring authority in their central office.[45] While this centralization of hiring authority would grow over time, captains long retained substantial influence in hiring, firing, and crew promotion.

Men were expected to do the work assigned, and if they failed to perform as the officers believed appropriate, they were quickly dismissed. As one chief engineer expressed it during the Depression to a newly hired fireman, "There's the coal pile. There's the shovel. There's the steam gauge. If you can't keep the steam up there's two hundred men ashore waitin' for your job."[46] Another Depression-era sailor recalled that as his ship approached port, a man called down from a bridge asking if there was any work. The mate answered that there were no jobs and then pointed out to the deckhands just how easily they could be replaced.[47]

For much of the century, fleet owners offered what they claimed was an enlightened and benevolent corporate labor policy that not only guaranteed good working conditions but also offered an ambitious young man a clear path to personal success. Rockefeller's Bessemer fleet, under the direction of L. M. Bowers, established a pattern of labor relations that would dominate on the lakes into the 1950s. Bowers, a self-made businessman, had never spent a day at sea, but was clear on how he wanted workers handled. To avoid employee turnover, which he saw as the root of several problems, he instituted a series of practices designed to encourage crew to stay aboard all season. He significantly improved crew quarters on all newly constructed Bessemer ships, and Sunday was declared a day of rest, with only those duties performed that were essential to operate the vessel. Various inducements were created to encourage crew to stay onboard for a season, including a year-end bonus. In addition, crew who showed both skill and loyalty to the company were to be given preference in promotion.[48]

Bowers's views regarding how workers were to be treated were echoed by the Pittsburgh fleet's manager Harry Coulby:

There is a human basis, on which to work industrially, now and in the future. We organize tremendous corporations and sometimes forget the men who are to make the corporations a success or a failure. We only see the financiers and managers. . . . Take my own business as an example. The Government deepens our channels and improves our harbors; marine architects build us monster ships; engineers invent marvelous loading and unloading machinery, but such things are not sufficient in themselves. We must have harmony, enthusiasm and hope among the men who do the real work. . . . The Human being in these days of immense combinations must be considered more than has been the rule heretofore.[49]

Coulby went on to say that, to achieve harmony, sailors in the Pittsburgh fleet "receive, in normal times, higher wages than any other sailors in the world, that they have better food and quarters than any other sailors in the world," and added that every man from a deckhand up was given an opportunity to grow. Coulby made no guarantee of success, however—merely of an opportunity to succeed. "There are no easy berths with us. No man is coddled. We say: 'Here is the opportunity. It is up to you to make good.'"[50]

Men like Bowers and Coulby came by their belief in relatively generous treatment of employees, and encouraging ambitious men to succeed, through personal experience. Both men had worked their way up from simple beginnings. Bowers had started life as a traveling salesman peddling soap. He would eventually become a partner in the soap business, move on to wholesale groceries, then to real estate and the sale of farm implements. In 1883 he began to spend some of his time as a confidential agent for John D. Rockefeller. Clearly Rockefeller took a liking to Bowers and in 1895 named him manager of the Bessemer fleet.[51] Coulby's first job had been as a stenographer with Pickands Mather & Co. He held a variety of posts of increasing responsibility within the firm, eventually becoming supervisor of the firm's vessels. Coulby became president of Great Lakes Towing Co. (which operated tug boats in most Great Lakes ports) before becoming the head of the Pittsburgh line.[52]

Bowers and Coulby were self-made men, and they had little use for men with less ambition than they had shown. Coulby summed up his philosophy about employees this way: "If I have a clerk who is satisfied to be a clerk, I get rid of him. When a mate tells me that he never wants the responsibilities of a captain, I strike his name sooner or later off the pay roll."[53] Both men sought to hire young men modeled on themselves: bright, ambitious lads willing to start at the bottom and who would, through talent and hard work, strive to become senior leaders within their companies.

The intense commitment to individual opportunity was paralleled by an equally intense opposition to anything that they believed would limit the individual's ability to advance. In particular, they opposed unions in general and contractual labor agreements in particular. Opposition to unionization was nothing new among shipowners. In the last years of the nineteenth century and the early years of the twentieth century, there had been efforts to unionize freighter crews, some of which met with temporary success. In 1890 an upturn in business made crews hard to find, and allowed unions to gain a foothold aboard ships. However, shipowners fundamentally opposed unionization and waged a long and bitter campaign to eliminate unions.[54]

The sailors themselves made the owners' anti-union efforts easier. Sailors divided along craft lines, creating many small and often bickering unions. In the 1880s, unions that represented crews of sailing vessels refused to organize men on steamships, whom they held in contempt. At the beginning of the twentieth century, firemen could not find a union home. The Sailors' Union had little interest in organizing the men in the boiler room. But when the Longshoremen's Union, which represented dockworkers, agreed to organize firemen, the Sailors' Union took offense. The American Federation of Labor (AFL), which both unions belonged to, intervened and decided that the dockworkers' union had no jurisdiction aboard ships. Galley crews found themselves in the middle of an argument over whether they were sailors or hotel workers. They eventually fell victim to an absurd compromise within the AFL: galley workers on oceangoing vessels were declared sailors by the AFL, while on the Great Lakes, the same jobs were to be placed under the jurisdiction of the hotel workers' union. The situation of various unions bickering over who should represent Great Lakes sailors continued long into the twentieth century. In the 1960s, although most non-licensed crew serving on the major fleets had been unionized, there was bitter hostility between the United Steel Workers (USW), which had signed contracts covering the majority of unlicensed crew members, and the International Seafarers Union (ISU), which represented a minority of Great Lakes unlicensed crew. The USW accused the ISU of a wide variety of unsavory tactics in an effort to persuade crew to change their allegiance from the USW to the ISU. This kind of divisiveness did little to forward union organization.[55]

In a few cases, a craft-based sailors' union did have the power to organize effectively. Marine engineers first organized a fraternal body in Buffalo in 1854, and by

1875 that body expanded to include engineers from several Great Lakes and Atlantic ports. In 1895 the Marine Engineers' Beneficial Association (MEBA) assumed the role of a labor union and began to seek collective bargaining agreements for its members. Although the owners refused to sign any written agreements, in 1899 a threatened MEBA strike resulted in engineers obtaining a substantial wage increase. MEBA continued to successfully bargain on behalf of engineers between 1901 and 1908, obtaining several concessions but never a signed agreement.[56] Deck officers, likely seeing the gains won by their counterparts in the engine room, also organized, and by 1903 they also had obtained substantial concessions from owners, but again not a signed contract.[57]

Although management granted temporary concessions to unions as a practical necessity, they did not accept the permanent presence of unions and continually looked for ways to eliminate union representation from their ships. In 1900 the LCA launched an unsuccessful effort to establish a company union. Its failure led to the reorganization of the LCA, with one of the new organization's goals being a more effective anti-union policy. In 1904 a slump in shipping gave the LCA a chance to attack the various unions. Wages were unilaterally cut. A two-month strike by deck officers was endured, while pro-union officers were systematically removed from the ships. The battle begun in 1904 continued for several years. In the fall of 1907 it was clear to all that the LCA was preparing to break the unions. Enough iron ore had been stockpiled to keep the steel mills running through September 1908. Very high fences were erected around the dock areas to make it easy to keep out strikers or protestors, and company police became visible and numerous on the docks.[58]

Having made its preparations, on April 9, 1908, the LCA announced that an open shop—that is, a workplace in which union membership is not required and which is not governed by a collective bargaining agreement—would prevail on the lakes. Harry Coulby told the captains, "If any man pulls a book of [union] rules on you, he is not an open shop man. Put him on the dock."[59] As an alternative to unionization, the LCA also announced a welfare plan for sailors. The plan was composed of four parts. First, hiring halls would be opened in principal port cities. The hall would also serve as a reading room and recreational center for men "on the beach." A nominal fee would be charged for use of the room. Second, men registered in the hall would be given preference in hiring. Although not a written rule, men not registered, or ineligible for registration, were not hired. Third, each registered sailor would receive a "continuous record book" that would be given to the captain of the ship when a sailor came aboard. When a person left the ship, if his record was fair to good, the captain would return the book and the individual would be eligible for rehiring. If the captain considered the person unsatisfactory, the captain would keep the book and the individual was not eligible to be rehired. The book was called "the fink book" by union men, and they claimed its real purpose was to blacklist pro-union sailors. Fourth, a modest death benefit was established for members of the association in good standing.[60]

Anticipating a poor shipping season in 1908 and observing the careful preparations made to mitigate the consequences of any strike, union leaders angrily accepted the LCA's actions. In 1909 the unions realized that even though the shipping season again looked to be poor, the unions had to take a stand or become completely irrelevant. MEBA called for a strike beginning May 1, and the strike was supported and honored by all of the ship-based unions. However, the longshoremen, who loaded and unloaded the ships, did not honor the picket lines. Although shipping was delayed for a few weeks, eventually enough nonunion workers were found to crew the ships, and cargo began to flow at acceptable levels. The strike was lost, and although they continued to exist in name, the unions had few continuing members and no influence aboard the ships.[61]

Having eliminated unions on the ships, the LCA, through its Welfare Plan and a variety of other actions, took steps that discouraged renewed unionization. The wages unilaterally established by the LCA were generally slightly better than those paid to seafarers on either coast. Aboard ships, more attention was paid to sanitary conditions and the quality of the food served the crew. Conditions were also regularly improved in the halls where sailors congregated and were hired. Finally advancement in the ranks was encouraged by free schools held during the winter that taught seamen the skills to pass the government tests that would make them either deck officers or engineers.[62]

World War I brought another union challenge to the open shop aboard Great Lakes freighters. The war created a labor shortage and sailors became hard to hire. Just as important, because of the war production needs, the government wanted labor peace at any price. Resurgent unions took advantage of the situation to again try to organize sailors on the Great Lakes. They took heart when a signed agreement with seafarers' unions on the Atlantic Coast led to considerable pressure to sign a similar agreement with unions on the Great Lakes. The LCA, however, resisted this idea. The LCA was willing to voluntarily match many of the terms of the East Coast contract, including raising wages. The LCA also agreed to allow a federal agency to investigate the continuous record books to determine the legitimacy of union complaints that the books were being used to blacklist union men. Eventually a government body concluded that the books had in fact been used to blacklist union men, and ordered that the books no longer be used. The LCA reluctantly accepted this decision, although it quickly adopted a new record-keeping system that accomplished the same purpose. But on the most important issue, the LCA implacably and successfully opposed a signed contract with any union.[63]

In the immediate postwar environment, unions continued to show some strength, and by 1920 they had signed agreements with a few small Great Lakes shipping lines that did not belong to the LCA. These contracts called for a 25 percent raise and the institution of an eight-hour-day/three-watch system, rather than the then common twelve-hour-day/two-watch system. Although the LCA held firm to the two-watch system, it more than matched the union-won wage increase by voluntarily increasing wages 30 percent. When 1921 proved to be a grim shipping season, as it had in the past the LCA struck back at sailors who had joined the unions. By 1922 the "fink book" was reintroduced, and once again all hiring was to take place through LCA halls, thus doing their best to weed out "union men." The unions struck, but as in 1909 the strike was broken, and as a consequence union members disappeared from the LCA ships, and the few contracts that had been signed were not renewed. This effectively ended unionization efforts on lake freighters until World War II.[64]

Just prior to and during the war, union organizers again appeared at Great Lakes ports and tried to organize sailors. Beginning in 1939 and continuing throughout the war, various unions won National Labor Relations Board (NLRB) elections certifying them as negotiating agents for the crews; but the LCA consistently avoided signing a contract through legal appeals, stonewalling negotiations, and direct appeals to workers.[65] The Pittsburgh line fought the hardest, mailing employees two different letters from its president. The first mailing offered for the sailors' thoughtful consideration a speech made on the floor of the Congress articulating reasons to oppose unionization. The company's second mailing was both unusual and cynical, although truthful. The company mailed at its own expense a union pamphlet issued by the National Maritime Union, entitled "The NMU Fights Jim Crow." The mailing informed sailors of the NMU's official position that crews should be racially integrated. NMU organizers had been less than forthcoming about the union's position on race when speaking to the white, and presumably racially prejudiced, crews on Great Lakes ships.

In 1942 a small crack appeared in the armor of the companies that owned freighters on the lakes when the Ford Motor Company, newly organized by the United Automobile Workers, allowed the NMU to organize its sailors. In 1943 the National War Labor Board required that all shippers give time-and-a-half pay for any work over eight hours, a standard union demand that had gone unrecognized.[66] By war's end, the NMU had managed to sign a few contracts with independent firms, and in 1946 an NMU strike won contracts from independent shipping lines that did not belong to the LCA, establishing union hiring halls to replace company hiring practices, and a guaranteed forty-four-hour workweek.[67]

Shortly after these modest victories, as a result of the Taft-Hartley Act's passage in 1947 and several court rulings, the unions were again put on the beach.[68] When officers in the NMU refused to sign affidavits required of them by the Taft-Hartley law stating that they were not Communists, the National Labor Relations Board (NLRB) refused to certify the NMU to represent sailors. Compounding the problem, the federal courts subsequently reversed an existing NLRB decision that the Pittsburgh line had engaged in unfair labor practices. Matters became even harder for the NMU when the NLRB, citing the Taft-Hartley Act, said that union-run hiring halls were illegal. As a result of these and other issues, by 1951 the NMU effectively abandoned organization efforts on the Great Lakes. Licensed officers (deck officers and engineers) were even more disadvantaged by the Taft-Hartley law. The legal definition of an employee who was covered by the federal regulations was changed such that officers no longer enjoyed any protection. Thus officers, unlike the rest of the crew, had no legal recourse for any alleged company discrimination in employment based on union membership.[69] As they had many years before, companies were now again free to fire officers simply for joining a union.

When it abandoned organizing efforts on the Great Lakes, the NMU, almost as an afterthought, granted jurisdiction to the United Steel Workers of America (USW) to organize crew who were not officers. This peculiar-sounding decision was based on the observation that the largest fleet on the lakes, the Pittsburgh line, was a subsidiary of United States Steel. Through the logic of the "industrial" union organizing principles that had come to predominate in parts of the union movement, the sailors in the Pittsburgh fleet could be seen as just another group of steelworkers. The USW took this responsibility seriously and created Local 5000 to organize sailors. To everyone's surprise, Local 5000 won an NLRB certification election in November 1953 and thus became the legal representative of the company's sailors who were not officers.[70]

The certification of USW Local 5000 to bargain on behalf of Pittsburgh's sailors laid the groundwork for unionization, but the union's goal of a signed contract with the Pittsburgh line would not be realized for three years. The year 1956 was a turbulent one on the lakes. It began with labor trouble on the Canadian side, which was settled by a new contract in May.[71] On May 28, crews on the U.S. side struck against Great Lakes Towing, the company that operated most of the tugs on the Great Lakes. Fifteen lake ports saw tug operations affected.[72] Without the aid of tugs, freighters of the era frequently could neither enter nor leave ports, particularly those ports with difficult turns and narrow passages. The tug strike continued for months. Bad as it was for shipping, it was quickly eclipsed by even larger strikes.

On July 1, some 600,000 steelworkers struck against the nation's major steel companies. The strike stopped approximately 85 percent of the nation's steel production. Although the steel strike did not include the bulk carrier fleet, because unloading facilities at the steel mills were closed, there was no way to unload the ships. The shipment of iron ore stopped and most of the fleet was tied up until the strike was settled.[73] On July 27 the steel strike ended with a three-year labor agreement. As part of the larger settlement, Local 5000 sailors were granted various new concessions, including higher pay and a forty-hour workweek. Ship officers, who were not members of Local 5000, became furious when the company would not offer comparable conditions to them but rather expected officers to continue working a fifty-six-hour week. As a result, engineers in MEBA struck against the Pittsburgh line. Local 5000 honored the MEBA picket lines and refused to crew ships the MEBA was striking. Some boats, using nonunion crews, did manage to get underway, but unionized railroad workers at two key ports put in place the final part needed to make the strike effective when they announced that they too would not cross the MEBA picket lines and refused to load cargo into the few vessels that had gotten underway with nonunion workers. In the end the strike idled more than 250 boats.

Perhaps overestimating the company's support among deck and engineering officers, and clearly not recognizing the level of immediate anger within this group, the Pittsburgh line voluntarily agreed to hold a government-supervised election among officers to determine if MEBA should represent officers in labor negotiations. One can only assume that the company's corporate culture had so internalized anti-unionism that its leaders truly believed a majority of "level-headed" officers would vote against unionization, and the strike, the work of a few alleged hotheads, would end. Instead, on August 27 the officers overwhelmingly voted in favor of a union.[74]

This unexpected result, undoubtedly coupled with pressure from its parent firm, U.S. Steel, to resume shipping as quickly as possible, forced the Pittsburgh line's leadership for the first time in a half-century to enter into direct labor negotiations. However, the company's long history of open-shop practices made its senior management ill equipped to negotiate a speedy end to the conflict. Having kept unions off their ships for fifty years, making contractual concessions to a union was simply not how they did business. From the parent firm's view, its resumption of operations was being stopped by one local union striking against a subsidiary over what were, from the national perspective, "local" concerns. To resolve the problem, USS replaced the Pittsburgh line's management at the bargaining table with two negotiators from the parent company who were given unilateral authority to settle the matter, and apparently ordered to do so quickly. On September 2, these negotiators signed, on behalf of the Pittsburgh line, a three-year contract with MEBA that granted the union most of its demands.

The agreement established a forty-hour workweek for officers and, despite the reduction in hours, a pay raise of just over 5 percent. Officers who opted to work the old fifty-six-hour schedule received time-and-a-half for the extra labor and an astounding 40 percent pay increase. For the first time on the lakes, paid holidays and vacations were established. In addition, although the custom of paying a bonus to sailors who stayed until the end of the season went back to the beginning of the century, for the first time the bonus, set at 10 percent, was contractually established.[75]

With the strike at the Pittsburgh line settled and a contract signed, most other companies quickly followed suit, also signing union contracts. On September 6 the tugboat strike was also settled on terms largely favorable to the strikers but different from those reached by MEBA with the Pittsburgh line. Three additional steamship lines quickly signed union contracts, modeled on the terms of the tugboat agreement.[76] No single "pattern contract" emerged for agreements with the various shipping companies, and a few companies continued to resist unionization. In 1963 Interlake Steamship Company remained nonunion.[77]

The contractual differences that existed between companies led the Steel Workers Union to create two local unions to represent Great Lakes sailors, Local 5000 and Local 7000. "Local 5," as it was often called, represented sailors in fleets directly affiliated with major steel manufacturers. Local 7000 represented sailors on independent fleets that were not owned by steel companies. Although wages were generally uniform, other contract terms varied. As the newspaper jointly published by Locals 5000 and 7000 explained, contracts "must be substantially different" depending on the fleet's owner, since "funds for fringe benefits from LSU members [local 7000] are not tied in with shoreside steel."[78] Simply put, large, prosperous steel companies included generous fringe-benefit packages in their contracts that smaller, independently owned shipping firms, lacking the deep pockets of the steel industry, could not afford to match.

The organization of the Pittsburgh fleet by the USW did not bring labor peace to the lakes. The USW routinely complained about what it felt were unfair practices on the part of management. In 1961, in a vehement statement, the union complained about anti-union officers aboard the ships, referring to them as "sick personalities" and "little Hitlers." Rather ominously, the union warned that if these officers continued in their anti-union ways, not only would they fail to thwart the union, "they will live to regret their ill-advised attempt."[79]

Over the next half-century, labor unions continued to impact lake shipping. In the 1960s and 1970s, Local 5000 and other lake unions were highly critical of the Coast Guard. Among other charges, they believed that the Coast Guard had unfairly entered into contractual issues when it changed crewing requirements to allow fleets to eliminate sailors. The unions complained bitterly about changes made by the Coast Guard in 1965 and in 1970 that allowed vessel owners to eliminate deck watches.[80]

These crewing complaints had their roots in the 1960s when the USW routinely objected to reductions in crew size created by various forms of automation. MEBA, however, took a more pragmatic line in the 1960s, accepting crew reduction if it were linked with training for the licensed officers who remained, qualifying them to use new equipment, and a liberalized retirement program to create a largely voluntary path that would reduce the pool of available engineers.[81] However, MEBA could draw a line. The organization bitterly contested a Coast Guard decision to allow "automated" vessels to sail with unattended engine rooms, thus eliminating the need for any engine-room crew. MEBA argued in court that this decision by the Coast Guard violated the USCG's own safety regulations. Eventually a federal judge found in MEBA's favor and issued an order reinstating the three-watch system in Engineering.[82] The first ship with a fully automated engine room did not sail until the twenty-first century.[83]

The unions also complained that while the Coast Guard had legal responsibility for enforcing federal health and safety laws aboard lake freighters, the USCG failed to address these matters in a systematic way. Union representatives pointed out, by way of example, that dockside longshoremen were entitled by Occupational Safety and Health Administration (OSHA) regulations to have safety nets strung below vertical ladders. Vertical ladders were also frequently used on ships, but the Coast Guard established no such regulation for safety equipment. Such obvious differences in the enforcement of the law between OSHA and the USCG led the Coast Guard to publicly concede that it had done little to enforce OSHA regulations. Enforcing occupational health and safety laws was a "low priority."[84] All this put together led unions during the 1970s to generally agree with an inflammatory statement penned by Congressman Philip Ruppe, who complained of the "blatant one sided behavior of the Coast Guard to favor vessel operators at the expense of the merchant seamen."[85]

As the union complaints about the Coast Guard made clear, as the twentieth century progressed, the government came to play a role in labor relations and all other aspects of Great Lakes shipping. Government involvement in shipping, however, was not something born in the mid to late twentieth century. Great Lakes shipping was, in fact, made practical by various government actions in the nineteenth and early twentieth centuries. One government action impacting shipping was the vast sums of money spent to modify the lakes themselves. Historically the federal government financed lake improvements from the Treasury's general fund. It was only in 1986 that Congress enacted the Harbor Maintenance Tax (HMT) to recover a portion of the money spent maintaining the nation's navigable waterways. The 1986 tax was intended to fund 40 percent of the nation's maintenance dredging costs. In 1990 Congress decided that, moving forward, 100 percent of all maintenance dredging expenses would be funded by the HMT. The effect of the tax was severe in the Great Lakes, where the many short trips tended to mean that the tax was disproportionately heavy when compared to that of oceangoing vessels.[86]

Paying for improvements to the lakes for most of the twentieth century was actually a continuation of a long history of government involvement that affected shipping on the Great Lakes. Although rarely mentioned, the first and most fundamental government activity involving lake commerce was international diplomacy. The navigable passages used by large ships within the Great Lakes regularly cross the international boundary line that divides the United States and Canada. An American flag ship traveling between Oswego, New York, and Duluth, Minnesota, travels through approximately 235 miles of Canadian waterways. A Canadian flag vessel traveling between Toronto and Fort William/Port Arthur on Lake Superior traverses 540 miles of American waterways.[87] If either nation enacted legislation that intentionally or unintentionally limited or banned foreign flag vessels from their coastal waterways, commerce on the lakes would come to a halt. Although in the twentieth century it was hard to imagine Canada and the United States not cooperating on the lakes, in the early years of the nineteenth century, with memories of the naval battles that had occurred during the War of 1812 fresh in mind, cooperation was not to be assumed.

Bilateral cooperation to ensure passage of vessels on the Great Lakes was first formally recognized in a treaty signed in 1842 between Great Britain and the United States.[88] All of the Detroit and St. Clair Rivers, as well as parts of the St. Lawrence River, were opened without restriction to vessels flying either nation's flag. In 1872 a subsidiary treaty granted U.S. flag vessels the right to sail the length of the St. Lawrence River to the sea, and Canadian flag vessels the right to freely sail in Lake Michigan.[89]

The final treaty governing passage of ships on the Great Lakes was signed between Canada and the United States in 1909. The Boundary Waters Treaty denationalized the lakes for American and Canadian flag vessels. Any ship from either nation was free to operate anywhere on the Great Lakes. The treaty stipulated that if either nation chose to charge tolls for the use of locks or other navigational devices within their national jurisdiction, fees were to be imposed "equally and without discrimination" on ships flying either flag. The treaty did allow the nations to retain certain rights. Each nation could ban ships flying the other's flag from "coastal trade"—that is, from transporting cargo from one port to another within the United States or Canada. Only U.S. ships could carry cargo between American ports. Similarly, only Canadian ships could carry cargo between Canadian ports. Each nation could also establish and enforce its own national safety regulations aboard ships flying their nation's flag.[90]

The 1909 treaty had two unanticipated effects. The first was that the United States routinely financed major improvements to navigation within Canadian national waters. Because American ships were guaranteed free navigation through these Canadian waters, the American government was willing to finance improvements to a navigational channel without regard to which side of the boundary the channel might traverse. Almost half of the work the American government paid for in the Detroit River actually took place within Canadian waterways. The second unanticipated effect of the treaty was to limit American diversion of water from the Great Lakes. The treaty stated that water could be removed from the lakes only for "domestic or sanitary" purposes.

That treaty language quickly was cited by Americans who wished to curb water flowing through the Chicago Sanitary and Ship Canal from Lake Michigan to the Mississippi River. As nature created it, the Chicago River flowed into Lake Michigan. The Sanitary and Ship Canal reversed the flow of the river. After its construction, water pumped out of Lake Michigan by Chicago no longer returned to Lake Michigan. Instead it flowed down the now-reversed Chicago River from the Great Lakes into the Mississippi River. This monumental task was first proposed as a public health measure. In the nineteenth century, Chicago's freshwater supply and sewage came from and went into Lake Michigan. As the city grew and the amount of sewage discharged into the lake increased, so too did fears that sewage could infiltrate the drinking water supply, potentially causing epidemics of typhoid fever, cholera, and dysentery. This fear was based on history, as Chicago had experienced cholera outbreaks in 1849, 1854, 1866, and 1867. A massive storm in 1885 pushed sewage far out into the lake and might have caused another outbreak, but good fortune intervened when persistent winds pushed the raw sewage away from the city's freshwater intakes.[91] Good fortune, however, might not always shine on the city.

Completed in 1900, the Sanitary and Ship Canal reversed the flow of the Chicago River. Instead of emptying into Lake Michigan, locks closed the river's entrance to the lake, and huge pumps pushed the water in the opposite direction—over the continental divide and into the drainage basin of the Mississippi River. Although the canal was conceived of as a public health measure, boosters of the idea quickly realized it also had a valuable commercial application. The canal created the only navigable water route between the Great Lakes and the Mississippi River. At a more subtle level, Mississippi River shipping interests saw the water being pumped out of Lake Michigan as a convenient way to raise the Mississippi River if the water level fell so low that commercial navigation was made difficult or impossible. Both the City of Chicago and the Mississippi River shipping interests argued for the right to divert water as they saw fit. Unrestricted pumping, however, was banned by repeated court rulings, including one from the United States Supreme Court that specifically cited the 1909 treaty as the reason why the flow of water through the Sanitary and Ship Canal could be limited in both purpose and quantity.[92]

Throughout the twentieth century, arguments over the diversion of water through the Sanitary and Ship Canal would be a constant subject of conversation, debate, and litigation, resulting in various settlements. As late as 1996, the City of

Chicago signed a settlement with the federal government and three states, agreeing that because of past "excess," the amount of water flowing through the canal would be limited to a maximum of 3,200 cubic feet per second. Over twenty-three years, this rate of flow would "restore" the amount of water that past practice had inappropriately allowed to flow through the canal.[93]

The government not only came to regulate the flow of water out of the lakes, it increasingly created rules that regulated the Great Lakes shipping industry. In general, navigation rules created by the government came about to codify into law established, voluntary industry agreements, and to force any last "holdouts" to comply. However there were times when industry and government did not agree on rules. After the opening of the St. Lawrence Seaway, an increasingly large number of "foreign vessels" (in this case, ships not registered in either the United States or Canada) entered the Great Lakes. It was not hard to prove that ocean captains unfamiliar with the special navigation rules of the Great Lakes frequently acted in ways that risked accidents.

A 1959 report noted that Great Lakes vessels passing through the Welland Canal experienced 4 accidents per 1,000 passages. Ocean vessels experienced 34 accidents per 1,000 passages.[94] One author claimed that in a two-week period in the late 1950s, ocean ships almost collided with three different passenger vessels: the *Aquarama*, then operating between Detroit and Cleveland, as well as the day excursion ships; the *Columbia* and the *Ste. Claire*, both of which made several ninety-minute journeys daily between downtown Detroit and Bob-Lo Island, an amusement park at the mouth of Lake Erie. As the author put it, "Rules of navigation, signals, and common sense alike are ignored by masters of foreign ships on the lakes."[95]

What was more difficult was to decide what to do about it. The LCA and most lake interests argued that vessels from countries other than the United States and Canada should be required to carry pilots while in the Great Lakes.[96] The idea, however, was strongly resisted by international shipping interests, who noted that pilotage could add $4,000 to the cost of a round trip between Montreal and Thunder Bay.[97] Rules regarding pilots continued a long tradition of government licensing and regulating of officers on the lakes' commercial ships. In 1852 Congress required the Steamboat Inspection Service, which had been created in 1838 to certify the safety of steam boilers on ships, to also issue licenses that assured the public that the engineers and the pilots of steam-powered passenger vessels were qualified to do their job. In 1871 the law was amended so that the master, chief mates, engineers, and pilots of all steam-powered vessels would be required to be licensed. Virtually all captains of cargo ships required licensing when Congress in 1898 extended the law to cover the master and chief mates of any vessel weighing more than 700 tons.[98] By 1900 all of the officers serving aboard a Great Lakes freighter were licensed by the government. The specific requirements needed for licensure were broadly outlined by the law, but the specific criteria were left to the discretion of the Board of Supervising Inspectors, part of the Steamboat Inspection Service, and the agency that wrote and graded the certification tests.[99] In 1915 the same board was given authority to regulate the minimum number of officers required on a ship.[100]

The same 1915 law that established regulations for a minimum number of officers also established for the first time a licensing procedure for crew members. The law did not require that all crew members be licensed, but the law did give the Supervising Inspectors authority to establish a minimum ratio of licensed to unlicensed crew.[101] In 1932 the Steamboat Inspection Service was merged with another federal agency to form the Bureau of Marine Inspection and Navigation within the Department of Commerce. In 1942 an executive order was signed by President Franklin Roosevelt temporarily placing the bureau under the jurisdiction of the United States Coast Guard. This action was made permanent in 1946. The Coast Guard continued to have responsibility for the licensing of crews for the remainder of the twentieth century.[102]

Over time, the knowledge required and the tests administered to qualify an individual for a license evolved to meet changing needs. In general, however, the initial tests and periodic exams required for relicensure (generally once every five years for officers) were graded in a way that demonstrated possession of the minimum skills necessary to sail a ship. They were not used as future-oriented tools requiring the learning of new information, or rigorous examinations used to weed out the minimally competent or mediocre, and thus create a more elite body of officers and licensed crew. Government testing and licensing created a basic level of skill all must meet, but it did not seek to raise the industry's skill level to new heights.

Government, unions, and most of all management played a shoreside role that greatly influenced what happened on the boats plying the lakes. But in the end, what mattered most was economics. The bulk carriers existed because of the need to move bulk cargo, and the realization that the least expensive way to do it was over the water. Comparison after comparison made the point. In 1929, it cost 75 cents per ton to move coal by water from Cleveland, Ohio, to Ashland, Wisconsin. The same trip by rail would cost $3.50 to $4.00 per ton.[103] Throughout the century, bulk cargo consistently moved at lower cost per ton on water than by rail, and these two means of transportation were both much more efficient at moving bulk goods than trucks. At century's end, it was estimated that the lakers could move bulk cargo at a cost savings of $10 to $20 per ton compared to their nearest competitor.[104]

Changes in the economy over time, however, created changes in basic fleet operations. For the first half of the twentieth century, iron ore moved almost exclusively from west to east: from mines in Minnesota and northern Michigan to steel mills on the southern shores of Lake Erie and Lake Michigan. This basic direction of trade was threatened, but eventually maintained, in the second half of the century. As World War II came to a close, the constant mining of ore from Michigan and Minnesota dramatically reduced the supply of easily obtained, high-grade iron ore. Ore shortages began to occur, and the steel industry began to seek a new source of raw material. A global search for iron ore began, with major resources discovered in Canada, Brazil, and Venezuela. Much of the Canadian ore was found in a remote area between Labrador and Quebec.

The opening of the St. Lawrence Seaway in 1959 created the infrastructure needed to exploit the ore between Labrador and Quebec and create an alternate east to west movement of ore. American and Canadian vessels experimented with loading ore mined in Quebec and Labrador at the port of Seven Islands (Sept-Îles) on the St. Lawrence River and moving it west to mills along the Great Lakes.[105] Canadian steel firms would eventually adopt this as their solution to the ore crisis, making Seven Islands at its height the second largest port (measured by tonnage shipped) in Canada. American steel companies, however, chose a different solution to the ore shortage, one that maintained the traditional downbound freighter traffic in ore.[106]

In the United States, taconite replaced raw iron ore. Taconite was manufactured at mine sites in Minnesota and Michigan from what was once considered ore too low in iron content to bother about, and it became the ore boats' principal downbound cargo. But from the shipper's viewpoint, manufactured taconite had an unanticipated negative effect. Manufactured taconite's high and consistent iron content, approximately 65 percent and higher than all but the best of raw ore, meant less taconite was needed to produce a pound of steel than was needed if raw ore was used.[107] It was a subtle shift, but all other things being equal one that lessened the total annual tonnage needed to generate the same amount of steel.[108] This change was a problem for the shipping industry, but the problem was dwarfed by a much greater change in the economy: the overall decline in America's manufacturing industries. As manufacturing declined in the last quarter of the twentieth century, so too did U.S. steel production and the size of the U.S. flag lake fleet in the Great Lakes.

In 1900 the country produced 11.2 million tons of steel. By 1910 the number had grown to 28.3 million tons, and by 1920, 46.2 million tons of steel were produced in America. To support this rapid increase in product required an equally rapid increase in the amount of ore shipped and a rapid growth in shipping capacity. Predictably, the U.S. shipping industry on the lakes saw its biggest construction boom in the twentieth century during these years. World War II and the years that followed saw another boom in steel production, reaching 79.7 million tons in 1945 and growing to 117 million tons by 1955. While production remained high into the 1970s, growth was modest, and production peaked at 150.8 million tons in 1973. In the last "good year," 1981, 120.8 million tons of steel were produced. The next year, 74.6 million tons of steel were made, and the industry entered into a decline that was only modestly reversed at the end of the century. Domestic steel production did not again top 100 million tons until 1993. In the last year of the century, 1999, the United States produced 107.4 million tons of steel.[109]

The decline in American steel production led to the end of the steel industry as it had been created at the beginning of the twentieth century. The *Encyclopedia of Chicago History* concisely explains the consequences:

> During the 1970s and 1980s, the U.S. steel industry suffered a sudden collapse that threw thousands out of work. U.S. Steel and other American steel companies that still depended upon large numbers of older, inefficient plants failed to withstand the combination of a decline in demand and the rise of international competition in the 1970s. The sudden decline of American steel stunned the employees of mills across the Chicago area. Between 1979 and 1986, about 16,000 Chicago-area steelworkers lost their jobs. Wisconsin Steel closed abruptly in 1980 after attempts at a financial bailout failed. South Works endured a prolonged shutdown before closing its doors in 1992. Inland Steel cut thousands of workers. Republic Steel dismissed half its employees. In 1984, it merged with LTV Steel, which declared bankruptcy in 1986. The closures left many steelworkers without jobs or health care and decimated communities in northwest Indiana and the Calumet district.
>
> During the final years of the twentieth century, the Chicago region continued to be a leading center of production in an American steel industry that was much weaker and smaller than it had been before. By the mid-1980s, the area was home to several "minimills," small-scale plants that used sophisticated electric furnaces to

recycle scrap metal. By the end of the 1980s, mills in Northern Indiana were making about a quarter of all the steel produced in the United States. While the region remained a center of steel production, the industry was no longer the powerhouse that had been a crucial part of the Chicago-area economy for over a century.[110]

The reorganization of the steel industry in Chicago mirrored what occurred across the Great Lakes. The ripple effect from massive consolidation caused the amount of cargo to decline and the number of ships to also decline.[111] The economy defined the need for, and number of, freighters.

The story regarding coal is somewhat different. For most of the century, coal was the second most important cargo on the lakes. It was a welcome load for U.S. ships. Iron ore moved downbound, from ports in Lake Superior to steel mills either at the southern end of Lake Michigan or located in various ports on the southern shore of Lake Erie. Coal moved upbound, shipped north by train from mines in Pennsylvania or West Virginia, then loaded aboard empty ore boats.[112] Unlike steel production, which declined after 1981, in the last decades of the twentieth century U.S. coal production grew to newfound heights, after having sagged in the 1960s and 1970s. At the beginning of the twentieth century, America produced approximately 270 million tons of coal. By 1950 that had grown to 560 million tons. By 1980 national production had reached approximately 830 million tons. In the 1990s production grew again, exceeding one billion tons in seven of the decade's ten years.[113] Although overall production increased, where this coal was produced, and where it was used, worked to the detriment of the Great Lakes shipping industry.

In 1950, about 524.4 million tons of coal were produced east of the Mississippi River, and a scant 36 million tons were produced west of the Mississippi. By the end of the century, in 1999, some 529.6 million tons of coals were produced east of the Mississippi and 570.8 million tons west of the river.[114] Much of this vast increase in western coal production resulted from the adoption of the Clean Air Act of 1970.[115] Electrical generating facilities and other industrial sites were required to lower emissions. One simple way to accomplish this was to burn coal low in sulfur. Pennsylvania and West Virginia coal, the traditional cargo of upbound lake boats, tended to be high in sulfur. Coal from America's West tended to be low in sulfur. Increasingly coal moved from west to east, reversing the traditional flow of the product.[116] At the same time as production was shifting, the home-heating market for coal was declining. The quick penetration of natural gas and fuel oil into the domestic heating market after World War II caused coal shipments to decline.[117]

The net result was an overall downturn in coal traffic on the lakes and a fundamental change in the direction coal traveled. The amount of coal shipped over the Great Lakes declined from 45.5 million tons to 33.0 million tons. The traditional coal ports along Lake Erie, particularly Toledo, lost substantial amounts of cargo.[118] In a sign of changing times, in 1987 Superior, Wisconsin, replaced Toledo as the lakes' leading coal port.[119]

Even stone, the most stable of the three core cargoes carried by lakers, experienced changes that affected the shipping industry. At century's close, stone continued to be an important cargo. Limestone made up 85 percent of this cargo, and the vast majority of it continued to come from Alpena, Michigan.[120] Like iron ore, stone generally moved "downbound," from Alpena to the mills at the southern end of Lakes Erie and Michigan. However, late in the twentieth century some stone began to move into Lake Superior to be used in "flux pellets," an improved form of taconite that premixed the flux provided by stone into the taconite.[121]

Although the grain trade on the lakes remained an important one in the twentieth century, it was a commodity that moved most frequently on Canadian ships. In the twentieth century, wheat tended to be loaded on Canadian ships docked on the Canadian shore of Lake Superior to be shipped to Canada's eastern cities. Prior to the Civil War, grain was the most common bulk product on the lakes. In the nineteenth and early twentieth centuries, much of the grain moved from American ports. As late as 1965, Buffalo, the Great Lakes' traditional grain port, had twenty-seven operating grain elevators. But by 1984 the number of operating elevators had declined to four.[122] Over time, the Great Lakes grain trade came to be largely dominated by Canadian and overseas vessels. Particularly after the opening of the St. Lawrence Seaway, more Canadian grain was shipped both to Eastern Canada and globally. Because the Seaway gave Canadian vessels an upbound cargo, ore for Canadian steel mills along Lake Huron, Canadian flag vessels found this a very profitable activity.[123]

Similarly, ocean vessels flying the flags of various nations could use the Seaway to enter the lakes and travel to the far end of Lake Superior to pick up a grain cargo destined for a foreign port.[124] By 1968 more than half of the grain shipped moved on foreign vessels rather than either U.S. or Canadian ships.[125] The Seaway also caused a temporary boom in U.S. grain traveling out of Great Lakes ports. In 1969, about 18 percent of all grain exported from the United States was loaded in a lake port, although most often not on an American ship, while 6 percent traveled out of a port along the Atlantic Ocean. The growth in the size of oceangoing vessels in the late twentieth century ended this boom. By 1982 only 7 percent of the nation's grain exports were loaded at a Great Lakes port, while 14 percent left the country along the Atlantic shoreline. The economies of scale achieved by massive new ocean vessels, too big to sail through the St. Lawrence Seaway, more than compensated for the additional railroad expenses needed to move grain from the Midwest to the Atlantic Seaboard.[126] In the last decade of the century, the Canadian grain trade on the lakes also diminished, as changing trade patterns sent more and more Canadian grain to Canada's Pacific coast, where it was loaded onto ships bound for Asia.[127]

All of these broad economic trends controlled both the profitability and the business of shipping. How much ore, coal, stone, and grain there was to move and the direction in which it flowed both profoundly affected shipping. But to say that the history of Great Lakes shipping in the twentieth century is simply about economic history somehow falls short of the mark. Knowing how the ships were ultimately controlled by economic forces located on the shore is not enough to understand the story of lake shipping.

James Oliver Curwood was right to say the ships were things of rough beauty. Fred Dutton was right to be transfixed by the crew's tales, even subtracting 20 percent for fiction. The ships and the crews that sailed them were part of economic history, but much more than just economic history. They are remembered best not by statistics regarding annual tonnage or for carefully calculated costs per mile, but by the words of a song:

> Bold sailors that follow the Lakes
> On an iron ore vessel, your living to make
> I shipped in Chicago, bid adieu to the shore
> Bound away to Escanaba for red iron ore
>
> In the month of September, the seventeenth day
> Two dollars and a quarter is all they would pay
> And on Monday morning the *Bridgeport* did take
> The *E.C. Roberts* out in the Lake
>
> The wind from the south'ard sprang up a fresh breeze
> And away through Lake Michigan the *Roberts* did sneeze
> And away through Lake Michigan the *Roberts* did roar

And on Friday morning we passed through death's door

This packet she howled across the mouth of Green Bay
And before her cutwater, there dashed a white spray
We rounded the sandpoint, our anchor let go
We furled in our canvas and the watch went below

Next morning we hove alongside the *Exile*
And soon was made fast to an iron ore pile
They lowered their chutes and like thunder did roar
They spouted into us that red iron ore

Some sailors took shovels while others got spades
And some took wheelbarrows—each man to his trade
We looked like red devils, our fingers got sore
And we cursed Escanaba and that damned iron ore

The tug *Escanaba* she towed out the *Minch*
The *Roberts* she thought she had left in a pinch
And as she passed by us she bid us goodbye
Saying, "We'll meet you in Cleveland next Fourth of July!"

Through Louse Island it blew a fresh breeze
We passed the Foxes, the Beavers, the Skillagalees
We flew by the *Minch* for to show her the way
And she ne'er hove in sight till we were off Thunder Bay

Across Saginaw Bay the *Roberts* did ride
With the deep and dark waters rolling over her side
And now for Port Huron the *Roberts* must go
Where the tug *Kate Williams* she took us in tow

We went through North Passage—O Lord, how it blew!
And all round the Dummy a large fleet there came too
The night being dark, Old Nick it would scare
And we hove up next morning and for Cleveland did steer

And now we're in Cleveland, made fast stem and stern
And over the bottle we'll spin a big yarn
But Captain Harvey Shannon, he ought to stand treat
For getting into Cleveland ahead of the fleet

Now my song is ended, I hope you won't scoff
Our dunnage is packed and all hands is paid off
Here's a health to the *Roberts*, she's staunch, strong and true
Not forgotten the bold boys that comprise her crew.[128]

NOTES

CHAPTER 1. REMAKING THE LAKES TO MOVE THE CARGO

1. Heather Steinberger, "Shipsitters," http://writeonllc.com/2011/08/shipsitters.

2. Clare J. Snider and Michael W. R. Davis, *The Ford Fleet* (Cleveland: Freshwater Press, 1994), 133–34.

3. The "Upper Lakes" refer to Superior, Michigan, Huron, and Erie. Lake Ontario is divided from the Upper Lakes by the Niagara River and, of course, Niagara Falls. The river drops approximately 326 feet (99 meters), about half of that at the Falls. Because of this impenetrable navigational barrier, Lake Ontario is separated from the Upper Lakes physically and usually not included in discussions of the "Upper Lakes."

4. Lauchlen P. Morrison, "Recollections of the Great Lakes, Part 7," *Inland Seas* 6, no. 3 (Fall 1950): 186.

5. Morrison, "Recollections of the Great Lakes, Part 7," 186; John W. Larson, *Essayons: A History of the Detroit District U.S. Army Corps of Engineers* (Detroit: U.S. Army Corps of Engineers, 1995), 87, 92, 119.

6. U.S. Army Corps of Engineers, *History of Dredging and Compensation St. Clair and Detroit Rivers, February 2009*, 8–12.

7. Alvin C. Gluek Jr., "The Lake Carriers' Association and the Origins of the International Waterways Commission, Part I," *Inland Seas* 36, no. 4 (Winter 1980): 238.

8. "Great Lakes Time Line," *Inland Seas* 41, no. 4 (Winter 1985): 291.

9. Kenneth Cottingham, "Erie—The Record of a Lake, Part II," *Inland Seas* 16, no. 3 (Fall 1960): 215.

10. Gordon W. Thayer, "Fifty Years Ago," *Inland Seas* 1, no. 3 (October 1945): 55.

11. F. A. Blust, "The Water Levels of Lake Erie," *Inland Seas* 19, no. 1 (Spring 1963): 29.

12. Cottingham, "Erie—The Record of a Lake, Part II," 215; N. Wilson Britt, "Pseudo Tides in Lake Erie," *Inland Seas* 10, no. 4 (Winter 1954): 294.

13. Today the Coast Guard uses automated devices to monitor the water's depth at Lime Kiln Crossing. Reports are radioed to vessels daily, but when the depth drops below the established minimum water level, reports are issued every half-hour.

14. William Ashworth, *The Late Great Lakes: An Environmental History* (New York: Alfred A. Knopf, 1986), 94.

15. Ashworth, *The Late Great Lakes*, 98. The ship *Challenge* had a hinged centerboard that could be raised to allow for navigation in shallow water, but lowered to increase stability in the open lake.

16. Secretary of the Treasury, *Statement of Appropriations and Expenditures for Public Buildings, Rivers and Harbors, Forts, Arsenals and Armories, and other Public Works, from March 4, 1789 to June 30, 1882* (Washington, DC: Government Printing Office, 1886), 159–225, 267, 271, 371–422.

17. Andrew T. Brown. "The Great Lakes, 1850–1861, pt. 5," *Inland Seas* 7, no. 3 (Fall 1951): 185.

18. Andrew T. Brown, "The Great Lakes, 1850–1861, pt. 4," *Inland Seas* 7, no. 2 (Summer 1951): 104.

19. Larson, *Essayons*, 54.

20. Richard A. Palmer, "'Towing the Line' at the St. Clair Flats," *Inland Seas* 66, no. 1 (Spring 2010): 29–30.

21. Bernie Arbic, *City of the Rapids: Sault Ste. Marie's Heritage* (Allegan Forest, MI: Priscilla Press, 2003), 120–21.

22. Arbic, *City of the Rapids*, 101.

23. Arbic, *City of the Rapids*, 120–21.

24. Arbic, *City of the Rapids*, 122.

25. Arbic, *City of the Rapids*, 95.

26. Secretary of the Treasury, *Statement of Appropriations*, 165.

27. Larson, *Essayons*, 77, 92.

28. Larson, *Essayons*, 94, 105.

29. Larson, *Essayons*, 107, 109.

30. Secretary of the Treasury, *Statement of Appropriations*, 165–66.

31. Elmer Eckroad, *The Soo Locks* (Detroit: National Lithograph Co., 1950), 14. In 1881 the Soo Locks also began to operate on a twenty-four-hour schedule. The state had operated the locks only during daylight hours. Larson, *Essayons*, 125.

32. Larson, *Essayons*, 125–27.

33. Larson, *Essayons*, 42; Arbic, *City of the Rapids*, 144; U.S. Army Corps of Engineers, "St. Mary's River," http://www.lre.usace.army.mil/Missions/GreatLakesInformation/Outflows/DischargeMeasurements/StMarysRiver.aspx.

34. Larson, *Essayons*, 140.

35. Mark L. Thompson, *Steamboats and Sailors of the Great Lakes* (Detroit: Wayne State University Press, 1991), 38.

36. Eckroad, *The Soo Locks*, 14.

37. "Sault Ste. Marie Canal National Historic Site," Parks Canada, http://www.pc.gc.ca/lhn-nhs/on/ssmarie/index.aspx. The Canadian lock was closed in 1987 because of a lock wall failure. In 1998 a new, smaller Canadian lock was opened. It was constructed within the confines of the 1895 lock and designed primarily for small, shallow-draft recreational boats.

38. Arbic, *City of the Rapids*, 228; F. Clever Bald, *The Sault Canal through 100 Years* (Ann Arbor: University of Michigan, 1954), notes on page 32 that an unsuccessful effort was made to name the lock after Chase Osborn.

39. "Channel Deepening Ceremony Marks Step Ahead on Lakes," *LCA Bulletin* 46, no. 2 (July 1957): 6, 22–23.

40. John J. Hartig, ed., *Honoring Our Detroit River: Caring for Our Home* (Bloomfield Hills, MI: Cranbrook Institute of Science, 2003), 6.

41. U.S. Army Corps of Engineers, Great Lakes and Ohio River Division, *Great Lakes System Dredged Material Management Long Term Strategic Plan*, (Cincinnati: U.S. Army Corps of Engineers, March 2010), 6, 22.

42. Lawrence A. Pomeroy Jr., "Reshaping Our Future: 1959 and Since," *Inland Seas* 22, no. 3 (Fall 1966): 314.

43. "A Century of Great Lakes Commerce," *Great Lakes Seaway Review* 37, no. 3 (January–March 2009): 81, includes a tabular summation of twentieth-century iron, coal, and stone commerce on the Great Lakes, compiled from the annual statistics found in the Lake Carriers' Association *Annual Reports*.

44. Al Miller, *Tin Stackers: The History of the Pittsburgh Steamship Company* (Detroit: Wayne State University Press, 1999), 135–36.

45. Thomas Andrew Sykora, "A Seventeen Year Old Looks at the Lakes," *Inland Seas* 3, no. 2 (April 1947): 80.

46. Bald, *The Sault Canal*, 29.

47. Miller, *Tin Stackers*, 18.

48. Miller, *Tin Stackers*, 18.

49. Thompson, *Steamboats*, 26.

50. Raymond A. Bawal Jr., *Superships of the Great Lakes: Thousand-Foot Ships on the Great Lakes* (Clinton Township, MI: Inland Expressions, 2011), 11.

51. Thompson, *Steamboats*, 20.

52. George J. Joachim, *Iron Fleet: The Great Lakes in World War II* (Detroit: Wayne State University Press, 1994), 18.

53. Bawal, *Superships*, 11.

54. Joachim, *Iron Fleet*, 18.

55. Snider and Davis, *The Ford Fleet*, 83; "Limestone for the Furnaces," *LCA Bulletin* 32, no. 2 (June 1944): unpaginated; U.S. Department of Transportation, *Status of the U.S. Flag Great Lakes Water Transportation Industry* (Washington, DC: U.S. Department of Transportation Maritime Administration, 2013), 11.

56. Reprint of a letter to the editor by R. C. Bristol, originally published in the *Chicago Daily Democrat*, May 5, 1849. *Inland Seas* 4, no. 3 (Fall 1948): 201.

57. Thompson, *Steamboats*, 26; David W. Francis, "Marine Casualties on the Great Lakes, 1863–1873: An Analysis," *Inland Seas* 42, no. 4 (Winter 1986): 261–62.

58. "Grain for the Hosts of Freedom," *LCA Bulletin* 32, no. 4 (August 1944): 11; George Dietrich, "Exciting Episodes in Grain Trade Climaxed by Epic Story of 1917–18," *LCA Bulletin* 39, no. 4 (August 1950): 1–4.

59. William Ashworth, *The Late Great Lakes* (New York: Knopf, 1986), 15.

CHAPTER 2. THE CREW

1. James Oliver Curwood published his first book in 1908. By the 1920s, he was consistently among the top-selling American authors. His most popular works were action adventure stories set in the Yukon or Alaska. When he died in 1927, at the age of forty-nine, he was said to be the most highly paid author in America.

2. Jay McCormick, *November Storm* (New York: Doubleday Duran, 1943), 82–83.

3. Patrick Livingston, *Eight Steamboats: Sailing through the Sixties* (Detroit: Wayne State University Press, 2004), 274.

4. R. W. England, "The Engineer," *Inland Seas* 1, no. 2 (April 1945): 12.

5. *LCA Bulletin* 32, no. 2 (June 1944): unpaginated.

6. Ray I. McGrath, *Great Lakes Stories* (Sault Ste. Marie, MI: Border Enterprises, 1996), 180.

7. Albert Bartlett Oral History Transcript, interview conducted September 1992, Albert A. Bartlett Collection, Box 3, Center for Archival Collections, Bowling Green State University, Ohio, 143.

8. England, "The Engineer," 12.

9. "Instructors of Long Experience Head Winter Schools," *LCA Bulletin* 32, no. 6 (October 1944): 14–15.

10. "Time to Start Training," *LCA Bulletin* 43, no. 5 (October 1946): 2–3. Classes in radar and gyrocompasses were apparently first offered in this year. "Radar School," Lake Carriers' Association, *Annual Report* [1950] (Rocky River, OH: 1950), 25.

11. Mark L. Thompson, *Steamboats and Sailors of the Great Lakes* (Detroit: Wayne State University Press, 1991), 105; *Inland Seas* 31, no. 1 (Spring 1975): 60.

12. Robert J. Blackwell, "The International Ship Masters Association Meeting, 1978," *Inland Seas* 34, no. 1 (Spring 1978): 9–11. A fathometer is a sonic device to determine the depth of water under a ship.

13. "Great Lakes Calendar," *Inland Seas* 3, no. 4 (October 1947): 256.

14. "Fleet Engineers Committee," Lake Carriers' Association, *Annual Report* [1958] (Rocky River, OH: 1958), 28; and "Fleet Engineers Committee," Lake Carriers' Association, *Annual Report* [1960] (Rocky River, OH: 1960), 16.

15. Gordon McLintock, "King Point Academy's Contribution to the American Merchant Marine," *Inland Seas* 6, no. 3 (Fall 1950): 144–48.

16. Memo of Minutes, Mutual Study Committee, September 13, 1977, United Steel Workers' Great Lakes Seamen Local 5000 Collection, box 1, Center for Archival Collections, Bowling Green State University, Ohio.

17. "Perspective," *LCA Bulletin* 58, no. 1 (April–May 1969): inside front cover; "Lake Maritime Academy—Training Lead to Officer Berth," *LCA Bulletin* 67, no. 3 (October–November 1978): 10–12; "Cadets Train for Great Lakes Career," *LCA Bulletin*, 71 no. 1 (June–July 1982): 3–9; "Great Lakes Maritime Academy," Northwestern Michigan College, https://www.nmc.edu.

18. Thompson, *Steamboats*, 100; "Great Lakes Calendar," *Inland Seas* 35, no. 2 (Summer 1979): 156.

19. Thompson, *Steamboats*, 231–32.

20. Esther Rice Battenfield, "In Grandpa's Wake," *Inland Seas* 9, no. 3 (Fall 1953): 195–99.

21. "Great Lakes Calendar," *Inland Seas* 33, no. 4 (Winter 1977): 340; "Women Sign on for Sailing Jobs," *LCA Bulletin* 66, no. 2 (July–August 1977): 13; "Great Lakes Calendar," *Inland Seas* 35, no. 4 (Winter 1979): 320; "Cadets Train for Great Lakes Career," *LCA Bulletin* 71, no. 1 (June–July 1982): 3; "Keeping Training on Course," *Great Lakes Seaway Review* 41, no.

1 (July–September 2012): 59; Undated newspaper clipping regarding Marjorie Murtaugh, Local 5000 Collection, box 2, Center for Archival Collections, Bowling Green State University, Ohio.

22. Kenneth F. London, "Civil Rights and Great Lakes Shipping," n.d., Local 5000 Collection, box 2, Center for Archival Collections, Bowling Green State University, Ohio.

23. Civil Rights Committee Minutes, June 1, 1976, Local 5000 Collection, Center for Archival Collections, Bowling Green State University, Ohio.

24. Statement of Martha Kogut, May 10, 1976, Local 5000 Collection, Center for Archival Collections, Bowling Green State University, Ohio.

25. Statement of Marie Dinoff, May 13, 1976, Local 5000 Collection, Center for Archival Collections, Bowling Green State University, Ohio.

26. Statement of Marie Dinoff, May 13, 1976, Local 5000 Collection, Center for Archival Collections, Bowling Green State University, Ohio.

27. Patrick D. Lapinski, "Legend of a Steamer: The *John J. Boland,*" *Inland Seas* 53, no. 1 (Spring 1997): 22.

28. Thompson, *Steamboats*, 120.

29. "No Longer an All-Male Profession," *Seaway Review* 19, no. 4 (April–June 1991): 77–79.

30. George J. Joachim, *Iron Fleet: The Great Lakes in World War II* (Detroit: Wayne State University Press, 1994), 15. Joachim is describing boats during the World War II era, but technology, which in later years would make it possible to reduce crew size, had yet to take significant effect.

31. Thompson, *Steamboats*, 102.

32. McGrath, *Great Lakes Stories*, 67–68.

33. Thompson, *Steamboats*, 112–13, 322–23; Nelson Haydamacker with Alan D. Millar, *Deckhand: Life on Freighters of the Great Lakes* (Ann Arbor: University of Michigan Press, 2009); "Hanna Pleads Poverty: Moves to Cut Crews," *Great Lakes Sailor*, April 1963, 3; "Local 7000 To Arbitrate Abolishment of Nite Cook Job on Steamer *Leon Falk,*" *Great Lakes Sailor*, December 1963, 4.

34. Thompson, *Steamboats*, 112; Livingston, *Eight Steamboats*, 128.

35. Thompson, *Steamboats*, 201.

36. Thompson, *Steamboats*, 21.

37. Bartlett Oral History, 48.

38. Haydamacker, *Deckhand: Life on Freighters of the Great Lakes*, 61.

39. Richard A. Belford, "Steamboating Forty Years Ago," *Inland Seas* 24, no. 4 (Winter 1968): 302.

40. Jacques LesStrang, *Lake Carriers* (Seattle: Salisbury Book Press, 1977), 127.

41. Battenfield, "In Grandpa's Wake," 97.

42. Clare J. Snider and Michael W. R. Davis, *The Ford Fleet* (Cleveland: Freshwater Press, 1994), 39; Kenneth R. Dickinson, "Henry Ford II," *Inland Seas* 62, no. 1 (Spring 2006): 9.

43. Al Miller, *Tin Stackers: The History of the Pittsburgh Steamship Company* (Detroit: Wayne State University Press, 1999), 179.

44. Miller, *Tin Stackers*, 178.

45. Miller, *Tin Stackers*, 177.

46. Livingston, *Eight Steamboats*, 174.

47. Nancy A. Schneider, "'Ob Gibson': Memories of the Great Lakes Waters," *Inland Seas* 57, no. 4 (Winter 2001): 291.

48. Thompson, *Steamboats*, 34–35, 43; Gregory W. Streb and William L. Wallace, "Care and Feeding of the Crew," *Inland Seas* 55, no. 2 (Summer 1999): 120.

49. "Complaints: Steamer *Robinson*," *Great Lakes Sailor*, November 1964, 7. Although the union did address the issue, the complaint was not contractual, since its target was a fellow union member rather than management.

50. Thompson, *Steamboats*, 22.

51. "Cliffs Steward Says Job is 'A Lot of Fun,'" *LCA Bulletin* 70, no. 3 (October–November, 1981): 3.

52. Streb and Wallace, "Care and Feeding of the Crew," 122.

53. Haydamacker, *Deckhand*, 39.

54. Thompson, *Steamboats*, 16, 144, 223, 319.

55. Bartlett Oral History, 98–99.

56. Thanksgiving 1947 Menu, Str. *Louis W. Hill*, BoatNerd, http://boatnerd.com/pictures/historic/perspectives/ValleyCamp2/default.htm.

57. Thanksgiving 1976 Menu, Str. *Charles M. White*, BoatNerd, http://www.boatnerd.com/news/newsthumbs/images-07–4/cmwhite11–25–76jpm-f.jpg.jpg.

58. Gregory W. Streb, "A Thanksgiving Vignette," *Inland Seas* 46, no. 1 (Spring 1990): 23.

59. McGrath, *Great Lakes Stories*, 74; Bartlett Oral History, 64.

60. McGrath, *Great Lakes Stories*, 45.

61. Fred Dutton, *Life on the Great Lakes: A Wheelsman's Story*, ed. William Donohue Ellis (Detroit: Wayne State University Press, 1991), 60–61.

62. Thompson, *Steamboats*, 63.

63. Haydamacker, *Deckhand*, 38.

64. Thompson, *Steamboats*, 43.

65. Haydamacker, *Deckhand*, 45.

66. Dutton, *Life on the Great Lakes*, 62.

67. Dutton, *Life on the Great Lakes*, 63; Snider and Davis, *The Ford Fleet*, 147.

68. DeForest Mellon, "A Great Lakes Memory," *Inland Seas* 12, no. 1 (Spring 1956): 72.

69. Livingston, *Eight Steamboats*, 279; Bartlett Oral History, 91.

70. Thompson, *Steamboats*, 43.

71. Thompson, *Steamboats*, 229–31.

72. "M.E.B.A. History," Marine Engineers' Beneficial Association, http://mebaunion.org/MEBA.

73. Bartlett Oral History, 133–34.

74. Bartlett Oral History, 134. Quote from Belford, "Steamboating Forty Years Ago," 297.

75. Edward A. Perrine, "Huron and On," *Inland Seas* 56, no. 1 (Spring 2000): 8.

76. Miller, *Tin Stackers*, 167.

77. Dutton, *Life on the Great Lakes*, 76–77.

78. Jack Farrell, "Clanging of Fireman's Shovel Disappearing on Great Lakes," *LCA Bulletin* 52, no. 3 (September–October 1963): 20–23. Harry F. Myers, "Remembering the 504's," *Inland Seas* 44, no. 2 (Summer 1988): 83, asserted the temperature rose to a mere 130 degrees, and then only on hot summer days.

79. Merwin Stone Thompson, *An Ancient Mariner Recollects* (Oxford, OH: Typoprint, Inc., n.d.), 36–38; Dutton, *Life on the Great Lakes*, 35.

80. James Oliver Curwood, *The Great Lakes and the Vessels That Plough Them: Their Owners, Their Sailors, and Their Cargoes* (New York: G.P. Putnam's Sons, 1909), 147–48.

81. Dutton, *Life on the Great Lakes*, 32; J. J. Garth, "Firehold University," *Inland Seas* 39, no. 3 (Fall 1983): 191; Myers, "Remembering the 504's," 90.

82. Dutton, *Life on the Great Lakes*, 34; Farrell, "Clanging of Fireman's Shovel," *LCA Bulletin* 52, no. 3 (September–October 1963): 20–23; William E. (Bill) Bardelmeier, "How to Steam a Steamboat: Sailing in Hand-Fired Lake Vessels in the WWII Era," *Inland Seas* 60, no. 3 (Fall 2004): 232, 235–36.

83. Bardelmeier, "How to Steam a Steamboat," 232, 236.

84. Myers, "Remembering the 504's," 90.

85. Dutton, *Life on the Great Lakes*, 32; Garth, "Firehold University," 191; Myers, "Remembering the 504's," 90.

86. Bardelmeier, "How to Steam a Steamboat," 236–37.

87. Dutton, *Life on the Great Lakes*, 33–34; Garth, "Firehold University," 190–91; Bardelmeier, "How to Steam a Steamboat," 237.

88. Dutton, *Life on the Great Lakes*, 32; Garth, "Firehold University," 91; Myers, "Remembering the 504's," 90.

89. Belford, "Steamboating Forty Years Ago," 300.

90. Dutton, *Life on the Great Lakes*, 35.

91. Miller, *Tin Stackers*, 138–39.

92. Snider and Davis, *The Ford Fleet*, 148; Farrell, "Clanging of Fireman's Shovel," *LCA Bulletin* 52, no. 3 (September–October 1963): 20–23.

93. "Hirshfield Cites Loss of Nine Ships to U.S. Fleet This Year," *LCA Bulletin* 53, no. 4 (October 1964): 5.

94. James L. Elliott, *Red Stacks over the Horizon: The Story of the Goodrich Steamboat Line* (Grand Rapids, MI: William B. Eerdmans Publishing Co., 1967), 199–200.

95. Snider and Davis, *The Ford Fleet*, 42–43.

96. Richard Hill, *Lake Effect: A Deckhand's Journey on the Great Lakes Freighters* (Sault Ste. Marie, MI: Gale Force Press, 2008), 27; Livingston, *Eight Steamboats*, 205, 277.

97. Myers, "Remembering the 504's," 91.

98. Hill, *Lake Effect*, 148–49; Livingston, *Eight Steamboats*, 278; Dutton, *Life on the Great Lakes*, 28.

99. Dutton, *Life on the Great Lakes*, 57.

100. Thompson, *Steamboats*, 194–95.

101. Haydamacker, *Deckhand*, 20.

102. Bartlett Oral History, 59–60, 86.

103. "Boom and Bosun's Chair Won Rapid Approval among Lake Crews," *LCA Bulletin*, 64, no. 2 (July–August 1975): 6.

104. Livingston, *Eight Steamboats*, 205; Dutton, *Life on the Great Lakes*, 28.

105. Bartlett Oral History, 63.

106. Bartlett Oral History, 84.

107. Haydamacker, *Deckhand*, 32.

108. Thompson, *Steamboats*, 27, 124; Livingston, *Eight Steamboats*, 205–6.

109. Haydamacker, *Deckhand*, 34.

110. Gary W. Schmidt, with Warren Gerds, *Real, Honest Sailing with a Great Lakes Captain* (Allouez, WI: Seaway Printing Co., 2013), 192.

111. Bill Herdter, *Old Sailor Bill* (Published by author, n.d., ca. 1997), 4; Hill, *Lake Effect*, 24.

112. Thompson, *An Ancient Mariner Recollects*, 34–35.

113. Haydamacker, *Deckhand*, 27.

114. Livingston, *Eight Steamboats*, 222.

115. Hill, *Lake Effect*, 137–38; Livingston, *Eight Steamboats*, 275.

116. Thompson, *An Ancient Mariner Recollects*, 39.

117. Thompson, *Steamboats*, 84–85.

118. Patrick Lapinski, "The Canadian Ambassador Captain Gerry Greig," *Inland Seas* 64, no. 2

(Summer 2008): 143–44.

119. Thompson, *Steamboats*, 83; McGrath, *Great Lakes Stories*, 113.

120. Knut Gjerset, *Norwegian Sailors on the Great Lakes* (Decorah, IA: Norwegian American Historical Association, 1928), 111.

121. McGrath, *Great Lakes Stories*, 113.

122. Thomas G. Matowitz Jr., "A Sailor's Life: The Story of Captain Harry Anderson," *Inland Seas* 62, no. 4 (Winter 2006): 320.

123. Miller, *Tin Stackers*, 197.

124. Thompson, *An Ancient Mariner Recollects*, 41–42.

125. Dutton, *Life on the Great Lakes*, 48–50; Livingston, *Eight Steamboats*, 146.

126. Dutton, *Life on the Great Lakes*, 56, 90–94.

127. Miller, *Tin Stackers*, 147.

128. Dutton, *Life on the Great Lakes*, 102.

129. Dutton, *Life on the Great Lakes*, 119.

130. Thompson, *Steamboats*, 77–78; Bartlett Oral History, 61.

131. Dutton, *Life on the Great Lakes*, 119.

132. Thompson, *Steamboats*, 62.

133. Thompson, *Steamboats*, 62–63. Samuel Plimsoll invented the system.

134. Miller, *Tin Stackers*, 197.

135. McGrath, *Great Lakes Stories*, 89–92.

136. Miller, *Tin Stackers*, 198; Dutton, *Life on the Great Lakes*, 135, 137.

137. Gjerset, *Norwegian Sailors*, 111.

138. Lapinski, "The Canadian Ambassador Captain Gerry Greig," 149.

139. Thompson, *An Ancient Mariner Recollects*, 34.

140. Frank T. Rice, "The Most Reluctant Lady of the Lakes," *Inland Seas* 8, no. 4 (Winter 1952): 230.

141. Mark Murphy, "The Bold Skippers of the Lakes," *Saturday Evening Post*, August 19, 1950, 35.

142. Walter Havighurst, *The Long Ships Passing: The Story of the Great Lakes* (New York: Macmillan, 1942), 248.

143. Roger M. Jones, "Crane Vessels of the Great Lakes," *Inland Seas* 62, no. 3 (Fall 2006): 187.

144. McGrath, *Great Lakes Stories*, 93.

145. McGrath, *Great Lakes Stories*, 106.

146. Bardelmeier, "How to Steam a Steamboat," 232.

147. Livingston, *Eight Steamboats*, 148–50, 154.

148. McGrath, *Great Lakes Stories*, 60, 63. See also Thompson, *Steamboats*, 28–29, for

continuation of drinking problems in the 1990s. See also Edward Perrine, "My Time on the *Frank Purnell,*" *Inland Seas* 63, no. 3 (Fall 2010): 254, for more on hard-drinking captains.

149. Edward A. Perrine, "Getting the *Stackhouse,*" *Inland Seas* 60, no. 3 (Fall 2004): 220.

150. Perrine, "Getting the *Stackhouse,*" 221–22.

151. Dutton, *Life on the Great Lakes*, 135.

152. Matowitz, "A Sailor's Life: The Story of Captain Harry Anderson," 321.

153. Miller, *Tin Stackers*, 179.

154. Gjerset, *Norwegian Sailors*, 110.

155. Snider and Davis, *The Ford Fleet*, 85.

156. Miller, *Tin Stackers*, 195.

157. Dutton, *Life on the Great Lakes*, 65; Thompson, *Steamboats*, 96.

158. Dutton, *Life on the Great Lakes*, 26, 32; Thompson, *Ancient Mariner*, 35–36.

159. McGrath, *Great Lakes Stories*, 164.

160. "Labor Conditions in Great Lakes Shipping," *Monthly Labor Review* of the Bureau of Labor Statistics, August 1937; reissued as Department of Labor Serial No. R. 609 (1937), 9; Myers, "Remembering the 504's," 90.

161. McGrath, *Great Lakes Stories*, 67–68.

162. Dutton, *Life on the Great Lakes*, 26.

163. Thompson, *An Ancient Mariner Recollects*, 31–32. He is describing his room aboard the *Roman* in 1893, which was a "state of the art" ship of that day. Gordon Macaulay, "The New Look on the Great Lakes," *Inland Seas* 9, no. 2 (Summer 1953): 96; Belford, "Steamboating Forty Years Ago," 299.

164. Battenfield, "In Grandpa's Wake," 198.

165. Thompson, *An Ancient Mariner Recollects*, 44; Macaulay, "The New Look on the Great Lakes," 96.

166. Thomas Andrew Sykora, "A Seventeen Year Old Looks at the Lakes," *Inland Seas* 3, no. 2 (April 1947): 77.

167. Thompson, *Steamboats*, 13, 24–25, 39; Gary S. Dewar, "Design Variations in Vessels for Great Lakes and Salt Water Vessels," *Inland Seas* 41, no. 3 (Fall 1985): 160.

168. Hill, *Lake Effect*, 148.

169. Hill, *Lake Effect*, 29.

170. Thompson, *Steamboats*, 165.

171. Bartlett Oral History, 113.

172. Haydamacker, *Deckhand*, 63. Windjammers could also deliver a blast of cold rainwater, should the weather take a turn for the worse.

173. Thompson, *Steamboats*, 275.

174. Dutton, *Life on the Great Lakes*, 25; Hill, *Lake Effect*, 161–62; Thompson, *Steamboats*, 165.

175. Murphy, "The Bold Skippers of the Lakes," 35.

176. Hill, *Lake Effect*, 167. Belford, "Steamboating Forty Years Ago," 300, recalls bedbugs.

177. Thompson, *Steamboats*, 57.

178. Bartlett Oral History, 38.

179. Thompson, *Steamboats*, 124–26.

180. Schmidt, *Real, Honest Sailing*, 124.

181. Livingston, *Eight Steamboats*, 151. Great Lakes ships were not unique in this regard. See U.S. Department of Commerce, *A Study of Human Resources in Ship Operations*, 54.

182. Haydamacker, *Deckhand*, 40.

183. Haydamacker, *Deckhand*, 26.

184. Livingston, *Eight Steamboats*, 275. By the twenty-first century, satellite television made it possible to receive a television signal anywhere on the lakes. Schmidt, *Real, Honest Sailing*, 38.

185. Claude E. Farmer, "Great Lakes Memories: Working on the Great Lakes, 1928–1938," *Inland Seas* 62, no. 4 (Winter 2006): 299.

186. Belford, "Steamboating Forty Years Ago," 298–99.

187. Streb and Wallace, "Care and Feeding of the Crew," 122; Janis Stein, "Cliff Kursinsky–Part 2," *Lake Shore Guardian*, March 2014, http://www.lakeshoreguardian.com/site/category/35/A-Great-Lakes-Sailor.

188. Livingston, *Eight Steamboats*, 144.

189. Dutton, *Life on the Great Lakes*, 141–42.

190. Haydamacker, *Deckhand*, 14; Bartlett Oral History, 74–75.

191. Edward A. Perrine, "It's the *Fitz*," *Inland Seas* 56, no. 3 (Fall 2000): 188.

192. Thompson, *Steamboats*, 28.

193. McGrath, *Great Lakes Stories*, 96.

194. Joachim, *Iron Fleet*, 16, citing a story published in the *Detroit Free Press*, December 22, 1941.

195. Bartlett Oral History, 45–46.

196. McGrath, *Great Lakes Stories*, 62–63, 107, 111.

197. Thompson, *Steamboats*, 65, 177.

198. Bartlett Oral History, 44–45.

199. Hill, *Lake Effect*, 164.

200. Hill, *Lake Effect*, 140–41.

201. Bartlett Oral History, 77–78.

202. Skip Gillingham, *Summer of '63 Memories: Working on the Lubrolake* (Vineland, Ontario: Glenaden Press, n.d.), 9.

203. Untitled boxed article re death of sailor, *LCA Bulletin* 32, no. 2 (June 1944): n.p.

204. Albert Bartlett Collection, box 1, folder 37, Center for Archival Collections, Bowling Green State University, Ohio.

205. Charles H. Hunger, "A Fifty Year Sailing Career on the Great Lakes, 1908–1958," *Inland Seas* 57, no. 2 (Summer 2001): 109.

206. Curwood, *The Great Lakes*, 155–56.

207. Haydamacker, *Deckhand*, 56–57.

208. Haydamacker, *Deckhand*, 16–17; Perrine, "Getting the *Stackhouse*," 224.

209. Perrine, "My Time on the *Frank Purnell*," 251–52.

210. McGrath, *Great Lakes Stories*, 133. The second assistant engineer was fired.

211. Victoria Brehm, "Refiguring a Literature of Place: The Economics of Great Lakes Maritime Literature" (PhD diss., University of Iowa, 1992), 125; "Here's What Coulby Discovered," *The Nation's Business*, April 1917, 37; Miller, *Tin Stackers*, 134.

212. Miller, *Tin Stackers*, 96.

213. Miller, *Tin Stackers*, 120.

214. Miller, *Tin Stackers*, 196.

215. Miller, *Tin Stackers*, 44.

216. William Lafferty and Valerie van Heest, *Buckets and Belts: Evolution of the Great Lakes Self-Unloader* (Holland, MI: In Depth Editions, 2009), 20.

217. Livingston, *Eight Steamboats*, 136.

218. Edward A. Perrine, "My Time on the *Frank Purnell*—Unexpected Promotion," *Inland Seas* 68, no. 3 (Fall 2012): 229.

219. Miller, *Tin Stackers*, 96; Herdter, *Old Sailor Bill*, 16–17.

220. Haydamacker, *Deckhand*, 47.

221. Thompson, *Steamboats*, 59–60. It should be added that the chief engineer was not beloved. He survived the attack, leading some crew members to suggest they take up a collection to buy the assailant a bigger knife.

222. Livingston, *Eight Steamboats*, 169.

223. McGrath, *Great Lakes Stories*, 107.

224. James P. Berry, "Evolution of Powered Work Boats," *Inland Seas* 57, no. 3 (Fall 2001): 203.

225. Haydamacker, *Deckhand*, 41.

226. Berry, "Evolution of Powered Work Boats," 203.

227. Livingston, *Eight Steamboats*, 156–59, 169–72, 175–76, 220–21, 270; McGrath, *Great Lakes Stories*, 107; Theodore N. Ferris, "Bumboats," *Inland Seas* 34, no. 1 (Spring 1978): 59–60.

228. "Vessel Personnel & Safety Committee," Lake Carriers' Association, *Annual Report* [*1986*] (Rocky River, OH: 1986), 19.

229. Maritime Consortium, Inc., "Drug Testing Regulations and Membership Questions," http://www.drugfreevessel.com. The final Coast Guard rule reflected a standard applied in many states to the operators of commercial vehicles, which established a blood alcohol level of .04 as the definition of driving under the influence of alcohol. Most states have established a blood alcohol level of .08 as the level at which individuals driving a private vehicle are considered intoxicated.

230. Perrine, "My Time on the *Frank Purnell*—Unexpected Promotion," 234–35.

231. "Great Lakes Calendar," *Inland Seas* 47, no. 3 (Fall 1991): 190–91. See also United States General Accounting Office, Report to the Chairman, Committee on Governmental Affairs, U.S. Senate, "Magnitude of Alcohol Problems and Related Maritime Accidents Unknown," GAO/RCED 90–150, May 1990, 2–6.

232. Schmidt, *Real, Honest Sailing*, 33.

233. Thompson, *Steamboats*, 226.

234. Thompson, *Steamboats*, 13.

235. Thompson, *Steamboats*, 24, 28–29, 32–33, 59–60, 95.

236. Thompson, *Steamboats*, 33.

237. Thompson, *Steamboats*, 346. If Dickens didn't say it, he should have.

238. Thompson, *Steamboats*, 133.

239. Livingston, *Eight Steamboats*, 277.

240. Hill, *Lake Effect*, 193.

241. Livingston, *Eight Steamboats*, 279.

242. Livingston, *Eight Steamboats*, 134, 152–53.

243. Livingston, *Eight Steamboats*, 274.

CHAPTER 3. THE SHIPS

1. Frank E. Kirby and A. P. Rankin, "The Bulk Freighter of the Great Lakes," *Inland Seas* 34, no. 3 (Fall 1978): 222.

2. Gary S. Dewar, "The Pittsburgh Supers," *Inland Seas* 48, no. 1 (Spring 1992): 2. Dewar notes that total tonnage in 1929 set the record at the time.

3. Bernard E. Ericson, "The Evolution of Great Lakes Ships, Part II—Steam and Steel," *Inland Seas* 25, no. 3 (Fall 1969): 203.

4. George Carrington Mason, "A Young Man's Experience of Great Lakes Ships and Shipbuilding during the Years 1895–1920," *Inland Seas* 10, no. 2 (Summer 1954): 88.

5. Alvin C. Gluek Jr., "The Lake Carriers' Association and the Origins of the International Waterways Commission, Part I," *Inland Seas* 36, no. 4 (Winter 1980): 239.

6. Al Miller, *Tin Stackers: The History of the Pittsburgh Steamship Company* (Detroit: Wayne State University Press, 1999), 104–6.

7. "Today in Great Lakes History, July 26," BoatNerd, July 26, 1998, http://www.boatnerd.com/news/archive/7–98.htm.

8. Lawrence A. Pomeroy Jr., "The Bulk Freighter," *Inland Seas* 2, no. 3 (July 1946): 197.

9. Mark L. Thompson, *Steamboats and Sailors of the Great Lakes* (Detroit: Wayne State University Press, 1991), 38.

10. Harry F. Myers, "Remembering the 504's," *Inland Seas* 44, no. 2 (Summer 1988): 79, 81–86.

11. Ericson, "The Evolution of Great Lakes Ships, Part II," 199.

12. W. Bruce Bowlus, "'Changes of Vast Magnitude': The Development of an Iron Ore Delivery System on the Great Lakes during the Nineteenth Century" (PhD diss., Bowling Green State University, 1992), 81.

13. Bowlus, "Changes of Vast Magnitude," 100. Only one steel vessel was built exclusively for the lumber trade, the *Erwin L. Fisher* in 1910.

14. Kenneth R. Kickson, "The Largest Schooner in the World Revisited," *Inland Seas* 42, no. 1 (Spring 1986): 4–5.

15. Bowlus, "Changes of Vast Magnitude," 94; Ericson, "The Evolution of Great Lakes Ships, Part II," 200.

16. Ericson, "The Evolution of Great Lakes Ships, Part II," 202–3.

17. Bowlus, "Changes of Vast Magnitude," 106, 109; "Last of the Composite Vessels," *LCA Bulletin* 34, no. 3 (August 1946): 17–18. The last operating composite ship, the *Yankcanuck*, originally named the *Manchester*, was abandoned in 1946. Thompson, *Steamboats*, 46.

18. U.S. Department of Transportation, *Status of the U.S. Flag Great Lakes Water Transportation Industry* (Washington, DC: U.S. Department of Transportation, Maritime Administration, 2013), 28.

19. Ericson, "The Evolution of Great Lakes Ships, Part II," 210.

20. Raymond A. Bawal Jr., *Superships of the Great Lakes: Thousand-Foot Ships on the Great Lakes* (Clinton Township, MI: Inland Expressions, 2011), 91.

21. Walter Havighurst, *The Long Ships Passing: The Story of the Great Lakes* (New York: Macmillan, 1942), 221; Thompson, *Steamboats*, 22.

22. Thompson, *Steamboats*, 314.

23. George Carrington Mason, "McDougall's Dream: The Whaleback," *Inland Seas* 9, no. 1 (Spring 1953): 9; "*Cliffs Victory*, US 247522," Marine Historical Society of Detroit, http://www.mhsd.org/photogallery/cliff.htm.

24. Raymond A. Bawal Jr., *Twilight of the Great Lakes Steamer* (Clinton Township, MI: Inland Expressions, 2009), 14; Dewar, "The Pittsburgh Supers," 2.

25. "Alexander Carnegie Kirk," in *Biographical Dictionary of the History of Technology*, ed. Lance Day and Ian McNeil, 402 (London: Routledge, 1996).

26. Pomeroy, "The Bulk Freight Vessel," 196.

27. Nelson Haydamacker, with Alan D. Millar, *Deckhand: Life on Freighters of the Great Lakes* (Ann Arbor: University of Michigan Press, 2009), 54.

28. Herbert W. Dosey, "What They Are Saying," *Inland Seas* 15, no. 2 (Summer 1959): 133.

29. "Engine Order Telegraph," Integrated Publishing, http://navyadministration.tpub.com/14067/css/14067_31.htm; and "The Basics of Engine Order Telegraph," Marine Insight, http://www.marineinsight.com.

30. Thompson, *Steamboats*, 60.

31. Miller, *Tin Stackers*, 139–40. The Bradley boats had used the turbines to generate electricity, which in turn powered huge electric motors that moved the ships.

32. "Charles Algernon Parsons," University of Cambridge, http://www-g.eng.cam.ac.uk/125/noflash/1875–1900/parsons2.html.

33. Thompson, *Steamboats*, 66.

34. "Boiler Automation: Modernization of Great Lakes Steamer Features Automatic Control of Boilers and Burners," *Great Lakes Sailor* (December 1964–January 1965): 7.

35. E. B. Williams, "Great Lakes Freighters Gradually Turn to Welding," *Ohio State Engineer* 22, no. 6 (May 1939): 19–20. See also *"William A. Irvin,"* Duluth Entertainment Convention Center, http://www.decc.org/william-a-irvin; "Great Lakes News and Rumors," BoatNerd, June 8, 1998, http://www.boatnerd.com; Miller, *Tin Stackers*, 131, 139.

36. Miller, *Tin Stackers*, 152.

37. Thompson, *Steamboats*, 26, 62; Ericson, "The Evolution of Great Lakes Ships, Part II," 204–5; Gary S. Dewar, "Rebuilding the Post-War Bulk Fleet," *Inland Seas* 42, no. 2 (Summer 1986): 85; Dewar, "The Pittsburgh Supers," 2–4; George H. Palmer Jr., Carlton E. Tripp, Richard Suehrstedt, and Joseph P. Fischer, "Rebuilding the U.S. Great Lakes Bulk Cargo Fleet and the Metamorphosis of the Self-Unloader, Pt. 1," *Inland Seas* 54, no. 1 (Spring 1998): 54.

38. Gary S. Dewar, "Changes in the Existing Bulk Fleet, 1945–1970," *Inland Seas* 45, no. 2 (Summer 1989): 96, 98.

39. Palmer et al., "Rebuilding the U.S. Great Lakes Bulk Cargo Fleet, Pt. 1," 54.

40. Dewar, "Changes in the Existing Bulk Fleet," 95–96.

41. Dewar, "Rebuilding the Post-War Bulk Fleet," 84–85; George H. Palmer Jr., Carlton E. Tripp, Richard Suehrstedt, and Joseph P. Fischer, "Rebuilding the U.S. Great Lakes Bulk

Cargo Fleet and the Metamorphosis of the Self-Unloader, Pt. II," *Inland Seas* 54, no. 2 (Summer 1998): 55.

42. Dewar, "Changes in the Existing Bulk Fleet, 1945–1970," 98, 103; Dewar, "Rebuilding the Post-War Bulk Fleet," 85; Myers, "Remembering the 504's," 86; Donald A. Gandre, "Recent Changes in Coal Traffic on the Great Lakes," *Inland Seas* 34, no. 1 (Spring 1978): 54.

43. Thompson, *Steamboats*, 66; George Wharton, "Great Lakes Fleet Page Vessel Feature— *Wilfred Sykes*," BoatNerd, http://www.boatnerd.com/pictures/fleet/sykes.htm. As of 1999 the Corps of Engineers allowed a vessel up to 730 feet in length to use the MacArthur Lock. Ericson, "The Evolution of Great Lakes Ships, Part II," 205.

44. George A. Cuthbertson, *Freshwater: A History and a Narrative of the Great Lakes* (New York: Macmillan Co., 1931), 256.

45. Pomeroy, "The Bulk Freighter," 196.

46. Thompson, *Steamboats*, 66.

47. Haydamacker, *Deckhand*, 53.

48. Palmer et al., "Rebuilding the U.S. Great Lakes Bulk Cargo Fleet, Pt. 1," 58.

49. "Hirshfield Cites Loss of Nine Ships to U.S. Fleet This Year," *LCA Bulletin* 53, no. 4 (October 1964): 5; "Great Lakes Calendar," *Inland Seas* 51, no. 3 (Fall 1995): 27; "Great Lakes Calendar," *Inland Seas* 38, no. 1 (Spring 1982): 69. The *Crapo*, however, was not the last coal-fired vessel on the lakes. The Lake Michigan ferry *Badger* continued to ply Lake Michigan well into the twenty-first century, although the ship's future was increasingly uncertain due to federal Environmental Protection Agency regulations forbidding the dumping of coal ash into the lake. Todd Spangler, "Future of S.S. *Badger* Ferry in Doubt as It Awaits EPA Approval to Continue Service," *Detroit Free Press*, December 20, 2012.

50. "Oil's Future as Lake Ship Fuel," *LCA Bulletin* 41, no. 7 (November 1952): 15–21. Kenneth R. Dickinson, "Henry Ford II," *Inland Seas* 62, no. 1 (Spring 2006): 4, claims the *Henry Ford II's* diesel engine had a peculiar but well-known rhythm that many swore sounded as if the ship was saying, "makin' money, makin' money, makin' money."

51. Clare J. Snider and Michael W. R. Davis, *The Ford Fleet* (Cleveland: Freshwater Press, 1994), 8.

52. Miller, *Tin Stackers*, 138–39, 164, 167–68, 202.

53. Bawal, *Twilight*, 2.

54. Bawal, *Twilight*, 3. The ship was scrapped in 2010. See "Great Lakes Calendar," *Inland Seas* 67, no. 1 (Spring 2011): 74.

55. John F. Devendorf, *Great Lakes Bulk Carriers, 1869–1985* (Niles, MI: J.F. Devendorf, 1995), 15.

56. Thompson, *Steamboats*, 57–58, 76.

57. Gary S. Dewar, "Conversion of WWII Ships for Great Lakes Service," *Inland Seas* 41, no. 1 (Spring 1985): 28–29.

58. "Historical Perspective Featured Lake Boat: *Cliffs Victory*," BoatNerd, http://www. boatnerd.com/pictures/historic/perspectives/cliffsvictory/default.htm.

59. Ernest Kirkwood, "From Salt to Fresh Water—or, the Story of *Cliffs Victory*," *Inland Seas* 16, no. 3 (Fall 1960): 203–5.

60. Dewar, "Conversion of WWII Ships," 30–31. See also Historical Perspective Featured Lake Boat: Cliffs Victory, BoatNerd.

61. Thompson, *Steamboats*, 46, 71–72; Dewar, "Conversion of WWII Ships," 33, 38; "Historical Perspective Featured Lake Boat: Cliffs Victory," BoatNerd; "*McKee Sons*," BoatNerd, http:// www.boatnerd.com/pictures/fleet/mckee.htm.

62. E. B. Williams, "Bow Thrusters Big Help at Dock, in Crooked Rivers," *LCA Bulletin* 51, no. 3 (August–September 1962): 18.

63. Frank Lanier, "How to Use a Bow Thruster, *BoatUS* (October–November 2014): n.p.

64. Williams, "Bow Thrusters," *LCA Bulletin* 51, no. 3 (August–September 1962): 18; Snider and Davis, *The Ford Fleet*, 120.

65. "Perspectives," *LCA Bulletin* 59, no. 2 (June–July 1970): inside cover.

66. "Great Lakes Calendar," *Inland Seas* 35, no. 2 (Summer 1979): 157.

67. Thompson, *Steamboats*, 82.

68. Gary W. Schmidt, with Warren Gerds, *Real, Honest Sailing with a Great Lakes Captain* (Allouez, WI: Seaway Printing Co., 2013), 1.

69. Palmer et al., "Rebuilding the U.S. Great Lakes Bulk Cargo Fleet, Pt. II," 62–63.

70. The freighter played a bit role in the 1980 film *The Blues Brothers*. Brothers Jake and Elwood successfully flew their Dodge over the 95th Street drawbridge, which was opening for the *Holloway*. Of the car, Elwood said, "It's got a cop motor, a four hundred and forty cubic inch plant, it's got cop tires, cop suspensions, cop shocks, it's a model made before catalytic converters, so it'll run good on regular gas." Elwood had no comments about the *Holloway*. Such is the fate of most lake freighters. An image and history of the freighter, including its role in the movie, is found under the heading "*W.W. Holloway* at the Cleveland Coal Dock," the "Ohio Guide Photographs," of the Ohio History Connection at OhioMemory.org.

71. Edward Perrine, "Up and Away on the Double 'W' Holloway," *Inland Seas* 55, no. 3 (Fall 1999): 200; both Holloway stories are on this page. See also Kenneth J. Blume, *Historical Dictionary of the U.S. Maritime Industry* (Lanham, MD: Scarecrow Press, 2012), 507.

72. Thompson, *Steamboats*, 80; Dewar, "Rebuilding the Post-War Bulk Fleet," 85.

73. Bawal, *Twilight of the Great Lakes Steamer* (Clinton Township, MI: Inland Expressions,

2009), 6.

74. Dewar, "Changes in the Existing Bulk Fleet, 1945–1970," 110.

75. Jenish, *The St. Lawrence Seaway*, 31.

76. Jenish, *The St. Lawrence Seaway*, 3. "Three Hundred Years of History," The Great Lakes St. Lawrence Seaway System, http://www.greatlakes-seaway.com.

77. Thompson, *Steamboats*, 74.

78. Bawal, *Superships*, 1–2.

79. Gary S. Dewar, "Canadian Bulk Construction, 1960–70," *Inland Seas* 43, no. 2 (Summer 1987): 104.

80. Gary S. Dewar, "Canadian Bulk Construction, 1945–59," *Inland Seas* 43, no. 1 (Spring 1987): 24–25.

81. Dewar, "Canadian Bulk Construction, 1945–59," 40.

82. Lawrence A. Pomeroy Jr., "Reshaping Our Future: 1959 and Since," *Inland Seas* 22, no. (Winter 1966): 316; Dewar, "Canadian Bulk Construction, 1960–70," 120; "Report of the President," Lake Carriers' Association, *Annual Report* [1961] (Rocky River, OH: 1961): 10–11; "Report of the President," Lake Carriers' Association, *Annual Report* [1987] (Rocky River, OH: 1987): 1, 20; Gary S. Dewar, "Changes in the Post-War Fleet: Part II," *Inland Seas* 45, no. 3 (Fall 1989): 179, 181.

83. "Algoisle," BoatNerd, http://www.boatnerd.com/pictures/fleet/algoisle.htm. The *Silver Isle* was unique in that it was constructed in Ireland and sailed across the Atlantic for service in the Great Lakes. The ship was sold for scrap in 2010. See "Great Lakes Calendar," *Inland Seas* 67, no. 1 (Spring 2011): 68. The use of overseas shipyards to build lake vessels resumed in the twenty-first century, when several new Canadian ships were constructed in yards located in the Far East.

84. "Vessel Construction," Lake Carriers' Association, *Annual Report* [1967] (Rocky River, OH: 1967): 38–40. Because the *Silver Isle* and the *Senneville* both operated through the St. Lawrence Seaway, the LCA designated the *Senneville* as the first ship of the design to operate "primarily" in the Great Lakes. Apparently the *Silver Isle* had spent most of its time east of the Seaway, whereas the *Senneville* operated primarily on the west side of the Seaway.

85. Thompson, *Steamboats*, 87.

86. "Orders for New Vessels Fill Builders Schedules," *LCA Bulletin* 63, no. 1 (May–June 1974): 8; George H. Palmer Jr., Carlton E. Tripp, Richard Suehrstedt, and Joseph P. Fischer, "Rebuilding the U.S. Great Lakes Bulk Cargo Fleet and the Metamorphosis of the Self-Unloader, Pt. III," *Inland Seas* 54, no. 2 (Summer 1998): 153.

87. "Orders for New Vessels, Fill Builders Schedules," *LCA Bulletin* 63, no. 1 (May–June

1974): 8; Bawal, *Superships*, 90–91. Twelve thousand-foot vessels were self-powered. The thirteenth, the *Presque Isle*, was a barge-tug combination that when united was 1,000 feet in length.

88. Bawal, *Superships*, 3.

89. Thompson, *Steamboats*, 86–87.

90. Bawal, *Superships*, 12, 90.

91. Patrick D. Lapinski, *Ships of the Great Lakes: An Inside Look at the World's Largest Inland Fleet* (Hudson, WI: Iconografix, 2011), 6.

92. Palmer et al., "Pt. III," 157; U.S. Department of Transportation, *Status of the U.S. Flag Great Lakes Water Transportation Industry*, 27.

93. Miller, *Tin Stackers*, 236.

94. Bawal, *Superships*, 70–77.

95. Bawal, *Superships*, 77. The *American Republic* measured 600 feet, 10 inches in length. "*Great Republic*," BoatNerd, http://www.boatnerd.com/pictures/fleet/greatrepublic.htm.

96. Sources give various dates for the last Canadian ship of the century.

97. Thompson, *Steamboats*, 97; Alan W. Sweigert, "Through the New Rear View Lens," *Inland Seas* 54, no. 3 (Fall 1998): 172. The *American Republic* was the culmination of experiences gained from several small ships that had plied the Cuyahoga River in the 1970s. Devendorf, *Great Lakes Bulk Carriers*, 15.

98. Devendorf, *Great Lakes Bulk Carriers*, 7.

99. "Barges Bid Lakes Adieu," *LCA Bulletin* 45, no. 5 (November 1956): 12; Carl C. Hanks, "The Pulpwood Fleet," *Inland Seas* 10, no. 2 (Summer 1954): 79–83.

100. D. S. Connelly, "*Presque Isle*," *Inland Seas* 30, no. 1 (Spring 1974): 35–36; Christine R. Robin-Tielke, "Pushing Cargo Along," *Great Lakes Seaway Review* 37, no. 3 (January–March 2009): 105; J. C. Rieger, "Wilson Marine Transit Smoothing Out Rough Spots in Tug-Barge 'Experiment,'" *LCA Bulletin* 52, no. 2 (July–August 1963): 12.

101. "U.S. Vessels Owners Continue to Wage Uphill Fight against Subsidized Canadian Fleet," *LCA Bulletin* 52, no. 1 (June 1963).

102. U.S. Department of Transportation, *Status of the U.S. Flag Great Lakes Water Transportation Industry*, 26.

103. Schmidt, *Real, Honest Sailing*, 32.

104. Bawal, *Superships*, 19; Patrick Lapinski, "Watching an Evolution: Tug-Barge Transportation on the Great Lakes Gets Nod from U.S. Fleet," *Great Lakes Seaway Review* 41, no. 1 (July–September 2012): 38.

105. Bawal, *Superships*, 21; Connelly, "*Presque Isle*," 36, 45. The *Presque Isle* itself was eventually chartered to U.S. Steel, which had "played it safe in building the Roger Blough,

and then found that because of orders placed by other lines for 1,000 footers, it could not have one constructed for four to five years."

106. Robin-Tielke, "Pushing Cargo Along," 106.

107. "Great Lakes Calendar," *Inland Seas* 38, no. 4 (Winter 1982): 297.

108. Robin-Tielke, "Pushing Cargo Along," 106–7.

109. Sweigert, "Through the New Rear View Lens"; Patrick Lapinksi, "The *E.M. Ford*," *Inland Seas* 55, no. 2 (Summer 1999): 94. The *E.M. Ford* and the *S.T. Crapo* were removed from active service in 1996, but both vessels served for many years as dockside storage units. The *Ford* was sold for scrap in 2008. "*E.M. Ford*," BoatNerd, http://www.boatnerd.com/pictures/fleet/emford.htm; David Young, "Tug Plus Barge Is More Than a Ship," *Chicago Tribune*, August 14, 1997. In 2004 the tug *Jacklyn M* was renamed the *G.L. Ostrander*. See "Ship's Log" The Barge *ATB Integrity* and Tug *G.L. Ostrander*," MLive, http://www.mlive.com/news/muskegon/index.ssf/2010/12/ships_log_atb_integrity_bargeg.html.

110. "*Pathfinder*," BoatNerd, http://www.boatnerd.com/pictures/fleet/pathfinder.htm. See also "The Christening of the Tug *Dorothy Ann* and Self-Unloading Barge *Pathfinder*," BoatNerd, http://www.boatnerd.com/pictures/fleet/dorothyannc.htm. See also Schmidt, *Real, Honest Sailing*, 15–19.

111. Bawal, *Superships*, 21; "Great Lakes Calendar," *Inland Seas* 55, no. 2 (Summer 1999): 141.

112. "Self-Unloading Barge under Construction," *Great Lakes Seaway Review* (January–March 1999), http://www.vtbarge.com/pressroom.html.

113. Lapinski, "Watching an Evolution: Tug-Barge Transportation," 38–39; U.S. Department of Transportation, *Status of the U.S. Flag Great Lakes Water Transportation Industry*, 26; Raymond A. Bawal Jr., *Ships of the St. Clair River* (Saint Clair, MI: Inland Expressions, 2008), 3, 8, 19, 57; David Young, "Tug Plus Barge Is More Than a Ship," *Chicago Tribune*, August 14, 1997.

114. Schmidt, *Real, Honest Sailing*, 2.

115. U.S. Department of Transportation, *Status of the U.S. Flag Great Lakes Water Transportation Industry*, 2; David Young, "Tug Plus Barge Is More Than a Ship," *Chicago Tribune*, August 14, 1997.

116. Bawal, *Superships*, 61.

117. Harry Benford, "Lament for a Lost Heritage," *Seaway Review* 9, no. 1 (Fall 1979): 22.

118. Edward A. Perrine, "The Northern Lights," *Inland Seas* 69, no. 2 (Summer 2013): 143.

119. Bill Armitage, chief engineer, *Algoma Montrealis*, as quoted in Patrick Lapinski, "Meet the Crew," *Great Lakes Seaway Review* 43, no. 2 (October–December 2014): 66.

120. Fred W. Dutton, *Life on the Great Lakes: A Wheelsman's Story*, ed. William Donohue Ellis (Detroit: Wayne State University Press, 1991), 171.

121. R. W. England, "The Engineer," *Inland Seas* 1, no. 2 (April 1945): 13.

122. Neil F. Morrison, "Lauchlen Maclean Morrison, Captain on the Great Lakes," *Inland Seas* 4, no. 1 (Spring 1948): 27.

123. James Oliver Curwood, *The Great Lakes and the Vessels That Plough Them: Their Owners, Their Sailors, and Their Cargoes* (New York: G. P. Putnam's Sons, 1909), 138.

CHAPTER 4. CHANGES ABOARD

1. Frank A. Blust, "The U.S. Lake Survey, 1841–1974," *Inland Seas* 32, no. 2 (Summer 1976): 92.

2. Blust, "The U.S. Lake Survey," 92–94; U.S. Army Corps of Engineers, United States Lake Survey. *The United States Lake Survey* (Detroit: United States Lake Survey, 1939), 35.

3. John W. Larson, *Essayons: A History of the Detroit District U.S. Army Corps of Engineers* (Detroit: U.S. Army Corps of Engineers, 1995), 141; Blust, "The U.S. Lake Survey," 95. The date survey work resumed is reported by Blust as 1889, by the *LCA Bulletin* as 1899, and by *The United States Lake Survey* (36) as 1900. I have incorporated the Lake Survey's date into this volume.

4. *The United States Lake Survey*, 2.

5. Fred Landon, "The Discovery of Superior Shoal," *Inland Seas* 15, no. 1 (Spring 1959): 50–54. "Discovery" in this case meant formally placing the shoal on government navigation charts. Fishermen seem to have been well aware of the shoal and visited it frequently in search of fish.

6. "Great Lakes Calendar," *Inland Seas* 15, no. 2 (Summer 1959): 145.

7. "Shoal Searchers," *LCA Bulletin* 47, no. 6 (November 1958): 11–13; "Lake Survey Center Closed," *LCA Bulletin* 65, no. 1 (June–July 1976): 11.

8. *The United States Lake Survey*, 26–27.

9. "84 Year Old 'Coast Pilot' Was Guide for Early Lake Mariners," *LCA Bulletin* 42, no. 3 (July 1953): 12.

10. Charles K. Hyde, *The Northern Lights: Lighthouses of the Upper Great Lakes* (Lansing, MI: Two Peninsula Press, 1986), 20.

11. Hyde, *Northern Lights*, 38.

12. Secretary of the Treasury, *Statement of Appropriations and Expenditures for Public Buildings, Rivers and Harbors, Forts, Arsenals and Armories, and Other Public Works, from March 4, 1789 to June 30, 1882* (Washington, DC: Government Printing Office, 1886), 409–21.

13. Mark L. Thompson, *Steamboats and Sailors of the Great Lakes* (Detroit: Wayne State University Press, 1991), 191. Range lights are sometimes referred to as "leading lights,"

particularly in England. Range or leads serve the same purpose as range lights, but are not illuminated. They are large, brightly colored objects that work in daylight exactly as range lights do at night.

14. "Grays Reef, MI," at LighthouseFriends.com, http://www.lighthousefriends.com/light. asp?ID=209.

15. David Lindley, *Degrees Kelvin: A Tale of Genius, Invention and Tragedy* (Washington, DC: Joseph Henry Press, 2003), 228.

16. Edward J. Dowling, "Captain William J. Taylor, Gentleman," *Inland Seas* 3, no. 3 (July 1947): 170.

17. "Great Lakes Calendar," *Inland Seas* 32, no. 4 (Winter 1976): 319.

18. Robert J. MacDonald, "Captain Gridley and the German Gas Buoy," *Inland Seas* 15, no. 4 (Winter 1959): 289.

19. Dowling, "Captain William J. Taylor," 170.

20. "Great Lakes Calendar," *Inland Seas* 33, no. 1 (Spring 1977): 81.

21. Herbert W. Dosey, "What They Are Saying," *Inland Seas* 15, no. 2 (Summer 1959): 131.

22. Al Miller, *Tin Stackers: The History of the Pittsburgh Steamship Company* (Detroit: Wayne State University Press, 1999), 108–9.

23. Gary W. Schmidt, with Warren Gerds, *Real, Honest Sailing with a Great Lakes Captain* (Allouez, WI: Seaway Printing Co., 2013).

24. "First Navigation Regulations Were Codified Century Ago," *LCA Bulletin* 48, no. 2 (November 1959): 16–19.

25. "Separate Courses Now on Five Lakes," *LCA Bulletin* 39, no. 1 (May 1950): 18.

26. "Meetings of Committees," Lake Carriers' Association, *Annual Report* [*1950*] (Rocky River, OH: LCA, 1950), 33. Even when separate courses for upbound and downbound vessels were established, by necessity the courses crossed in several places, requiring special prudence while navigating through those areas. See John C. Murray, "Close Navigation on Lakes Needs Constant Caution," *LCA Bulletin* 48, no. 1 (June 1959): 3; "Joint U.S., Canadian Efforts Bring Improved Charts to Lakes," *LCA Bulletin* 66, no. 1 (May–June 1977): 10.

27. Thompson, *Steamboats*, 56; L. A. Bauer, *United States Magnetic Declination Tables and Isogonic Charts for 1902* (Washington, DC: U.S. Department of Commerce and Labor, Coast and Geodetic Survey, 1903), 62–63.

28. Bartlett Oral History, Albert Bartlett Collection (GLMS 103), Center for Archival Collections, Bowling Green State University, Ohio, 52–53.

29. Lindley, *Degrees Kelvin*, 240–52.

30. Thomas Parke Hughes, *Elmer Sperry: Inventor and Engineer* (Baltimore: The John Hopkins Press, 1971), 130–51.

31. Jewell R. Dean, "The Wilson Fleet, Freight Pioneers," *Inland Seas* 2, no. 3 (July 1946): 163.

32. O. B. Whitaker, "Recalling How the Gyro-Compass First Came to the Great Lakes," *LCA Bulletin* 37, no. 6 (September 1948): 1–4.

33. Clare J. Snider and Michael W. R. Davis, *The Ford Fleet* (Cleveland: Freshwater Press, 1994), 119.

34. G. N. Roberts, "Trends in Marine Control Systems," *Annual Reviews in Control* 32 (2008): 263.

35. Roberts, "Trends in Marine Control Systems," 263.

36. Hughes, *Elmer Sperry*, 278–79; Roberts, "Trends in Marine Control Systems," 264; Tom Allensworth, "A Short History of Sperry Marine," rbmn.free.fr/Sperry.htm.

37. Hughes, *Elmer Sperry*, 278–79; Roberts, "Trends in Marine Control Systems," 264; Allensworth, "A Short History of Sperry Marine."

38. S. Bennett, *A History of Control Engineering, 1800–1930* (London: Peter Peregrinus, Ltd., 1979), 130.

39. Edward A. Perrine, "It's the *Fitz* Continued," *Inland Seas* 56, no. 4 (Winter 2000): 270–71.

40. S. A. Lyons, "The *J.H. Sheadle* in the Great Storm of 1913," *Inland Seas* 12, no. 1 (Spring 1956): 20; Miller, *Tin Stackers*, 144.

41. Thompson, *Steamboats*, 149; Miller, *Tin Stackers*, 159.

42. Thompson, *Steamboats*, 57.

43. Louis Brown, *A Radar History of World War II: Technical and Military Imperatives* (Philadelphia: Institute of Physics Publishing, 1999). For a more readable account of Anglo-American radar efforts see Robert Buderi, *The Invention That Changed the World: How a Small Group of Radar Pioneers Won the Second World War and Launched a Technological Revolution* (New York: Simon and Schuster, 1996).

44. "Great Lakes Calendar," *Inland Seas* 3, no. 1 (January 1947): 44.

45. "Great Lakes Calendar," *Inland Seas* 3, no. 3 (July 1947): 187.

46. "Common Sense View of Radar," *LCA Bulletin* 35, no. 3 (July 1947): 19.

47. "Radar Charts Coming," *LCA Bulletin* 37, no. 7 (November 1948): 22; George J. Joachim, *Iron Fleet: The Great Lakes in World War II* (Detroit: Wayne State University Press, 1994), 46–47; *Inland Seas* 4, no. 4 (Winter 1948): 272.

48. "Progress of Electronics Program," Lake Carriers' Association, *Annual Report* [1950], 36; Thompson, *Steamboats*, 66.

49. Mark Denny, *The Science of Navigation: From Dead Reckoning to GPS* (Baltimore: The John Hopkins University Press, 2012), 213–16; "Great Lakes Calendar," *Inland Seas* 36, no. 3 (Fall 1980): 220. United States Coast Guard and Federal Aviation Administration, *Loran C: An Introduction and Users Guide* (Cambridge, MA: Center for Navigation/DTS-52

February 1993).

50. "Trimble Sees Much Work Ahead to Make Year Round Shipping Routine," *LCA Bulletin* 64, no. 1 (May–June 1975): 5–6.

51. "Loran C Welcome Aboard," *LCA Bulletin* 69, no. 1 (May–June 1980): 2.

52. Miller, *Tin Stackers*, 257.

53. Schmidt, *Real, Honest Sailing*, 59–64. In 2010 GPS completely replaced Loran C. The first ECPIN system was installed on a laker in 1993. Patrick D. Lapinski, *Ships of the Great Lakes: An Inside Look at the World's Largest Inland Fleet* (Hudson, WI: Iconografix, 2011), 62.

54. Fredrick Gary Hareland, "Shipboard Radio Communications," *PowerShips* 283 (Fall 2012): 39–41.

55. Richard Gebhart, "The Reluctant Acceptance of Wireless Use on the Great Lakes," *Inland Seas* 49, no. 2 (Summer 1993): 149.

56. Gebhart, "The Reluctant Acceptance of Wireless," 152.

57. Gebhart, "The Reluctant Acceptance of Wireless," 152.

58. Paul C. LaMarre III, "Iron Elegance: The History of the SS *Col. James M. Schoonmaker*," *Inland Seas* 64, no. 1 (Spring 2008): 6; "*Col. James M. Schoonmaker*," Great Lakes Historical Society, http://www.inlandseas.org/museum/col-james-m-schoonmaker.

59. Gebhart, "The Reluctant Acceptance of Wireless," 152–53; Charlie J. Bunton, *Rogers City: A History of a Nautical City* (Published by author, 2013), notes on page 407 that the Bradley fleet placed radio transmitters and receivers on their ships in the early 1920s, after installing used World War I radio equipment in their home office in 1922.

60. H. N. Burke, "Weather on the Great Lakes," *Inland Seas* 13, no. 2 (Summer 1957): 138. "Magnetic telegraph" was a nineteenth-century term for what today is simply called the telegraph.

61. Burke, "Weather on the Great Lakes," 138.

62. Burke, "Weather on the Great Lakes," 138.

63. Michael Schumacher, *November's Fury: The Deadly Great Lakes Hurricane of 1913* (Minneapolis: University of Minnesota Press, 2013), 11.

64. Thompson, *Steamboats*, 56.

65. Hareland, "Shipboard Radio Communications," 41.

66. "Lorrain's Radio Station Remodeled to Speed VHF Channels," *LCA Bulletin* 42, no. 4 (August 1953): 3.

67. "Lorrain's Radio Station Remodeled to Speed VHF Channels," *LCA Bulletin* 42, no. 4 (August 1953): 1, 19.

68. Burke, "Weather on the Great Lakes," 138–39.

69. "Electronics Committee," Lake Carriers' Association, *Annual Report* [*1956*] (Rocky River, OH: LCA, 1956), 36–37.

70. "Electronics Committee," Lake Carriers' Association, *Annual Report* [*1960*] (Rocky River, OH: LCA, 1960), 27.

71. "Lorrain's Radio Station Remodeled to Speed VHF Channels," *LCA Bulletin* 42, no. 4 (August 1953): 3.

72. "Improved Radiotelephone System Being Readied for Lake Test," *LCA Bulletin* 62, no. 3 (October–November 1973): 3; "All VHF Radiotelephone Offers Improved Communication Service," *LCA Bulletin* 63, no. 1 (May–June 1974): 3–4; "Trimble Sees Much Work Ahead to Make Year Round Shipping Routine," *LCA Bulletin* 64, no. 1 (May–June 1975): 3–6.

73. Raymond A. Bawal Jr., *Superships of the Great Lakes: Thousand-Foot Ships on the Great Lakes* (Clinton Township, MI: Inland Expressions, 2011), 57.

74. Thompson, *Steamboats*, 57.

75. Hareland, "Shipboard Radio Communications," 41–42.

76. U.S. Department of Commerce, Maritime Administration, *Domestic Waterborne Shipping Market Analysis—Legal and Regulatory Constraints—Great Lakes, August 1974*, Report No. MA-RD-940–75020 (Reproduced by the National Technical Information Service, Springfield, Virginia), 4–5.

77. Lawrence A. Pomeroy Jr., "Life Line of America," *Inland Seas* 7, no. 1 (Spring 1951): 14–15.

78. Thompson, *Steamboats*, 156–58; "Lake Vessels Outfitting with Latest Emergency Gear," *LCA Bulletin* 56, no. 4 (November–December 1967): 12.

79. Thompson, *Steamboats*, 158; "Survival Suits Approved for Shipboard Uses," *LCA Bulletin* 66, no. 3 (September–November 1977): 8.

80. Testimony of Melvin H. Pelfrey, vice president, Marine Engineers' Beneficial Association on July 14, 1977, before the U.S. House of Representatives Merchant Marine and Fisheries Committee, Subcommittee on Coast Guard and Navigation, USW Great Lakes Seamen Local 5000 Collection, box 4, Bowling Green State University, Ohio.

81. Frank T. Rice, "The Most Reluctant Lady of the Lakes," *Inlands Seas* 8, no. 4 (Winter 1952): 230. The "rules of the road" in question likely refer to the first separate courses plotted on the lakes for upbound and downbound freighters.

82. Miller, *Tin Stackers*, 148.

83. Ray I. McGrath, *Great Lakes Stories* (Sault Ste. Marie, MI: Border Enterprises, 1996), 109–10.

84. Thompson, *Steamboats*, 62, 201.

85. John J. Kelley, "An Historic Thirty-Six Hours of Superior Seamanship," *Inland Seas* 40, no. 2 (Summer 1984): 82–88.

86. Fred W. Dutton, *Life on the Great Lakes: A Wheelsman's Story*, ed. William Donohue Ellis (Detroit: Wayne State University Press, 1991), 152–57.

87. Edward A. Perrine, "Huron and On," *Inland Seas* 56, no. 1 (Spring 2000): 13.

88. Thompson, *Steamboats*, 183; Nelson Haydamacker, with Alan D. Millar, *Deckhand: Life on Freighters of the Great Lakes* (Ann Arbor: University of Michigan Press, 2009), 24.

89. Schmidt, *Real, Honest Sailing*, 97.

90. "Great Lakes Calendar," *Inland Seas* 8, no. 2 (Summer 1952): 129.

91. Thompson, *Steamboats*, 183; Stuart Sheill, "More on the Ice Jam of '84," *Inland Seas* 42, no. 2 (Summer 1986): 127–29.

92. Licensed Tugmen's Protective Association of America, *Directory and Manual of the Licensed Tugmen's Protective Association of America* (Toledo, OH: Hadley Printing and Paper Co., 1917), 94.

93. Thompson, *Steamboats*, 184–85.

94. Thompson, *Steamboats*, 186.

95. Thompson, *Steamboats*, 186–87.

96. Paul E. Trimble, "Year-round Navigation on the Great Lakes," *Inland Seas* 32, no. 4 (Winter 1976): 250.

97. Miller, *Tin Stackers*, 230.

98. "Great Lakes Calendar," *Inland Seas* 32, no. 1 (Spring 1976): 77.

99. "Great Lakes Calendar," *Inland Seas* 32, no. 1 (Spring 1976): 77.

100. "Great Lakes Calendar," *Inland Seas* 33, no. 2 (Summer 1977): 164.

101. Raymond A. Bawal Jr., *Twilight of the Great Lakes Steamer* (Clinton Township, MI: Inland Expressions, 2009), 43. For typical examples of "rear-end" accidents, see Bawal, *Twilight*, 65; Bawal, *Ships of the St. Clair River* (Saint Clair, MI: Inland Expressions, 2008), 26; or Miller, *Tin Stackers*, 232.

102. Bawal, *Superships*, 50; Miller, *Tin Stackers*, 237. It was eventually decided that the loss of the rudder was caused by a shipyard construction error, although the conclusion was long contested by the shipyard, who blamed the ice.

103. "Great Lakes Calendar," *Inland Seas* 32, no. 2 (Summer 1976): 156.

104. Miller, *Tin Stackers*, 233; "LCA Fleets Committed to Extended Navigation Season," *LCA Bulletin* 72, no. 2 (January 1984): 2–7.

105. Dutton, *Life on the Great Lakes*, 171.

106. Dutton, *Life on the Great Lakes*, 171–72.

107. Dutton, *Life on the Great Lakes*, 172.

CHAPTER 5. LOADING AND UNLOADING

1. W. Bruce Bowlus, "'Changes of Vast Magnitude': The Development of an Iron Ore Delivery System on the Great Lakes during the Nineteenth Century" (PhD diss., Bowling Green State University, 1992), 246.

2. Frank E. Kirby and A. P. Rankin, "The Bulk Freighter of the Great Lakes," *Inland Seas* 34, no. 3 (Fall 1978): 222; Al Miller, *Tin Stackers: The History of the Pittsburgh Steamship Company* (Detroit: Wayne State University Press, 1999), 59.

3. Kirby and Rankin, "The Bulk Freighter of the Great Lakes," 221.

4. Eric Hirsimaki, "The Ore Docks," *Inland Seas* 47, no. 3 (Fall 1991): 165.

5. Hirsimaki, "The Ore Docks," 169–70.

6. Hirsimaki, "The Ore Docks," 167; Bowlus, "Changes of Vast Magnitude," 210–11; Mark L. Thompson, *Steamboats and Sailors of the Great Lakes* (Detroit: Wayne State University Press, 1991), 21.

7. Mike Schafer and Mike McBride, *Freight Train Cars* (Osceola, WI: MBI Publishing Co., 1999), 74–79.

8. "Ore Jennies," American-Rails, http://www.american-rails.com. See also Mike Schafer with Mike McBride, *Freight Train Cars* (Osceola, WI: MBI Publishing Company, 1999), 78.

9. Miller, *Tin Stackers*, 135–36.

10. Fred W. Dutton, *Life on the Great Lakes: A Wheelsman's Story*, ed. William Donohue Ellis (Detroit: Wayne State University Press, 1991), 115.

11. Dutton, *Life on the Great Lakes*, 116.

12. Thompson, *Steamboats*, 32; Dutton, *Life on the Great Lakes*, 29.

13. Dutton, *Life on the Great Lakes*, 116–18.

14. Dutton, *Life on the Great Lakes*, 64.

15. A bollard is a short, vertical post, firmly anchored into the dock. Docks usually have a large number of bollards. Ropes or metal cables holding a ship to the dock are attached to the bollards.

16. Dutton, *Life on the Great Lakes*, 116; Patrick Livingston, *Eight Steamboats: Sailing through the Sixties* (Detroit: Wayne State University Press, 2004), 209–10.

17. Thomas Andrew Sykora, "A Seventeen Year Old Looks at the Lakes," *Inland Seas* 3, no. 2 (April 1947): 79.

18. Nelson Haydamacker, with Alan D. Millar, *Deckhand: Life on Freighters of the Great Lakes* (Ann Arbor: University of Michigan Press, 2009), 69; George J. Joachim, *Iron Fleet: The Great Lakes in World War II* (Detroit: Wayne State University Press, 1994), 19.

19. Bert A. Beldin, "Ohio Editor Fondly Recalls Sailing Lakes 40 Years Ago," *LCA Bulletin* 47, no. 2 (July 1958): 3.

20. Joseph P. Fischer, "Hatch Covers," *Great Lakes Seaway Review* 38, no. 1 (July–September 2009): 45–46.

21. Bartlett Oral History, Albert Bartlett Collection (GLMS 103), Center for Archival Collections, Bowling Green State University, Ohio, 106–8; Richard Hill, *Lake Effect: A Deckhand's Journey on the Great Lakes Freighters* (Sault Ste. Marie, MI: Gale Force Press, 2008), 159–60; Bill Herdter, *Old Sailor Bill* (Published by author, n.d., ca. 1997), 7; "Automation Assumes Important Ship Safety Role," *LCA Bulletin* 53, no. 5 (November 1964): 6.

22. Fischer, "Hatch Covers," 45–46.

23. Thompson, *Steamboats*, 48.

24. Ann Myers, "The Mysterious Legacy of the Cyprus," *Inland Seas* 66, no. 2 (Summer 2010): 150–54. Quotations from the *Port Colborne Leader*, 152.

25. Miller, *Tin Stackers*, 138–39; Herdter, *Old Sailor Bill*, 7; Livingston, *Eight Steamboats*, 210; Thompson, *Steamboats*, 60; Gary S. Dewar, "Changes in the Existing Bulk Fleet, 1945–1970," *Inland Seas* 45, no. 2 (Summer 1989): 98; Fischer, "Hatch Covers," 45–46; Bartlett Oral History, 75.

26. Livingston, *Eight Steamboats*, 273. Hill, *Lake Effect*, 26–27, recalls eighty to ninety clamps per hatch cover. "Automation Assumes Important Ship Safety Role," *LCA Bulletin* 53, no. 5 (November 1964): 6.

27. Livingston, *Eight Steamboats*, 205; Thompson, *Steamboats*, 61.

28. Patrick Lapinski, "The Canadian Ambassador Captain Gerry Greig," *Inland Seas* 64, no. 2 (Summer 2008): 143.

29. Raymond A. Bawal Jr., *Ships of the St. Clair River* (Saint Clair, MI: Inland Expressions, 2008), 67. The *Maumee* was operating in 2008. Built in 1929 as the *William G. Clyde* (1929), in 2000 it sailed as *Calcite II*.

30. Fischer, "Hatch Covers," 45–46.

31. Eric Hirsimaki, "The Hulett Story," *Inland Seas* 47, no. 2 (Summer 1991): 90.

32. Bowlus, *Changes of Vast Magnitude*, 209; John A. Burke, "Barrels to Barrows, Buckets to Belts: 120 Years of Iron Ore Handling on the Great Lakes," *Inland Seas* 31, no. 4 (Winter 1975): 268–71.

33. "Mechanical Elephants," *LCA Bulletin*, 32, no. 5 (September 1944): 7–8; Burke, "Barrels to Barrows," 268–71.

34. Hirsimaki, "The Hulett Story," 84–85; Burke, "Barrels to Barrows," 268–71.

35. "Mechanical Elephants," *LCA Bulletin* 32, no. 5 (September 1944): 8–9.

36. C. E. Van Syckle, "A Half Century with Iron Ore," *LCA Bulletin* 43, no. 3 (August 1954): 1.

37. Hirsimaki, "The Hulett Story," 87–89.

38. Hirsimaki, "The Hulett Story," 88–89.

39. J. H. Stratton, "The Development of Ore Unloading on the Great Lakes," *Journal of the Cleveland Engineering Society* 6 (July 1913): 15; ASME International, "Hulett Iron-Ore Unloaders: Historic Mechanical Engineering Landmark" (Cleveland, Ohio, August 2, 1998), 10.

40. ASME International, "Hulett Iron-Ore Unloaders," 4, 11. Only two Hulett machines were built outside of the Great Lakes, one in New York City and the other in Sandy Hook, New Jersey. Hulett unloaders were not useful on the seacoasts because they could not easily adjust for tides.

41. "Mechanical Elephants," *LCA Bulletin* 32, no. 5 (September 1944): 10–12; Kirby and Rankin, "The Bulk Freighter of the Great Lakes," 220–21; Miller, *Tin Stackers*, 59.

42. Hirsimaki, "The Hulett Story," 94.

43. Clare J. Snider and Michael W. R. Davis, *The Ford Fleet* (Cleveland: Freshwater Press, 1994), 137.

44. ASME International, "Hulett Iron-Ore Unloaders," 12.

45. Livingston, *Eight Steamboats*, 205; Snider and Davis, *The Ford Fleet*, 125.

46. Nancy A. Schneider, "'Ob Gibson': Memories of the Great Lakes Waters," *Inland Seas* 57, no. 4 (Winter 2001): 289.

47. Richard J. Wright, "Conneaut Harbor, Part 2," *Inland Seas* 15, no. 1 (Spring 1959): 31–35.

48. Carrie Hatler, "Taconite Harbor: Lake Superior's Once-Upon-a-Time Town," Forgotten Minnesota, http://forgottenminnesota.com/2012/01/the-north-shores-once-upon-a-time-town; Haydamacker, *Deckhand*, 28–29.

49. Victoria Brehm, "Refiguring a Literature of Place: The Economics of Great Lakes Maritime Literature" (PhD diss., University of Iowa, 1992), 117.

50. John A. Burke, "Lake Erie Coal Dumping Machines, Origins and Evolution," *Inland Seas* 61, no. 3 (Fall 2005): 183.

51. Burke, "Lake Erie Coal Dumping Machines," 183–84.

52. Burke, "Lake Erie Coal Dumping Machines," 185–92.

53. Raymond A. Bawal Jr., *Twilight of the Great Lakes Steamer* (Clinton Township, MI: Inland Expressions, 2009), 86.

54. Snider and Davis, *The Ford Fleet*, 83, 125.

55. Snider and Davis, *The Ford Fleet*, 81–82, 86.

56. "Great Lakes Calendar," *Inland Seas* 13, no. 1 (Spring 1957): 57; "Great Lakes Calendar," *Inland Seas* 13, no. 4 (Winter 1957): 317.

57. Haydamacker, *Deckhand*, 29.

58. Raymond A. Bawal Jr., *Superships of the Great Lakes: Thousand-Foot Ships on the Great*

Lakes (Clinton Township, MI: Inland Expressions, 2011), 29; Hirsimaki, "The Ore Docks," 171.

59. Hirsimaki, "The Hulett Story," 94; *Inland Seas* 48, no. 4 (Winter 1992): 276.

60. Burke, "Lake Erie Coal Dumping Machines," 192.

61. William Lafferty and Valerie van Heest, *Buckets and Belts: Evolution of the Great Lakes Self-Unloader* (Holland, MI: In Depth Editions, 2009), 40–41, 49; Mark L. Thompson, *Queen of the Lakes* (Detroit: Wayne State University Press, 1994), 135.

62. Lafferty and van Heest, *Buckets and Belts*, 40–41, 49, 74–75.

63. Joachim, *Iron Fleet*, 18.

64. Snider and Davis, *The Ford Fleet*, 83; "Limestone for the Furnaces," *LCA Bulletin* 32, no. 2 (June 1944): n.p.

65. Edward A. Perrine, "Huron and On," *Inland Seas* 56, no. 1 (Spring 2000): 13–14.

66. Roger M. Jones, "Maneuvering an Intricate Self-Unloader Discharge in East Chicago, Indiana," *Inland Seas* 57, no. 3 (Fall 2001): 188–91.

67. Lafferty and van Heest, *Buckets and Belts*, 164.

68. Joachim, *Iron Fleet*, 19.

69. Thompson, *Steamboats*, 45.

70. Roger M. Jones, "Crane Vessels of the Great Lakes," *Inland Seas* 62, no. 3 (Fall 2006): 182–83. The last U.S. flagged crane vessels disappeared from the lakes around 1980.

71. Cement is a powdery substance made with lime and clay. It is mixed with water to form mortar, or mixed with sand, gravel, and water to make concrete.

72. Roy L. Peck, "Cement Afloat," *Inland Seas* 21, no. 1 (Spring 1965): 36–40. See also "Great Lakes Calendar," *Inland Seas* 24, no. 2 (Summer 1968): 153, regarding the *Medusa Challenger*.

73. "The Cement Trade," *Seaway Review* 16, no. 3 (July–September 1987): 67–68.

74. Valerie van Heest and William Lafferty, "Buckets and Belts," *Great Lakes Seaway Review* 37, no. 3 (January–March 2009): 101–3. In 1999, the *McGiffin* was substantially modified and rechristened the *CSL Niagara*. See BoatNerd, http://www.boatnerd.com/pictures/fleet/cslniagara.htm.

75. Gary W. Schmidt, with Warren Gerds, *Real, Honest Sailing with a Great Lakes Captain* (Allouez, WI: Seaway Printing Co., 2013), 193–94.

76. J. V. Petill, "SS *Philip R. Clarke* 'Silver Stack Pride,'" *Inland Seas* 58, no. 1 (Spring 2002): 5. When the *Clarke* was originally launched in 1951, it was 647 feet long. During the 1974–1975 layover, a 120-foot-long section was added to the ship.

77. U.S. Department of Transportation, *Status of the U.S. Flag Great Lakes Water Transportation Industry* (Washington, DC: U.S. Department of Transportation Maritime

Administration, 2013), 24.

78. Thompson, *Steamboats*, 78.

79. Bawal, *Superships*, 70–72. With eight rudders and bow and stern thrusters, the *American Republic*, renamed the *Great Republic* in 2011, remains one of the most maneuverable ships in the world. "*Great Republic*," BoatNerd, http://www.boatnerd.com/pictures/fleet/greatrepublic.htm.

80. Thompson, *Steamboats*, 16.

81. Snider and Davis, *The Ford Fleet*, 12, 143.

82. "Great Lakes Time Line," *Inland Seas* 41, no. 4 (Winter 1985): 272, 295.

83. Randall E. Rohe, "The Upper Great Lakes Lumber Era," *Inland Seas* 40, no. 1 (Spring 1984): 27.

84. Rohe, "The Upper Great Lakes Lumber Era," 26.

85. Carl E. Krog, "Lumber Ports of Marinette-Menominee in the Nineteenth Century," *Inland Seas* 28, no. 4 (Winter 1972): 277; Fred Dutton, "The William C. Moreland," *Inland Seas* 5, no. 2 (Summer 1949): 84, 90; W. R. Williams, "Lumber Carriers of the Lakes," *Inland Seas* 11, no. 3 (Fall 1955): 204–6. Lumber floats were occasionally seen on the lakes as late as 1973, when an 800-foot-long float pulled by two tugs locked through the Soo. "Great Lakes Calendar," *Inland Seas* 29, no. 3 (Fall 1973): 211. Regarding Ford boats carrying lumber, see Irl V. Beall, "East Indian of Detroit," *Inland Seas* 29, no. 3 (Fall 1973): 21; and "Great Lakes Calendar," *Inland Seas* 43, no. 3 (Fall 1987): 220, regarding a log raft in Lake Superior in June 1987.

86. Theodore S. Charrney, "The Potato Ships of Lake Michigan," *Inland Seas* 44, no. 1 (Spring 1988): 46–51.

87. Miller, *Tin Stackers*, 174.

88. Miller, *Tin Stackers*, 174.

89. Gregory W. Streb and William L. Wallace, "Care and Feeding of the Crew," *Inland Seas* 55, no. 2 (Summer 1999): 122.

90. Miller, *Tin Stackers*, 173–74.

91. Miller, *Tin Stackers*, 175.

92. Richard Belford, "The Butchers, the Bakers, the Paint and Thing Makers," *Inland Seas* 27, no. 2 (Summer 1971): 108–10.

93. Miller, *Tin Stackers*, 175.

94. "Timeline," J.W. Westcott Co., http://www.jwwestcott.com/timeline.html.

CHAPTER 6. ASHORE

1. Ron Chernow, "The Deal of the Century," *American Heritage* 59, no. 4 (July–August 1998): 12; W. Bruce Bowlus, "'Changes of Vast Magnitude': The Development of an Iron Ore Delivery System on the Great Lakes during the Nineteenth Century" (PhD diss., Bowling Green State University, 1992), 106; Al Miller, *Tin Stackers: The History of the Pittsburgh Steamship Company* (Detroit: Wayne State University Press, 1999), 19–20.

2. Miller, *Tin Stackers*, 22–24; Chernow, "The Deal of the Century," 12.

3. Miller, *Tin Stackers*, 24–26.

4. Chernow, "The Deal of the Century," 12. See "United States Steel Corporation History," Funding Universe, www.fundinguniverse.com/company-histories/united-states-steel-corporation-history. See also "U.S. Steel Corp.," *Encyclopedia of Chicago*, http://www.encyclopedia.chicagohistory.org/pages/2882.html.

5. As quoted in Miller, *Tin Stackers*, 29.

6. Miller, *Tin Stackers*, 28–29.

7. Miller, *Tin Stackers*, 42.

8. Miller, *Tin Stackers*, 38–39.

9. Miller, *Tin Stackers*, 13, 29, 54.

10. Miller, *Tin Stackers*, 56–59, 63.

11. Miller, *Tin Stackers*, 92–93.

12. Miller, *Tin Stackers*, 94–95.

13. Miller, *Tin Stackers*, 119.

14. Miller, *Tin Stackers*, 121.

15. Miller, *Tin Stackers*, 130–31, 169–71.

16. Miller, *Tin Stackers*, 130–31.

17. Miller, *Tin Stackers*, 204–5.

18. Miller, *Tin Stackers*, 159.

19. Miller, *Tin Stackers*, 194–95.

20. Miller, *Tin Stackers*, 194–96.

21. Miller, *Tin Stackers*, 61.

22. Roger M. Jones, "Passenger Quarters on the Old Lakers," *Inland Seas* 57, no. 2 (Summer 2001): 90–97.

23. Both quotes from Miller, *Tin Stackers*, 179.

24. Miller, *Tin Stackers*, 178.

25. Kenneth R. Dickinson, "Henry Ford II," *Inland Seas* 62, no. 1 (Spring 2006): 6–9.

26. Dickinson, "Henry Ford II," 6–9.

27. Miller, *Tin Stackers*, 177.

28. Patrick Lapinksi, "'Fair Weather and All the Best': The Maritime Life of Richard D. Bibby," *Inland Seas* 59, no. 4 (Winter 2003): 302–3.

29. Miller, *Tin Stackers*, 116–17.

30. Miller, *Tin Stackers*, 206–10.

31. "House Flags of U.S. Shipping Companies," CRW Flags, http://www.crwflags.com/fotw/flags/us~hfph.html#pittsburgh; Miller, *Tin Stackers*, 87.

32. Miller, *Tin Stackers*, 243–44.

33. Miller, *Tin Stackers*, 250–54.

34. *"John J. Munson,"* BoatNerd, http://www.boatnerd.com/pictures/fleet/munson.htm.

35. U.S. Department of Transportation, *Status of the U.S. Flag Great Lakes Water Transportation Industry* (Washington, DC: U.S. Department of Transportation Maritime Administration, 2013), 22; Howard Dicus, "Rough Sailing for Shipping: Cloudy Future for the Jones Act," *Pacific Business Review* 39, no. 33 (October 26, 2001): 20.

36. Fred Dutton, "The *William C. Moreland,*" *Inland Seas* 5, no. 2 (Summer 1949): 82; "Cabotage Laws (The Jones Act)," Lake Carriers' Association, *Annual Report* [*1987*] (Rocky River, OH: 1987): 19.

37. "Report of the President," Lake Carriers' Association, *Annual Report* [*1987*] (Rocky River, OH: 1987): 1; "Cabotage Laws (The Jones Act)," 19–20.

38. N. R. Danielian, "The St. Lawrence Seaway," *Inland Seas* 6, no. 1 (Spring 1950): 6–8.

39. "Great Lakes Calendar," *Inland Seas* 4, no. 4 (Winter 1948): 273.

40. "Labor Conditions in Great Lakes Shipping," *Monthly Labor Review* of the Bureau of Labor Statistics, August 1937; reissued as Department of Labor Serial No. R. 609 (1937), 3.

41. William L. Wallace, "Up the Grades on Ore Boats: From Coal Passer to Wheelsman to Third Mate," *Inland Seas* 53, no. 3 (Fall 1997): 178.

42. George J. Joachim, *Iron Fleet: The Great Lakes in World War II* (Detroit: Wayne State University Press, 1994), 15; "Labor Conditions in Great Lakes Shipping," 3; Fleetwood K. McKean, "Oscar Wing: A Captain of the Lakes," *Inland Seas* 22, no. 2 (Summer 1966): 137–41.

43. Charles P. Larrowe, *Maritime Labor Relations on the Great Lakes* (East Lansing: Michigan State University, 1959), 40.

44. "Labor Conditions in Great Lakes Shipping" (1937), 4.

45. Cletus P. Schneider, "War and Depressions, 1916–1945: Great Lakes Shipping as Remembered by A.E.R. Schneider," *Inland Seas* 61, no. 1 (Spring 2005): 22.

46. Joachim, *Iron Fleet*, 23.

47. Wallace, "Up the Grades on Ore Boats," 182.

48. Victoria Brehm, "Refiguring a Literature of Place: The Economics of Great Lakes Maritime

Literature" (PhD diss., University of Iowa, 1992), 121–25.

49. Harry Coulby, quoted in James B. Morrow, "Here's What Coulby Discovered," *The Nation's Business* 5, no. 4 (April 1917): 36.

50. Harry Coulby, quoted in *The Nation's Business* 5, no. 4 (April 1917): 36.

51. Lamont Montgomery Bowers Papers, 1847–1941, Binghamton University Libraries, http://128.226.37.53/index.php?p=collections/collections.

52. "Harry Coulby," MarineLink.com, http://www.marinelink.com/history/harry-coulby.

53. Harry Coulby, quoted in *The Nation's Business* 5, no. 4 (April 1917): 36.

54. Larrowe, *Maritime Labor Relations*, 14.

55. Larrowe, *Maritime Labor Relations*, 20–23; "USW-SIU Meeting Fails, Hall Walk Out," *Great Lakes Sailor*, "Office Employees Union Leader Accuses SIU Lack of Principles," *Great Lakes Sailor*, May 15, 1961, 1–2, 6; "Seafarers All Out against Trade Union Principles," June 15, 1961, 4, 8.

56. Larrowe, *Maritime Labor Relations*, 24–25.

57. Larrowe, *Maritime Labor Relations*, 25–28; "M.E.B.A History," Marine Engineers' Beneficial Association, http://mebaunion.org/MEBA/m-e-b-a-history.

58. Larrowe, *Maritime Labor Relations*, 31–32.

59. Larrowe, *Maritime Labor Relations*, 33.

60. Larrowe, *Maritime Labor Relations*, 35–36.

61. Larrowe, *Maritime Labor Relations*, 37–38.

62. Larrowe, *Maritime Labor Relations*, 39.

63. Larrowe, *Maritime Labor Relations*, 42–44.

64. Larrowe, *Maritime Labor Relations*, 42–58.

65. The National Labor Relations Board (NLRB) is an independent federal agency created by law in 1935. Its responsibility is to investigate and rule upon complaints regarding "unfair labor practices" as defined by the same law as created the agency. It is also empowered to require "certification" elections within companies upon receiving a petition signed by 30 percent or more of the company's employees. Should the workers choose to be represented by a union in an NLRB certification election, the company is legally obliged to enter into "good faith" negotiations with the union of the employees' choosing. All decisions by the NLRB have the force of law. "Our History," The National Labor Relations Board, https://www.nlrb.gov/who-we-are/our-history.

66. The National War Labor Board was created by order of President Franklin Roosevelt on January 12, 1942. In order to avoid disruption of critical wartime production, the NWLB was empowered to arbitrate any dispute between a manufacturer and a union that would otherwise lead to a strike affecting the manufacturing of material for the war effort. The

decisions of the NWLB were binding on all parties. The board was dissolved December 31, 1945. "Our History," The National Labor Relations Board, https://www.nlrb.gov/who-we-are/our-history.

67. Larrowe, *Maritime Labor Relations*, 58–68.

68. The Taft-Hartley Act amended the National Labor Relations Act of 1935 in ways that limited the rights granted to unions by that law. Union leaders at the time routinely referred to the Taft-Hartley legislation as the "slave-labor bill."

69. Larrowe, *Maritime Labor Relations*, 69–76.

70. Larrowe, *Maritime Labor Relations*, 76–79.

71. "Great Lakes Calendar," *Inland Seas* 12, no. 3 (Fall 1956): 203.

72. "Great Lakes Calendar," *Inland Seas* 12, no. 3 (Fall 1956): 204.

73. "Great Lakes Calendar," *Inland Seas* 12, no. 4 (Winter 1956): 293.

74. Larrowe, *Maritime Labor Relations*, 79–80.

75. Larrowe, *Maritime Labor Relations*, 80–81; "Great Lakes Calendar," *Inland Seas* 12, no. 4 (Winter 1956): 293.

76. "Great Lakes Calendar," *Inland Seas* 12, no. 4 (Winter 1956): 293.

77. "Steelworkers Issue Call for Unity among Remaining Great Lakes Sailors," *Great Lakes Sailor*, May 1963, 4.

78. "More Insurance, Increased SVP, Better Hospitalization Coverage Is Featured in Local 5000 Settlement," "Negotiations without Re-Opener Announced by Armour Following Meetings with Shipping Companies," "Local 7000 Contract Negotiations Continue," *Great Lakes Sailor*, July 1963, 1.

79. "An Open Letter to Certain Captains and Chief Engineers," *Great Lakes Sailor*, August 15, 1961, 1.

80. "Coast Guard Moves to Abolish Deck Watches," *Great Lakes Sailor*, May 1965, 6; Testimony of Jack Bluitt, Seafarers International Union, July 14, 1977, Local 5000 Collection, box 3, folder 4, pp. 2–7, Bowling Green State University, Ohio.

81. "Automation Poses Threat," *Great Lakes Sailor*, August 15, 1961, 2, "Distant Early Warning in Automation Scheme," *Great Lakes Sailor*, August 15, 1961, 8; "Seamen Question Wilson Barge Plan," *Great Lakes Sailor*, April 1963, 3; "Two Unions Meet Automation Threats," *Great Lakes Sailor*, August 3, 1962, 4; "Local 7000 to Arbitrate Abolishment of Nite Cook Job on Steamer Leon Falk," *Great Lakes Sailor*, December 1963, 4.

82. Testimony of Melvin H. Pelfrey, vice president, Marine Engineers' Beneficial Association on July 14, 1977, before the Subcommittee on Coast Guard and Navigation of the House Merchant Marine and Fisheries Committee, 7–8; U.S. District Court for the Northwest District of Ohio–Western Division, Memorandum and Order C77–370, dated November

18, 1977; respectively in box 4, folder 7, and box 7, folder 31, Local 5000 Collection, Bowling Green State University, Ohio.

83. The *Cason J. Callaway* was the first ship that had engines directly controlled from the pilothouse. The automation was completed at the end of 2001. Patrick D. Lapinski, *Ships of the Great Lakes: An Inside Look at the World's Largest Inland Fleet* (Hudson, WI: Iconografix, 2011), 21.

84. Testimony of Jack Bluitt, Seafarers International Union, July 14, 1977, 9–10.

85. Testimony of Jack Bluitt, Seafarers International Union, July 14, 1977, 7.

86. Richard D. Stewart, "Great Lakes Marine Transportation System: White Paper Prepared for the Midwest Freight Corridor Study," 9, Western Upper Peninsula Center for Science, Mathematics and Environmental Education, http://wupcenter.mtu.edu/education/ great_lakes_maritime/lessons; Jean C. Godwin, "Infrastructure Finance: Who Pays, Who Doesn't, Who Should and How Much," American Association of Port Authorities, October 27, 1998, http://www.aapa-ports.org/Issues/content.cfm?ItemNumber=1016.

87. Gilbert R. Johnson, "United States–Canadian Treaties Affecting Great Lakes Commerce and Navigation, Part 1," *Inland Seas* 3, no. 4 (October 1947): 203.

88. At the time, what is today the nation of Canada was a number of separate colonies, all of which were part of the British Empire. The Dominion of Canada was established as an independent nation in 1861.

89. Johnson, "United States–Canadian Treaties, Part 1," 206–7.

90. Gilbert R. Johnson, "United States–Canadian Treaties, Part 2," *Inland Seas* 4, no. 2 (Summer 1948): 113–14.

91. Cynthia Dizikes, "Chicago Sanitary and Ship Canal Named to National Register of Historic Places," *Chicago Tribune Business News*, February 18, 2012. "Chicago's Legendary Epidemic," *Chicago Tribune*, August 22, 2007.

92. Johnson, "United States–Canadian Treaties, Part 2," 115.

93. "Great Lakes Calendar," *Inland Seas* 53, no. 1 (Spring 1997): 52–53.

94. "Great Lakes Calendar," *Inland Seas* 16, no. 4 (Winter 1960): 315.

95. Haviland F. Rivers, "'Happy Landing' on the Lakes," *Inland Seas* 15, no. 2 (Summer 1959), 112–13.

96. "Great Lakes Calendar," *Inland Seas* 12, no. 1 (January 1956): 62.

97. "Great Lakes Calendar," *Inland Seas* 29, no. 2 (Summer 1973): 132.

98. Lloyd M. Short, *Steamboat Inspection Service: Its History, Activities and Organization* (New York: Appleton & Co., 1922), 53.

99. Short, *Steamboat Inspection Service*, 55.

100. Short, *Steamboat Inspection Service*, 60.

101. Short, *Steamboat Inspection Service*, 57–59.

102. United States Coast Guard, "U.S. Steamboat Inspection Service and the History of Merchant Vehicle Inspection," http://www.uscg.mil/history/articles/Steamboat_Inspection_Service.asp; National Maritime Center, "History of the National Maritime Center," http://www.uscg.mil/nmc/about_us/brochures/history.pdf.

103. Guy Burnham, *The Lake Superior County in History and Story* (Boston: Chapple Publishing, 1930), 232.

104. U.S. Department of Transportation, *Status of the U.S. Flag Great Lakes Water Transportation Industry*, 11.

105. Lawrence A. Pomeroy Jr., "Reshaping our Future: 1959 and Since," "Great Lakes Calendar," *Inland Seas* 22, no. 3 (Fall 1966), 315; "Great Lakes Calendar," *Inland Seas* 25, no. 1 (Spring 1969): 65.

106. "Great Lakes Calendar," *Inland Seas* 12, no. 2 (Summer 1956): 130; "Great Lakes Calendar," *Inland Seas* 15, no. 3 (Fall 1959): 235; Bertram B. Lewis, "The Great Lakes: Molders of Industry," *Inland Seas* 23, no. 1 (Spring 1967): 28–32; Mark Shumaker, "Wilson's *Westriver*," *Inland Seas* 66, no. 1 (Spring 2010): 43.

107. Commercially usable iron ore can be made up of anywhere from 16 to 70 percent pure iron, mixed with a variety of other substances. After the manufacturing process is complete, taconite usually contains 65 percent pure iron. In its natural state, taconite contains less than 15 percent iron and is not considered commercially useful.

108. Pomeroy, "Reshaping Our Future: 1959 and Since," 315.

109. For statistics regarding the annual U.S. steel production, consult U.S. Census Bureau, *Statistical Abstract of the United States*. For the purposes of this book, see the abstracts from 1974, 742; 1982–83, 791; 1987, 744; 1993, 760; 1999, 836; and 2001, 630.

110. "Iron and Steel," *Encyclopedia of Chicago*, http://www.encyclopedia.chicagohistory.org/pages/653.html.

111. U.S. Department of Transportation, *Status of the U.S. Flag Great Lakes Water Transportation Industry*, 41–42.

112. Joachim, *Iron Fleet*, 18.

113. U.S. Census Bureau, *Statistical Abstract of the United States*, 1999, 886; and U.S. Energy Information Administration, *Annual Energy Review 2011*, 201.

114. U.S. Energy Information Administration, *Annual Energy Review 2011*, 201.

115. "Lake Erie Coal Trade Feels Winds of Change," *Great Lakes Seaway Review* 21, no. 2 (October–December 1992): 22.

116. Raymond A. Bawal Jr., *Ships of the St. Clair River* (Saint Clair, MI: Inland Expressions, 2008), 36, 83.

117. *Great Lakes Seaway Review* 25, no. 1 (July–September 1994): 9.

118. Donald A. Gandre, "Recent Changes in Coal Traffic on the Great Lakes," *Inland Seas* 34, no. 1 (Spring 1978): 53–58.

119. "Great Lakes Calendar," *Inland Seas* 44, no. 1 (Spring 1988): 60.

120. U.S. Department of Transportation, *Status of the U.S. Flag Great Lakes Water Transportation Industry*, 48–49.

121. Miller, *Tin Stackers*, 254. In the steelmaking process, limestone fuses with various impurities that must be removed from the steel. The result, called "slag," is lighter than iron and, when both are still molten, literally floats on top of the liquid iron and can be skimmed off.

122. "Great Lakes Calendar," *Inland Seas* 40, no. 4 (Winter 1984): 292.

123. Raymond A. Bawal Jr., *Twilight of the Great Lakes Steamer* (Clinton Township, MI: Inland Expressions, 2009), 5; "Grain for the Hosts of Freedom," *LCA Bulletin* 32, no. 4 (August 1944): 11; George Dietrich, "Exciting Episodes in Grain Trade Climaxed by Epic Story of 1917–18," *LCA Bulletin* 39, no. 4 (August 1950): 1–4.

124. Mark L. Thompson, *Steamboats and Sailors of the Great Lakes* (Detroit: Wayne State University Press, 1991), 76, 139–40.

125. "Great Lakes Time Line," *Inland Seas* 41, no. 4 (Winter 1985): 273.

126. "Great Lakes Calendar," *Inland Seas* 39, no. 1 (Spring 1983): 71.

127. Bawal, *Twilight*, 102.

128. Brehm, "Refiguring a Literature of Place," 117.

BIBLIOGRAPHY

SAILOR NARRATIVES

Although often idiosyncratic, the published accounts of the men who crewed the vessels are almost always the most compelling. When reading the tales of sailors, however, one is wise to recall the words of Fred Dutton. A sailor himself, Dutton enjoyed immensely the stories he heard aboard ship. But he knew better than to believe every word that came off a sailor's tongue. In a moment of candor, Dutton noted that he loved the best tales, "even subtracting 20 percent for fiction."

Sailor narratives appear as both books and articles.

BOOKS

Dutton, Fred W. *Life on the Great Lakes: A Wheelsman's Story*. Edited by William Donohue Ellis. Detroit: Wayne State University Press, 1991.

Gillingham, Skip. *Summer of '63 Memories: Working on the Lubrolake*. Vineland, Ontario: Glenaden Press, n.d.

Haydamacker, Nelson, with Alan D. Millar. *Deckhand: Life on Freighters of the Great Lakes*. Ann Arbor: University of Michigan Press, 2009.

Herdter, Bill. *Old Sailor Bill*. Published by author, n.d., ca. 1997.

Hill, Richard. *Lake Effect: A Deckhand's Journey on the Great Lakes Freighters*. Sault Ste. Marie,

MI: Gale Force Press, 2008.

Livingston, Patrick. *Eight Steamboats: Sailing through the Sixties*. Detroit: Wayne State University Press, 2004.

McGrath, Ray I. *Great Lakes Stories*. Sault Ste. Marie, MI: Border Enterprises, 1996.

Schmidt, Gary W., with Warren Gerds. *Real, Honest Sailing with a Great Lakes Captain*. Allouez, WI: Seaway Printing Co., 2013.

Thompson, Mark L. *An Ancient Mariner Recollects*. Oxford, OH: Typoprint, Inc., n.d.

———. *Queen of the Lakes*. Detroit: Wayne State University Press, 1994.

———. *A Sailor's Logbook: A Season aboard Great Lakes Freighters*. Detroit: Wayne State University Press, 1999.

———. *Steamboats and Sailors of the Great Lakes*. Detroit: Wayne State University Press, 1991.

Thompson, Merwin Stone. *An Ancient Mariner Recollects*. Oxford, OH: Typoprint, Inc., n.d.

ARTICLES

Bardelmeier, William E. "Bill." "How to Steam a Steamboat: Sailing in Hand-Fired Lake Vessels in the WWII Era." *Inland Seas* 60, no. 3 (Fall 2004): 232–37.

Belford, Richard A. "Steamboating Forty Years Ago." *Inland Seas* 24, no. 4 (Winter 1968): 297–302.

Farmer, Claude E. "Great Lakes Memories: Working on the Great Lakes, 1928–1938." *Inland Seas* 62, no. 4 (Winter 2006): 287–300.

Hunger, Charles H. "A Fifty Year Sailing Career on the Great Lakes, 1908–1958." *Inland Seas* 57, no. 2 (Summer 2001): 107–11.

Mason, George Carrington. "A Young Man's Experience of Great Lakes Ships and Shipbuilding during the Years 1895–1920." *Inland Seas* 10, no. 2 (Summer 1954): 84–95.

Mellon, DeForest. "A Great Lakes Memory." *Inland Seas* 12, no. 1 (Spring 1956): 72–73.

Morrison, Lauchlen P. "Recollections of the Great Lakes." Serialized in *Inland Seas* 6, no. 2 (Summer 1950): 105–10, and 6, no. 3 (Fall 1950): 184–88.

Myers, Harry F. "Remembering the 504's." *Inland Seas* 44, no. 2 (Summer 1988): 76–93.

Perrine, Edward A. "Getting the *Stackhouse*." *Inland Seas* 60, no. 3 (Fall 2004): 211–25.

———. "Huron and On." *Inland Seas* 56, no. 1 (Spring 2000): 3–19.

———. "It's the *Fitz*." *Inland Seas* 56, no. 3 (Fall 2000): 178–91.

———. "It's the *Fitz*, Continued." *Inland Seas* 56, no. 4 (Winter 2000): 268–83.

———. "My Time on the *Frank Purnell*." *Inland Seas* 63, no. 3 (Fall 2010): 242–56.

———. "My Time on the *Frank Purnell*—Unexpected Promotion." *Inland Seas* 68, no. 3 (Fall 2012): 228–40.

———. "Up and Away on the Double 'W' Holloway." *Inland Seas* 55, no. 3 (Fall 1999): 192–210.

Sykora, Thomas Andrew. "A Seventeen Year Old Looks at the Lakes." *Inland Seas* 3, no. 2 (April 1947): 77–82.

Wallace, William L. "Up the Grades on Ore Boats: From Coal Passer to Wheelsman to Third Mate." *Inland Seas* 53, no. 3 (Fall 1997): 178–91.

CONTEMPORARY PUBLICATIONS AND PRIMARY SOURCES

Throughout the twentieth century, the Lake Carriers' Association (LCA) has represented the interests of shipowners. The LCA's publications, although they exclusively represent a business perspective, nevertheless form an invaluable, ongoing source of documentation regarding commercial activity on the lakes. Although this volume was largely written out of secondary sources, in addition to contemporary trade and union publications, a few manuscript collections were accessed:

Albert Bartlett Collection (GLMS 103). Center for Archival Collections, Bowling Green State University, Ohio.

Great Lakes Sailor, published jointly by the United Steelworkers Locals 5000 and 7000 Duluth, Minnesota.

Lake Carriers' Association. *Annual Report(s)*. Rocky River, OH.

Lake Carriers' Association. *LCA Bulletin*. Rocky River, OH.

Licensed Tugmen's Protective Association of America. *Directory and Manual of the Licensed Tugmen's Protective Association of America*. Toledo, OH: Hadley Printing and Paper Co., 1917.

United Steel Workers, Great Lakes Seamen Local 5000 Collection (GLMS 50), Center for Archival Collections, Bowling Green State University, Ohio.

SECONDARY WORKS

There are surprisingly few book-length secondary works that discuss some aspect of the history of Great Lakes shipping, or mention commercial vessels as part of a broader narrative. Much more informative is the periodical literature on the subject.

BOOKS

Arbic, Bernie. *City of the Rapids: Sault Ste. Marie's Heritage*. Allegan Forest, MI: Priscilla Press, 2003.

Ashworth, William. *The Late Great Lakes: An Environmental History*. New York: Alfred A. Knopf,

1986.

Bald, F. Clever. *The Sault Canal through 100 Years*. Ann Arbor: University of Michigan, 1954.

Bawal, Raymond A., Jr. *Ships of the St. Clair River*. Saint Clair, MI: Inland Expressions, 2008.

———. *Superships of the Great Lakes: Thousand-Foot Ships on the Great Lakes*. Clinton Township, MI: Inland Expressions, 2011.

———. *Twilight of the Great Lakes Steamer*. Clinton Township, MI: Inland Expressions, 2009.

Bennett, S. *A History of Control Engineering, 1800–1930*. London: Peter Peregrinus, Ltd., 1979.

Blume, Kenneth J. *Historical Dictionary of the U.S. Maritime Industry*. Lanham, MD: Scarecrow Press, 2012.

Bunton, Charlie J. *Rogers City: A History of a Nautical City*. Published by author, 2013.

Burnham, Guy. *The Lake Superior County in History and Story*. Boston: Chapple Publishing, 1930.

Curwood, James Oliver. *The Great Lakes and the Vessels That Plough Them: Their Owners, Their Sailors, and Their Cargoes*. New York: G. P. Putnam's Sons, 1909.

Cuthbertson, George A. *Freshwater: A History and a Narrative of the Great Lakes*. New York: Macmillan, 1931.

Devendorf, John F. *Great Lakes Bulk Carriers, 1869–1985*. Niles, MI: John F. Devendorf, 1995.

Eckroad, Elmer. *The Soo Locks*. Detroit: National Lithograph Co., 1950.

Elliott, James L. *Red Stacks over the Horizon: The Story of the Goodrich Steamboat Line*. Grand Rapids, MI: William B. Eerdmans Publishing Co., 1967.

Gjerset, Knut. *Norwegian Sailors on the Great Lakes*. Decorah, IA: Norwegian American Historical Association, 1928.

Hartig, John J., ed. *Honoring our Detroit River: Caring for Our Home*. Bloomfield Hills, MI: Cranbrook Institute of Science, 2003.

Havighurst, Walter. *The Long Ships Passing: The Story of the Great Lakes*. New York: Macmillan, 1942.

Hughes, Thomas Parke. *Elmer Sperry: Inventor and Engineer*. Baltimore: Johns Hopkins University Press, 1971.

Jackson, John N. *Welland and the Welland Canal*. Belleville, Ontario: Mika Publishing Co., 1975.

Jenish, D'Arcy. *The St. Lawrence Seaway: Fifty Years and Counting*. Manotick, Ontario: St. Lawrence Seaway Management Corp., 2009.

Joachim, George J. *Iron Fleet: The Great Lakes in World War II*. Detroit: Wayne State University Press, 1994.

Lafferty, William, and Valerie van Heest. *Buckets and Belts: Evolution of the Great Lakes Self-Unloader*. Holland, MI: In Depth Editions, 2009.

Lapinski, Patrick D. *Ships of the Great Lakes: An Inside Look at the World's Largest Inland Fleet*.

Hudson, WI: Iconografix, 2011.

Larrowe, Charles P. *Maritime Labor Relations on the Great Lakes*. East Lansing: Michigan State University, 1959.

Larson, John W. *Essayons: A History of the Detroit District, U.S. Army Corps of Engineers*. Detroit: U.S. Army Corps of Engineers, 1995.

LesStrang, Jacques. *Lake Carriers*. Seattle: Salisbury Book Press, 1977.

McCormick, Jay. *November Storm*. New York: Doubleday Duran, 1943.

Miller, Al. *Tin Stackers: The History of the Pittsburgh Steamship Company*. Detroit: Wayne State University Press, 1999.

Schafer, Mike, and Mike McBride. *Freight Train Cars*. Osceola, WI: MBI Publishing Co., 1999.

Schumacher, Michael. *November's Fury: The Deadly Great Lakes Hurricane of 1913*. Minneapolis: University of Minnesota Press, 2013.

Short, Lloyd M. *Steamboat Inspection Service: Its History, Activities and Organization*. New York: D. Appleton & Co., 1922.

Snider, Clare J., and Michael W. R. Davis. *The Ford Fleet*. Cleveland: Freshwater Press, 1994.

ARTICLES

Unlike the monographic literature, there is a rich periodical literature describing sailing on the Great Lakes. Special acknowledgment is due to the journal *Inland Seas*. First published in 1945, it is an invaluable source of information regarding the history of shipping on the lakes. Also valuable to the researcher is the *Great Lakes Seaway Review* (http://www.greatlakes-seawayreview.com). An industry publication, the *Review* often offers a snapshot of a given issue at a particular time. The *Review* also recognizes that many of its readers have an interest in lake history, and thus runs the occasional retrospective article that nicely summarizes some aspect of the industry.

Both *Inland Seas* and the *Great Lakes Seaway Review* publish unattributed reports, often in regular columns, as a part of each issue. Found under various titles, these "Comings and Goings" often include otherwise unavailable information about Great Lakes shipping.

It should be noted that much of the periodical literature is both specialized and detailed. Thus it is of greater interest to someone devoted to the history of the lakes rather than to a general reader.

ATTRIBUTED ARTICLES

ASSE International. "Hulett Iron-Ore Unloaders." ASME International History and Heritage Program, (1998).

Battenfield, Esther Rice. "In Grandpa's Wake." *Inland Seas* 9, no. 3 (Fall 1953): 195–99.

Beall, Irl V. "*East Indian* of Detroit." *Inland Seas* 29, no. 3 (Fall 1973): 21.

Belford, Richard. "The Butchers, the Bakers, the Paint and Thing Makers." *Inland Seas* 27, no. 2 (Summer 1971): 107–12.

Benford, Harry. "Lament for a Lost Heritage." *Seaway Review* 9, no. 1 (Fall 1979): 22.

Berry, James P. "Evolution of Powered Work Boats." *Inland Seas* 57, no. 3 (Fall 2001): 193–206.

Blackwell, Robert J. "The International Ship Masters Association Meeting, 1978." *Inland Seas* 34, no. 1 (Spring 1978): 4–12.

Blust, Frank A. "The U.S. Lake Survey, 1841–1974." *Inland Seas* 32, no. 2 (Summer 1976): 91–104.

———. "The Water Levels of Lake Erie." *Inland Seas* 19, no. 1 (Spring 1963): 27–29.

Britt, N. Wilson. "Pseudo Tides in Lake Erie." *Inland Seas* 10, no. 4 (Winter 1954): 294.

Brown, Andrew T. "The Great Lakes, 1850–1861, pt. 4." *Inland Seas* 7, no. 2 (Summer 1951): 99–104.

———. "The Great Lakes, 1850–1861, pt. 5." *Inland Seas* 7, no. 3 (Fall 1951): 185–89.

Burke, John A. "Barrels to Barrows, Buckets to Belts: 120 Years of Iron Ore Handling on the Great Lakes." *Inland Seas* 31, no. 4 (Winter 1975): 268–77.

———. "Lake Erie Coal Dumping Machines, Origins and Evolution." *Inland Seas* 61, no. 3 (Fall 2005): 182–92.

Burke, H. N. "Weather on the Great Lakes." *Inland Seas* 13, no. 2 (Summer 1957): 138–40.

Charrney, Theodore S. "The Potato Ships of Lake Michigan." *Inland Seas* 44, no. 1 (Spring 1988): 46–51.

Chernow, Ron. "The Deal of the Century." *American Heritage* 59, no. 4 (July–August 1998): 12.

Connelly, D. S. "*Presque Isle.*" *Inland Seas* 30, no. 1 (Spring 1974): 35–36.

Cottingham, Kenneth. "Erie—The Record of a Lake, Part II." *Inland Seas* 16, no. 3 (Fall 1960): 215–23.

Danielian, N. R. "The St. Lawrence Seaway." *Inland Seas* 6, no. 1 (Spring 1950): 3–9.

Dean, Jewell R. "The Wilson Fleet, Freight Pioneers." *Inland Seas* 2, no. 3 (July 1946): 159–64.

Dewar, Gary S. "Canadian Bulk Construction, 1945–59." *Inland Seas* 43, no. 1 (Spring 1987): 24–42.

———. "Canadian Bulk Construction, 1960–1970." *Inland Seas* 43, no. 2 (Summer 1987): 102–23.

———. "Changes in the Existing Bulk Fleet, 1945–1970." *Inland Seas* 45, no. 2 (Summer 1989): 95–106.

———. "Changes in the Post-War Fleet: Part II." *Inland Seas* 45, no. 3 (Fall 1989): 165–82.

———. "Conversion of WWII Ships for Great Lakes Service." *Inland Seas* 41, no. 1 (Spring 1985): 28–45.

———. "Design Variations in Vessels for Great Lakes and Salt Water Vessels." *Inland Seas* 41, no. 3 (Fall 1985): 158–61.

———. "The Pittsburgh Supers." *Inland Seas* 48, no. 1 (Spring 1992): 2–19.

———. "Rebuilding the Post-War Bulk Fleet." *Inland Seas* 42, no. 2 (Summer 1986): 84–101.

Dickinson, Kenneth R. "*Henry Ford II*." *Inland Seas* 62, no. 1 (Spring 2006): 2–20.

Dosey, Herbert W. "What They Are Saying." *Inland Seas* 15, no. 2 (Summer 1959): 131–35.

Dowling, Edward J. "Captain William J. Taylor, Gentleman." *Inland Seas* 3, no. 3 (July 1947): 169–72.

Dutton, Fred. "The *William C. Moreland*." *Inland Seas* 5, no. 2 (Summer 1949): 76–92.

England, R. W. "The Engineer." *Inland Seas* 1, no. 2 (April 1945): 11–13.

Ericson, Bernard E. "The Evolution of Great Lakes Ships, Part II—Steam and Steel." *Inland Seas* 25, no. 3 (Fall 1969): 199–212.

Ferris, Theodore N. "Bumboats." *Inland Seas* 34, no. 1 (Spring 1978): 59–60.

Fischer, Joseph P. "Hatch Covers." *Great Lakes Seaway Review* 38, no. 1 (July–September 2009).

Francis, David W. "Marine Casualties on the Great Lakes, 1863–1873: An Analysis." *Inland Seas* 42, no. 4 (Winter 1986): 261–69.

Gandre, Donald A. "Recent Changes in Coal Traffic on the Great Lakes." *Inland Seas* 34, no. 1 (Spring 1978): 51–58.

Garth, J. J. "Firehold University." *Inland Seas* 39, no. 3 (Fall 1983): 188–92.

Gebhart, Richard. "The Reluctant Acceptance of Wireless Use on the Great Lakes." *Inland Seas* 49, no. 2 (Summer 1993): 149–53.

Gluek, Alvin C., Jr. "The Lake Carriers' Association and the Origins of the International Waterways Commission, Part I." *Inland Seas* 36, no. 4 (Winter 1980): 236–45.

———. "The Lake Carriers' Association and the Origins of the International Waterways Commission, Part II." *Inland Seas* 37, no. 1 (Spring 1981): 24–32.

Hanks, Carl C. "The Pulpwood Fleet." *Inland Seas* 10, no. 2 (Summer 1954): 79–83.

Hareland, Fredrick Gary. "Shipboard Radio Communications." *PowerShips* 283 (Fall 2012): 38–41.

Hirsimaki, Eric. "The Hulett Story." *Inland Seas* 47, no. 2 (Summer 1991): 82–95.

———. "The Ore Docks." *Inland Seas* 47, no. 3 (Fall 1991): 165–78.

Johnson, Gilbert R. "United States–Canadian Treaties Affecting Great Lakes Commerce and Navigation, Part 1." *Inland Seas* 3, no. 4 (October 1947): 203–7.

———. "United States–Canadian Treaties Affecting Great Lakes Commerce and Navigation, Part 2." *Inland Seas* 4, no. 2 (Summer 1948): 113–17.

Jones, Roger M. "Crane Vessels of the Great Lakes." *Inland Seas* 62, no. 3 (Fall 2006): 182–87.

———. "Maneuvering an Intricate Self-Unloader Discharge in East Chicago, Indiana." *Inland Seas* 57, no. 3 (Fall 2001): 188–92.

————. "Passenger Quarters on the Old Lakers." *Inland Seas* 57, no. 2 (Summer 2001): 90–103.

Kelley, John J. "An Historic Thirty-Six Hours of Superior Seamanship." *Inland Seas* 40, no. 2 (Summer 1984): 82–88.

Kickson, Kenneth R. "The Largest Schooner in the World Revisited." *Inland Seas* 42, no. 1 (Spring 1986): 4–5.

Kirby, Frank E., and A. P. Rankin. "The Bulk Freighter of the Great Lakes." *Inland Seas* 34, no. 3 (Fall 1978): 218–23.

Kirkwood, Ernest. "From Salt to Fresh Water—or, The Story of *Cliffs Victory*." *Inland Seas* 16, no. 3 (Fall 1960): 203–5.

Krog, Carl E. "Lumber Ports of Marinette-Menominee in the Nineteenth Century." *Inland Seas* 28, no. 4 (Winter 1972): 272–80.

LaMarre III, Paul C. "Iron Elegance: The History of the SS *Col. James M. Schoonmaker*." *Inland Seas* 64, no. 1 (Spring 2008): 6.

Landon, Fred. "The Discovery of Superior Shoal." *Inland Seas* 15, no. 1 (Spring 1959): 50–54.

Lapinski, Patrick. "The *Canadian Ambassador* Captain Gerry Greig." *Inland Seas* 64, no. 2 (Summer 2008): 143–44.

————. "The *E.M. Ford*." *Inland Seas* 55, no. 2 (Summer 1999): 91–95.

————. "'Fair Weather and All the Best': The Maritime Life of Richard D. Bibby." *Inland Seas* 59, no. 4 (Winter 2003): 297–306.

————. "Legend of a Steamer: The *John J. Boland*." *Inland Seas* 53, no. 1 (Spring 1997): 15–27.

————. "Watching an Evolution: Tug-Barge Transportation on the Great Lakes Gets Nod from U.S. Fleet." *Great Lakes Seaway Review* 41, no. 1 (July–September 2012): 38.

Lewis, Bertram B. "The Great Lakes: Molders of Industry." *Inland Seas* 23, no. 1 (Spring 1967): 28–32.

Lyons, S. A. "The *J.H. Sheadle* in the Great Storm of 1913." *Inland Seas* 12, no. 1 (Spring 1956): 16–23.

Macaulay, Gordon. "The New Look on the Great Lakes." *Inland Seas* 9, no. 2 (Summer 1953): 92–97.

MacDonald, Robert J. "Captain Gridley and the German Gas Buoy." *Inland Seas* 15, no. 4 (Winter 1959): 288–90.

Matowitz, Thomas G., Jr. "A Sailor's Life: The Story of Captain Harry Anderson." *Inland Seas* 62, no. 4 (Winter 2006): 318–23.

McKean, Fleetwood K. "Oscar Wing: A Captain of the Lakes." *Inland Seas* 22, no. 2 (Summer 1966): 137–41.

McLear, Patrick. "Rivalry between Chicago and Wisconsin Lake Ports for Control of the Grain Trade." *Inland Seas* 24, no. 3 (Fall 1968): 225–33.

McLintock, Gordon. "King Point Academy's Contribution to the American Merchant Marine." *Inland Seas* 6, no. 3 (Fall 1950): 144–52.

Morrison, Neil F. "Lauchlen Maclean Morrison, Captain on the Great Lakes." *Inland Seas* 4, no. 1 (Spring 1948): 22–28.

Morrow, James B. "Here's What Coulby Discovered." *The Nation's Business* 5, no. 4 (April 1917): 34–37.

Murphy, Mark. "The Bold Skippers of the Lakes." *Saturday Evening Post*, August 19, 1950.

Myers, Ann. "The Mysterious Legacy of the *Cyprus*." *Inland Seas* 66, no. 2 (Summer 2010): 144–58.

Myers, Harry F. "Remembering the 504's." *Inland Seas* 44, no. 2 (Summer 1988): 76–93.

Palmer, George H., Jr., Carlton E. Tripp, Richard Suehrstedt, and Joseph P. Fischer. "Rebuilding the U.S. Great Lakes Bulk Cargo Fleet and the Metamorphosis of the Self-Unloader, Pt. I." *Inland Seas* 54, no. 1 (Spring 1998): 52–60.

———. "Rebuilding the U.S. Great Lakes Bulk Cargo Fleet and the Metamorphosis of the Self-Unloader, Pt. II." *Inland Seas* 54, no. 1 (Spring 1998): 61–67.

———. "Rebuilding the U.S. Great Lakes Bulk Cargo Fleet and the Metamorphosis of the Self-Unloader, Pt. III." *Inland Seas* 54, no. 2 (Summer 1998): 149–65.

Palmer, Richard A. "'Towing the Line' at the St. Clair Flats." *Inland Seas* 66, no. 1 (Spring 2010): 29–39.

Peck, Roy L. "Cement Afloat." *Inland Seas* 21, no. 1 (Spring 1965): 36–40.

Perrine, Edward A. "The Northern Lights." *Inland Seas* 69, no. 2 (Summer 2013): 143.

Petill, J. V. "SS *Philip R. Clarke* 'Silver Stack Pride.'" *Inland Seas* 58, no. 1 (Spring 2002): 2–6.

Pomeroy, Lawrence A., Jr. "The Bulk Freight Vessel." *Inland Seas* 2, no. 3 (July 1946): 191–200.

———. "Life Line of America." *Inland Seas* 7, no. 1 (Spring 1951): 13–20.

———. "Reshaping Our Future: 1959 and Since." *Inland Seas* 22, no. 4 (Winter 1966): 313–17.

Rice, Frank T. "The Most Reluctant Lady of the Lakes." *Inland Seas* 8, no. 4 (Winter 1952): 229–34.

Rivers, Haviland F. "'Happy Landing' on the Lakes." *Inland Seas* 15, no. 2 (Summer 1959): 106–13.

Roberts, G. N. "Trends in Marine Control Systems." *Annual Reviews in Control* 32 (2008): 263.

Rohe, Randall E. "The Upper Great Lakes Lumber Era." *Inland Seas* 40, no. 1 (Spring 1984): 16–29.

Robin-Tielke, Christine R. "Pushing Cargo Along." *Great Lakes Seaway Review* 37, no. 3 (January–March 2009): 105.

Schneider, Cletus P. "War and Depressions, 1916–1945: Great Lakes Shipping as Remembered by A.E.R. Schneider." *Inland Seas* 61, no. 1 (Spring 2005): 22.

Schneider, Nancy A. "'Ob Gibson': Memories of the Great Lakes Waters." *Inland Seas* 57, no. 4 (Winter 2001): 285–92.

Sheill, Stuart. "More on the Ice Jam of '84." *Inland Seas* 42, no. 2 (Summer 1986): 127–29.

Shumaker, Mark. "Wilson's *Westriver*." *Inland Seas* 66, no. 1 (Spring 2010): 43–54.

Stratton, J. H. "The Development of Ore Unloading on the Great Lakes." *Journal of the Cleveland Engineering Society* 6 (July 1913): 3–26.

Streb, Gregory W. "A Thanksgiving Vignette." *Inland Seas* 46, no. 1 (Spring 1990): 23.

Streb, Gregory W., and William L. Wallace. "Care and Feeding of the Crew." *Inland Seas* 55, no. 2 (Summer 1999): 119–23.

Sweigert, Alan W. "Through the New Rear View Lens." *Inland Seas* 54, no. 3 (Fall 1998): 170–73.

Trimble, Paul E. "Year-round Navigation on the Great Lakes." *Inland Seas* 32, no. 4 (Winter 1976): 248–54.

United States Coast Guard and Federal Aviation Administration. *Loran C: An Introduction and Users Guide* (Center for Navigation/DTS-52: Cambridge, MA, February 1993).

Van Heest, Valerie, and William Lafferty. "Buckets and Belts." *Great Lakes Seaway Review* 37, no. 3 (January–March 2009).

Wallace, William L. "Up the Grades on Ore Boats: From Coal Passer to Wheelsman to Third Mate." *Inland Seas* 53, no. 3 (Fall 1997): 178.

Williams, E. B. "Great Lakes Freighters Gradually Turn to Welding." *Ohio State Engineer* 22, no. 6 (May 1939): 19–20.

Williams, W. R. "Lumber Carriers of the Lakes." *Inland Seas* 11, no. 3 (Fall 1955): 204–6.

Wright, Richard J. "Conneaut Harbor, Part 2." *Inland Seas* 15, no. 1 (Spring 1959): 29–35.

UNATTRIBUTED ARTICLES ARRANGED BY HEADLINE

"The Cement Trade." *Seaway Review* 16, no. 3 (July–September 1987): 67–68.

"Keeping Training on Course." *Great Lakes Seaway Review* 41, no. 1 (July–September 2012): 59.

"Lake Erie Coal Trade Feels Winds of Change." *Seaway Review* 21, no. 2 (October–December 1992): 22.

"No Longer an All-Male Profession." *Seaway Review* 19, no. 4 (April–June 1991): 77–79.

UNPUBLISHED SECONDARY WORKS AND GOVERNMENT DOCUMENTS

Much detailed information about Great Lakes commerce is found in relatively obscure government documents. Although sometimes difficult to locate, the government publications are helpful for understanding the way the navigational system was created and is maintained, as well as, of course, the role of government regulation in the Great Lakes shipping industry.

DISSERTATIONS

Bowlus, W. Bruce. "'Changes of Vast Magnitude': The Development of an Iron Ore Delivery System on the Great Lakes during the Nineteenth Century." PhD diss., Bowling Green State University, 1992.

Brehm, Victoria. "Refiguring a Literature of Place: The Economics of Great Lakes Maritime Literature." PhD diss., University of Iowa, 1992.

GOVERNMENT DOCUMENTS

Bauer, L. A. *United States Magnetic Declination Tables and Isogonic Charts for 1902.* Washington, DC: U.S. Department of Commerce and Labor, Coast and Geodetic Survey, 1903.

"Labor Conditions in Great Lakes Shipping." *Monthly Labor Review* of the Bureau of Labor Statistics, August 1937. Reissued as Department of Labor Serial No. R. 609 (1937).

U.S. Army Corps of Engineers, Great Lakes and Ohio River Division. "Great Lakes System Dredged Material Management Long Term Strategic Plan," March 2010.

U.S. Census Bureau. *Statistical Abstract of the United States* (1999).

U.S. Department of Commerce, Maritime Administration, Office of Commercial Development. *A Study of Human Resources in Ship Operations, Phase 1 Report,* 1979 (National Maritime Research Center, 200).

U.S. Department of Commerce, Maritime Administration. *Domestic Waterborne Shipping Market Analysis—Legal and Regulatory Constraints—Great Lakes August 1974.* Report No. MA-RD-940–75020. Reproduced by the National Technical Information Service, Springfield, Virginia.

U.S. Department of Transportation. *Status of the U.S. Flag Great Lakes Water Transportation Industry.* Washington, DC: U.S. Department of Transportation Maritime Administration, 2013.

U.S. Department of the Treasury. *Statement of Appropriations and Expenditures for Public Buildings, Rivers and Harbors, Forts, Arsenals and Armories, and Other Public Works, from March 4, 1789 to June 30, 1882.* Washington, DC: Government Printing Office, 1886.

U.S. Energy Information Administration. *Annual Energy Review 2011.* DOE/EIA-0384(2011).

United States General Accounting Office. Report to the Chairman, Committee on Governmental Affairs, U.S. Senate, "Magnitude of Alcohol Problems and Related Maritime Accidents Unknown." GAO/RCED 90–150, May 1990.

United States Lake Survey. *The United States Lake Survey.* Detroit: United States Lake Survey, 1939.

WEBSITES

A contemporary author would be foolish to ignore the wealth of information available through the Internet. Although many critics complain about the accuracy of information found on the Web, it is fair to say that all sources, whether available in traditional print form or exclusively in an electronic format, must be used critically, and that there is no inherent reason why information gleaned from the Web is more, or less, likely to be accurate than that found in a printed source.

The primary limitation that is inherent to websites over printed matter is the unfortunately unpredictable, and often surprisingly short, length of time that information, or for that matter an entire website, can be found.

Allensworth, Tom. "A Short History of Sperry Marine." Rbmn.free.fr/Sperry.htm.

"*American Republic*." BoatNerd. Http://www.boatnerd.com/pictures/fleet/greatrepublic.htm.

Chadburn Society. Http://www.chadburntelegraphs.com.

"The Christening of the Tug *Dorothy Ann* and Self-Unloading Barge *Pathfinder*." BoatNerd.
     Http://www.boatnerd.com/pictures/fleet/dorothyannc.htm.

"*Col. James M. Schoonmaker*." Great Lakes Historical Society. Http://www.inlandseas.org/
     museum/col-james-m-schoonmaker.

"*E.M. Ford*." BoatNerd. Http://www.boatnerd.com/pictures/fleet/emford.htm.

Great Lakes Maritime Academy. Https://www.nmc.edu/maritime.

"*Harry Coulby*." MarineLink.com. Http://www.marinelink.com/history/harry-coulby.

Hatler, Carrie. "Taconite Harbor: Lake Superior's Once-Upon-a-Time Town." Forgotten
     Minnesota. Http://forgottenminnesota.com/2012/01/the-north-shores-once-upon-a-time-
     town.

"Iron and Steel." Encyclopedia of Chicago. Http://www.encyclopedia.chicagohistory.org/
     pages/653.html.

"*John J. Munson*." BoatNerd. Http://www.boatnerd.com/pictures/fleet/munson.htm.

Maritime Consortium, Inc. Drug Testing Regulations and Membership Questions. Http://www.
     drugfreevessel.com.

"M.E.B.A. History." Marine Engineers' Beneficial Association (MEBA). Http://mebaunion.org/
     MEBA.

Michigan Department of Natural Resources. Http://www.michigan.gov/dnr.

"History of the NMC–USCG National Maritime Center." Https://www.uscg.mil/nmc/about_us/
     brochures/history.pdf.

"*Pathfinder*." BoatNerd. Http://www.boatnerd.com/pictures/fleet/pathfinder.htm. See also
     http://www.boatnerd.com/pictures/fleet/dorothyannc.htm.

Pittsburgh Steamship Company. Http://www.crwflags.com/fotw/flags/us~hfph.
html#pittsburgh.

Sault St. Marie Canal National Historic Site. Parks Canada. Http://www.pc.gc.ca/lhn-nhs/on/
ssmarie/index.aspx.

"Steamboat Inspection Service History." United States Coast Guard. Http://www.uscg.mil/
history/articles/Steamboat_Inspection_Service.asp.

Stein, Janis. "Cliff Kursinsky." *Lake Shore Guardian*. http://www.lakeshoreguardian.com/site/
category/35/A-Great-Lakes-Sailor.

Steinberger, Heather. "Shipsitters." Http://writeonllc.com/2011/08/shipsitters.

Thanksgiving 1947 Menu, Str. *Louis W. Hill*. BoatNerd. Http://www.boatnerd.com/pictures/
historic/perspectives/ValleyCamp2/default.htm.

Thanksgiving 1976 Menu, Str. *Charles M. White*. BoatNerd. Http://www.boatnerd.com/news/
newsthumbs/images-07–4/cmwhite11–25–76jpm-f.jpg.jpg.

U.S. Army Corps of Engineers. "St. Mary's River." Http://www.lre.usace.army.mil.

United States Steel Corporation History. Http://www.fundinguniverse.com/company-histories/
united-states-steel-corporation-history.

U.S. Steel Corp. *Encyclopedia of Chicago*. Http://www.encyclopedia.chicagohistory.org/
pages/2882.html.

INDEX